QUEER LATINO *TESTIMONIO*, KEITH HARING, AND JUANITO XTRAVAGANZA

Hard Tails

Arnaldo Cruz-Malavé

palgrave
macmillan

QUEER LATINO *TESTIMONIO*, KEITH HARING, AND JUANITO XTRAVAGANZA
Copyright © Arnaldo Cruz-Malavé, 2007.

Cover: Drawing by Keith Haring on the steps of Henry Chalfant's studio on Grand Street, New York, where the city's graffiti writers used to congregate. Photo by Henry Chalfant, 1982; courtesy Henry Chalfant.

First published in 2007 by
PALGRAVE MACMILLAN™
175 Fifth Avenue, New York, N.Y. 10010 and
Houndmills, Basingstoke, Hampshire, England RG21 6XS
Companies and representatives throughout the world.

PALGRAVE MACMILLAN is the global academic imprint of the Palgrave Macmillan division of St. Martin's Press, LLC and of Palgrave Macmillan Ltd. Macmillan® is a registered trademark in the United States, United Kingdom and other countries. Palgrave is a registered trademark in the European Union and other countries.

ISBN-13: 978–1–4039–7747–2 (HC)
ISBN-10: 1–4039–7747–X (HC)
ISBN-13: 978–1–4039–7748–9 (pbk)
ISBN-10: 1–4039–7748–8 (pbk)

Library of Congress Cataloging-in-Publication Data

Cruz, Arnaldo.
      Queer latino testimonio, Keith Haring, and Juanito Xtravaganza : hard tails / by Arnaldo Cruz-Malave.
            p. cm.—(New directions in Latino American cultures series)
      Includes bibliographical references and index.
            ISBN 1–4039–7747–X (alk. paper)—ISBN 1–4039–7748–8 (alk. paper)
            1. Rivera, Juan, 1957– 2. Hispanic American gays—Biography. 3. Gay men—United States—Biography. 4. Haring, Keith. 5. Homosexuality, Male—United States—Biography. 6. New York (N.Y.)—Biography. I. Title.

HQ75.8.R58C78 2007
306.76'62092—dc22   2007005287
[B]

A catalogue record for this book is available from the British Library.

Design by Newgen Imaging Systems (P) Ltd., Chennai, India.

First edition: October 2007

10 9 8 7 6 5 4 3 2 1

Printed in the United States of America.

for Greg, the artist
for Lersie, because love also survives

CONTENTS

LIST OF FIGURES

ACKNOWLEDGMENTS

This book was born from the commotion that is to listen—to truly listen—to someone else's voice. But it was shaped through fits and starts by the active listening and reading of those whom I am blessed to call my friends. It exists because they, including Juan, wouldn't let me forget it. I first read portions of what would become Juan's interview to Mayra Santos Febres and Rubén Ríos Avila during a summer in San Juan in what now seems a utopianly gay decade, the 1990s, as we drank and tried to upstage one another by telling each other tales of real and imagined love woes. For the next ten years they wouldn't stop asking me about Juan's story, insisting that I develop it into a manuscript. Early one morning during this period, Doris Sommer, who had been staying overnight with us after attending an important meeting in New York, was enjoying a Spartan breakfast (we didn't have much) when I surprised her with a reading of what would become "Hard Tails: The Life and Times of Juanito Xtravaganza." Many of the ethical concerns about the *testimonio* genre and the limits of listening to others that I would agonize over for years to come may be traced to this early morning exchange. One night years later I would literally sequester Larry LaFountain-Stokes. He needed a place to stay in New York, and I would make him pay for his stay by reading my manuscript, which he diligently did, generously following up his reading with astutely informed conversation and myriad e-mails on all aspects of my project, as is his wont. The text was now growing after years of dormancy but I couldn't tell where it should go when I sent it off to Beatriz Jaguaribe in Rio, secretly hoping perhaps that Iemanjá's legendarily potent New Year's Eve waves would abscond with it. Instead it returned to me with Bia's unfailingly sensitive notes pointing out some gaps, suggesting leads, and urging me on. Later on that summer as I watched Insectavora in one of old Coney Island's sideshows with my partner Gregory de Silva and friends (Lina Meruane, José del Valle, Javier Jiménez-Belmonte, Luz Lenis, Wael Hibri, and Ivelisse Jiménez), Lina would offer to read my manuscript, which she did meticulously, annotating its pages with suggestive, thought-provoking questions and comments.

By the fall of that year the manuscript had begun to take definitive shape and I approached Licia Fiol-Matta and over lychee martinis under the Hudson Bar's Francesco-Clemente-painted ceiling explained my project to her. She (and José Quiroga through her) enthusiastically encouraged me to submit it to Palgrave Macmillan's *New Directions in Latino American Cultures* series. She would later read the entire manuscript, and my book would benefit greatly from her affectionate forthrightness and the nuance of her thought. A Fordham course reduction would allow me to work on the manuscript, and the text was more or less in its final state, so I thought, when Robert Reid-Pharr applied to it his sharp-as-a-scalpel, critical tough love and Arnaldo López his more delicately phrased yet equally incisive critique. In a way, both Robert's more forceful reading ("Naldo, boo, stop beating around the bush! Just say it! Risk it! Show yourself!") and Arnaldo's more gently phrased critique would confirm each other and force me to restructure the book. The book was now restructured when José del Valle, Luz Lenis, and Cristian Aquino applied their acute linguistic expertise and acumen to my "Spanglish Glosses," confirming to my relief most of its intuitions. Henry Chalfant, the great urban photographer and filmmaker, and Annelise Ream from the Keith Haring Foundation would generously grant permission to use the book's images. And Tess O'Dwyer's unerring eye would review the final manuscript before I delivered it into the capable hands of my editor Gabriella Georgiades, her editorial assistant Joanna Mericle, and production manager Katie Fahey, who would pass it on to the culturally sensitive staff of Maran Elancheran of Newgen Imaging Systems in Chennai, India, for copyediting and typesetting.

Along the way, I had shared a thousand-and-one stories from the book with those poor, unfortunate souls who, like Martin Manalansan, Dara Goldman, Hilda Nieto, Marvette Pérez, Elba Serrano, Antonio de Moya, Carmen Milagros Concepción, Ivelisse Jiménez, Angel Rodríguez-Díaz, Myrna García Calderón, Angelo Pitillo, Wael Hibri, Gerald Blaszczak, Giannina Braschi, Gayatri Gopinath, Gerard Fergerson, Judith Halberstam, Javier Jiménez-Belmonte, Luisita López Torregrosa, Viviane Mahieux, and Diamela Eltit, had opened that Pandora's box with the simple and innocuous question, "So what's your book about?" Somehow I could never tell them without launching into yet another story from the book, to which they graciously (and smilingly) listened over Indian and Thai dinners, academic receptions, birthday parties and picnics, and breakfasts. Along the way I had benefited from the insight and vast knowledge of New York popular culture of Ricardo Montez and from conversations with

filmmakers and ballroom culture documentarians, Félix Rodríguez
and Wolfgang Busch. And as the project developed, lingered, stalled,
haunting me, I can't say that I was beyond asking for divine intervention, as Iemanjá in Rio, the Virgen de Regla in Cuba, and Obatalá and
Ochún along the East River and the Hudson all know. But I won't
dwell on my indebtedness to them, for they know what I owe. I would
be remiss however if I didn't once more thank, explicitly now and in a
different key, Juan for his patience ("Naldo, *papo*, you think you'll be
able to finish *this* before I croak?"), Gregory de Silva, my partner of
thirty years, whose breath of intelligence or *aire* sustained me throughout the writing and infused my prose (to the extent that it contains
such) with lightness and joy, and Lersie, *mi hermana del alma*, to
whom this book is also dedicated, for every word in it, I would later
come to know, was written missing you.

CHAPTER 1

Listening Speaks (I)

An Introduction

Listening, your heart is in your throat.

—Wayne Koestenbaum, *The Queen's Throat*

Some ten years ago I was living in the Washington Heights area of New York City, in what local Dominican New Yorkers refer to as affectionately as *Quisqueya* Heights, when I received a call from someone I'd known nearly twenty years earlier. It was Juan Rivera, whom I'd known from my years as an undergraduate at Yale. I belonged then to a student organization, significantly named after a Puerto Rican independence rallying call, *¡Despierta Boricua!*, had an insurrectional afro, and political ideals to match; and as part of our community outreach, we'd go into the New Haven Puerto Rican neighborhood to tutor students at the local high school.

It was a community of recent immigrants from the rural interior of the Island, where I too had came from, and we, unbelievably the first class of "mainland" Puerto Rican students on the Yale campus, would often go there to attend political meetings, patronize cultural events, and search for good Puerto Rican music and food. To get there we'd have to cross the highway and the train tracks, which divided New Haven's expensive downtown shopping area from its poor inner-city neighborhoods, for the Puerto Rican community was literally on the other side of the tracks. We'd cross the highway, the train tracks, and walk up Congress Ave., or as it was both derisively and affectionately known to locals then, The Congo.

On the other side of The Congo, was the Puerto Rican neighborhood, The Hill, an isolated tangle of streets, a town in itself, strewn with Catholic and Pentecostal churches, where entire extended families lived in dilapidated Victorians facing each other, attentive to *el qué dirán*, to each other's every word and gaze. A town not unlike the town where I'd been raised in, in the heartland of Puerto Rico's volcanic rock interior, and where I'd migrated from four years earlier to New York—that incredibly and gaily named *San Sebastián del Pepino*—oh, yes, Saint Sebastian . . . of the Cucumber.

I must have seen Juan then while tutoring at the local high school or serving as a counselor for the Puerto Rican Youth Services program of the local antipoverty agency, *Junta*. I must have seen Juan at some community festival or on the stoops of this agency just hanging out. And he must have caught my eye, like so many of the handsome boys and girls who were initiating an identity then, as first-generation stateside Puerto Ricans with stridently beautiful afros, tropical polyester printed shirts, and prominently displayed Puerto Rican flags—on their butts.

But it was surely at the town's gay bar, the not unsuggestively named *The Neuter Rooster*, where we must have first met. For I too was initiating an identity then not only as a stateside Puerto Rican but as gay. And it was in these New Haven bars where I took my first steps. It was there where we, the Puerto Rican and black gay students at Yale, would often go after marathon meetings in which we'd strategize about building the most powerful third world student movement on the East Coast. And it was there where we'd continue planning for the Revolution in another key and under the glare of a different light—the disco ball.

And though we were Yale students, and as such privileged, we'd often have to devise the most elaborate plans to elude the racial quotas being enforced in the gay clubs then. We'd match the lightest skin of us to the darkest and try to enter in couples that way. But still every so often we'd be wandering outside the club perplexed at the failure of our flawlessly designed plan. Any rational racist would have approved, we thought. Once inside, however, we'd take over the dance floor with our expansive moves, and we'd dance salsa to disco and the reverse. Once inside, a sort of family, one of those extended Puerto Rican families that crisscross social classes and races, in which the stuck-up society lady shares uncomfortably the same lineage with the unemployed and the single mom, began to form on the basis of shared space, furious and elegant turning, deep dish, and desiring sweaty bodies.

Nearly twenty years later I was a professor at Fordham, a Jesuit University in New York, specializing in Latin American and U.S. Latino literatures, on the board of the Center for Lesbian and Gay

Studies of C.U.N.Y.'s Graduate Center, and writing my first essays on Puerto Rican and Latin/o American queerness, when I received Juan's call. I'd heard in the intervening years that Juan had been living in New York, gone through a series of odd jobs, been the lover of a famous artist, hung out with the rich and famous, traveled around the world. But now on the other side of the phone, he sounded distressed. He had developed AIDS and had recently come out of the hospital, and was looking for a way to make a living, to rebuild his life, looking for some direction, some way out, when he'd run into an old friend of mine from New Haven who'd given him my phone.

He also had a story to tell: something urgent to communicate— he'd been wronged, he knew it, and was looking for some vindication, to set the record straight. He visited me and he handed me a book, *Keith Haring: The Authorized Biography* by John Gruen, which he could barely read, where his name appeared—besmirched. After all, I was a Yale graduate, a university professor . . . I should know.

I listened to Juan's irresistibly tangled tale with no small measure of awe and rage, and quickly agreed that his story had to be heard. It had to be heard in its own right, first and foremost for Juan's sake. But it also resonated with so many of the issues queer studies was grappling with then, as it attempted to move toward its intersection with ethnic, racial, and gender studies, as it placed, so to speak, the margins of lesbian and gay identity at the center of a queer studies agenda. And it spoke similarly to questions that were beginning to be raised then in Latin/o American and Puerto Rican studies, as these fields moved from the analysis of national formations to an exploration of the nation's migrant borders. And it shed light on the vexed relations between popular and high culture and on discussions of consumerism and the appropriation of resistant vernacular forms that so preoccupied American cultural studies throughout the 1990s.

Juan had been lover and partner of the famous American 1980s Pop artist Keith Haring during some of the most frenetically productive years of his career, from 1986 to shortly before his death in February of 1990. They had met at the Paradise Garage, the legendary underground disco where black and Latino gay youth, vogueing drag queen divas, straight-identified "banjee" boys, and homeless and thrown-away kids stomped, sweated, and swirled with music business insiders and up-and-coming media celebrities (see chapter three, "A Love Interlude: The Paradise Garage"), and Haring, then at the peak of his internationalizing career, had been instantly smitten by his looks: "One night, at . . . the Paradise Garage, . . . I see this incredibly beautiful boy. I look at him and see that he's the man of my dreams. I convince myself that should he look at me . . . then *that's* going to be *it*! I will have found my new love," he would recall (Gruen 1991 138–39). And indeed Juan seemed then, as pictured in photos of the period in Haring's posthumous *Journals* and John Gruen's "authorized biography," perfectly made for this moment in Haring's rapidly ascending international career—not only "street" or urban New York and handsomely photogenic, but of a certain equivocal Puerto Rican cast and hue that would make him appear, paradoxically, internationally indigenous or local, as Haring, barely disguising his envy, would remark, "Juan, forever handsome with a chameleon face that adapts to every place we go, making him look Brazilian, Moroccan, or . . . Japanese" (Haring 1997 211–12) (see figure 1.1).

Like Keith Haring, Juan had arrived in New York toward the end of the 1970s, escaping the conservative turn of small-town and suburban America against the values of liberation and personal freedom emblematized by the 1960s, chief among them sexual self-expression.

Figure 1.1 Juan Rivera and Keith Haring around the time they met in 1986 at the Paradise Garage. Courtesy Juan Rivera.

But unlike Haring, he had arrived there as a runaway kid. He had run away from the then homophobically oppressive, small-town environment of his impoverished New Haven Puerto Rican neighborhood, The Hill, which, like so many other inner-city communities all over the United States, had been devastated by the flight of manufacturing from the cities and toward the suburbs and the state's disinvestment in inner-city neighborhoods in an attempt to dismantle the legacy of the 1960s and the "welfare state." He hadn't really been in search of the famed New York City lights, for as he says, he knew nothing about New York. But like so many other kids who were coming to New York then, like Keith Haring himself, he had been propelled by a simple affirmation of life, of a mysterious yet concrete and verifiable, life-sustaining, and abiding queer desire that others in his milieu, even himself, had considered "demonic." Movingly embracing what others would demonize in him, he had arrived in New York with nothing— or worse than nothing: the legacy of a deficient education that had left him functionally illiterate, and had ended up inadvertently trapped in a truly demonic space, the 42nd St. of the late 1970s, drawn, as he would say, by its evil force.

New York was then a polarized city. It had emerged out of a fiscal crisis that had pushed it to the brink of bankruptcy in 1975 to become a global, postindustrial capital of real estate, insurance, and finance. Yet many of its inner-city neighborhoods remained a devastated war zone of abandoned and burned-out buildings and vacant lots, overrun by the drug trade and patrolled by an unsympathetic police that identified their impoverished, working-class residents, mostly Latino and black, as the cause, rather than the victims, of their neighborhoods' decline.

And none more devastated than Times Square's 42nd St. Facing competition from the newly created home video technology, the row of 42nd St. "grind" movie theaters, which had subsisted there since the Depression days, had turned to porno and built out of the decaying old grand dames of Broadway theater a far-reaching and intensive sexual emporium, fed by a surplus of impoverished, runaway, mostly inner-city kids, and fueled by drugs. In fact, as the drug trade increased during this period, the rhythm of sexual transactions would accelerate as well, a vial of crack becoming the price of almost any act, the most common (yet ephemeral) currency of exchange (see chapter five, "Times Square and the Sex Trade"). It was this world that Juan Rivera would arrive in during the late 1970s, "falling," as he would say, into it and becoming trapped. Perhaps no one has captured the desperation of this moment in the lives of Latino, mostly Puerto Rican, young men hustling in the Square as eloquently, if problematically, as the controversial photographer Larry Clark in his book, *Teenage Lust* (1983) (see chapter five, "Times Square and the Sex Trade").

During the following years as Juan attempted to work his way out of what he would come to think of as this netherworld of hustling, he would become a house painter, an apartment construction worker, a maintenance man, a driver and partner in a limousine service company, and lover and partner of Keith Haring, for whom he would stretch canvases, fill in paintings, drive, cook, and keep house. And yet it seemed somehow that no matter how hard he tried to rise above that netherworld of hustling or, as he would call it simply, *that* he would always end up in the ensuing years, because of his lack of education, because of his functional illiteracy, falling right back into it, and he would be left once more, as he would certainly be after Keith Haring's death, destitute and depressed. Still, as he tried each time, he would always be fortified by the faith, a faith fed by a kind of Puerto Rican popular Catholicism, and the spirit of the times, that one could assume and transform the "demonic," redeem oneself, as it were, by finally seeing one's image in one's lover's validating eyes.

Unlike Juan, Keith Haring had had the benefits of a solidly middle-class, American-dream type of upbringing and education. And yet like Juan, he had also felt "suffocated" (Gruen 1991 20), stifled by the socially and sexually conservative ("redneck," he would call it; 10) environment of his small Pennsylvania-Dutch-country town. It was a racially and culturally segregated, mutedly homophobic, and reassuringly uniform environment, and Haring, feeling that both his sexual desire and his mission as an artist lay elsewhere than in the fixed, safe familial ground, that it lay instead in the spontaneous, unscripted, unquantifiable, and uncharted territory of otherness, would leave his hometown, Kutztown, to study art in New York City and, as he would put it in his *Journals*, live, "just live" (Haring 1997 2).

He would arrive in a New York whose inner-city neighborhoods were not only devastated from deindustrialization and disinvestment but also populated and crisscrossed by the multiple alternative and coded languages, movements, and sounds of hip-hop. And as he walked the streets on his way to museums and galleries, or traveled in the subways, he would fantasize over the dark boys he saw around him (with their "dark eyes, dark hair and gorgeous bodies, [and] penetrating gaze"; Haring 1997 70), and study the graffiti art he encountered. And it was this desire both for the racial and cultural other that would excite and incite him, inducing him to engage, to commune, and to communicate.

Inspired by the graffiti writers' work and his desire for them, Haring would elaborate a pictogramatic artistic vocabulary whose first icon, the ur-icon, as it were, which kept reappearing in all his subsequent work, was a 1950s drawing of a flying saucer, which looked like, in Haring's words (Gruen 1991 57), a Mexican *sombrero*, and which went about radiating or zapping humans, animals, and things with its ominous, alien beam of energy. In one of the original series of panels he would produce, this flying saucer would zap a dog with a rectangular muzzle, which would then pass on the beam of energy to an outlined male human figure through anal sex, setting off a chain reaction in which anyone or anything contaminated with, and penetrated by, the alien ray would be transformed and glow. The chain of mutations set off by the flying saucer and transmitted through this "doggy style" sex would be subsequently reinforced by a frieze at the bottom of the panel where the images of the dog and the silhouetted male figure, now on all fours, would alternate, thus giving birth to what would henceforth be known as Haring's world-famous identificatory tag, his radiated, crawling "radiant baby."

Drawn on city walls and on vacant subway ad panels, Haring's crawling "radiant baby" would appear then as a cipher for his ability to receive, embrace, and incorporate the purportedly unnatural, demonized alien other, which was for him both the devastated urban environment and the black and Latino youth cultures that had emerged in response to it. Coming at a time when the city was trying to rid itself of graffiti as a sign not only of the fiscal crisis it had just experienced but of a supposedly broader social decline it was transcending as well, Haring's art seemed to argue instead for the value and significance of the demonized other not as a destructive but a procreative force, as if art were itself somehow a call to be invaded, or penetrated, by an ominous alien other in order to become an-other, to be transformed, to glow (see chapter three, "A Radiated Radiant Baby").

Like the work of the queer avant-garde artists Haring considered his predecessors, Gysin, Burroughs, and Warhol, as well as that of Genet and of East Village underground artists such as Charles Ludlam and Jack Smith, artists for whom homosexual desire was an access to difference, theirs and others', rather than an affirmation of identity or sameness, his art would seek to embrace the alien other in the hope that abjection could be turned into a glowing image (his own), violence and banishment into visibility and joy.

Hard Tails is the story of this desiring, loving encounter with the abject other, Haring's as well as Juan's. But it is also the tale of the seductions and limitations of that quasi-religious trope of transformation and redemption that seemed to undergird so much popular as well as high-cultural production during the 1980s. I myself would be seduced by the trope. I myself would become, as I would call it (Cruz-Malavé 1996), entangled in it. And for more than ten years, as I followed the t(r)ail of Juan's relationship with Haring, I would agonize about the distressingly unseemly seductions of retelling his tale. And though I felt uncomfortable with, and inadequate to, the task of retelling—a task that had somehow befallen me and that kept tugging at my heart and conscience, insistently—I couldn't let it go.

What if I was secretly feeding a prurient interest—mine as well as others'—for Latino lives under duress? What if I was aestheticizing—and thereby neutralizing—sheer wretchedness? What if I was turning into palatable, tasty entertainment truncated lives? What if I was assuaging someone's guilt, my own included, about living, just living or going about one's daily life while entire populations were being reconnoitered and targeted? Or even worse: what if I was providing someone with a walk on the wild side so that that someone, me included, could finally feel, could *com-probar*, both confirm and taste that joyous sigh of relief, that jolt that may be experienced at reliving "lesser" lives at a distance, safely sconced at home, in one's comfortable armchair, with one's ubiquitous cup of coffee by one's side, as is thematized in the Argentine author Julio Cortázar's short story "Continuity of Parks"? "He could taste the almost perverse pleasure of disengaging himself . . . from his surroundings," of immersing himself in the "sordid" scene that the novel he was reading was recounting, says Cortázar's narrator of his protagonist's adventure in reading. And yet: "[H]e could feel at the same time that his head was resting comfortably on the velvet of his armchair's high back, that his cigarettes remained within easy reach of his hand" (11).

Coming in the wake of the 1980s Latin American boom in testimonial writing and of American critics' promotion of *testimonio* at universities, it was only natural—and necessary—that such questions about *use* be raised. Critics had so invested in *testimonio*'s counter-hegemonic discourse as a means of intervening in the university's culture wars that when, by the mid-1990s, *testimonio* had become canonical and institutionalized at American universities, they began to wonder about the value, and ethics, of reducing subaltern discourses to internal, American university struggles over cultural politics. And a generalized sense of guilt, a collective *mea culpa*, began to pervade academic writing.

Such contextualization helped to shed light on the caution some of my academic friends were advising, but it certainly gave me no relief. Quite the contrary, a feeling I can only retrospectively name over-powered me—shame.

So for about ten years the transcription of Juan's interviews lay there in my study, dormant and partially edited, sleeping, as one would say in Puerto Rican Spanish, *el sueño de los justos*, the righteous' uninterrupted, otherworldly sleep. And then, in the meantime, as in a Latin American *Boom* novel, the original tapes were lost.

CHAPTER 2

The Life and Times of JUANITO XTRAVAGANZA

As Told by Juan Rivera and Retold by Arnaldo Cruz-Malavé

Mi voz puede volar . . . (My voice can also fly . . .)

—Celia Cruz, *Yo Viviré* (I Will Survive)

The following interviews were conducted at multiple sessions in the City of New York during the years 1994–1996. Some of the names of the people that appear in them have been omitted, in order to protect the not-so-innocent; others have been retained, as they belong to the public domain. These interviews have been edited and their order modified to conform to the spirit of Juan Rivera's involved story-telling, of his always detouring voice, as is explained in the editor's introductory comments, "Listening Speaks (II)." Supplemental information on the people, the places, and the terms referred to in them has been added in chapter five "What's in a Name." Notes on Spanish-English, or Spanglish, code-switching have been provided as glosses to Rivera's creative bilingualism. And references have been supplied for the curious reader, who might want to follow up on the story's many bifurcating leads.

FLY, ROBIN, FLY

JR: When I knew you back then I always thought 'cause of your voice and 'cause you were timid that you were gay.
AC-M: Because I was timid?

JR: Very timid. And 'cause of the way you spoke—very soft, Puerto Rican . . .

AC-M: I was timid?

JR: You were shy. And I've always been attracted to guys that are shy.

AC-M: I'm still shy . . .

JR: You still are . . . and you still got that look. But back then you never made an attack, so I assumed it was 'cause I was young or some shit like that. I don't know.

AC-M: Yeah, I was a *mess* . . . I was a mess back then.

JR: I thought you were adorable and I figured at some point you were gonna make the first attack . . .

AC-M: . . . I was in college and you were in high school, and to me that made a difference then. I mean, I was only two years older, and I'd just been in high school two years before that myself, but that made a difference back then. You see, I was in this Puerto Rican student organization, and we were supposed to be role models for Puerto Rican men—we weren't supposed to be sleeping around with them.

JR: Those were the vibes I picked up from you back then.

AC-M: It was silly . . . but I really bought into it back then.

JR: Did you know I was gay? I mean, did you have a sense I was gonna be gay?

AC-M: I thought so.

JR: Why? 'Cause I was messing with M . . .?

AC-M: No, I didn't know *that* . . . but one night I saw you walking around campus and we locked eyes and we talked.

JR: At Yale?

AC-M: Yeah.

JR: Oh, yeah, that was around the time I disappeared and came to New York.

AC-M: Right. I was trying to get over this relationship I'd had with this guy, this Hawaiian guy.

JR: Oh, yeah . . .

AC-M: It was this *tortured* relationship . . .

JR: Oh, yeah . . . I remember him . . .

AC-M: Yeah?

JR: It was this Chinese guy—*nice, smooth, gymnast's body, hairless skin* . . .

AC-M: Hm . . .

JR: I think he came on to me once.

AC-M: Hm . . .

JR: But I don't recall if he was your piece then . . .

AC-M: Probably.

JR: He was *hot.* I mean, I never thought I'd get into *un chino* but . . . Yeah, I remember . . . This guy *was* cute.

AC-M: He *was* cute . . . But then I saw him many years later . . . and oh, boy, had he changed! Anyway, I had this feeling I was responsible for . . . *the world*. I was a counselor in this college-bound program for minority students, and I was supposed to be a role model. So I couldn't. I wouldn't.

JR: You just didn't know how to have your cake and eat it too!

AC-M: I guess . . . that's always been my problem—too much consistency.

JR: Me too . . . I too was insecure back then. Even having had a few pieces, I didn't know how to be . . . I mean, it was more of a lust kind of thing.

AC-M: But at least you were free, free with your body.

JR: Weren't you out?

AC-M: Yeah, I was . . . I knew I was gay, and if we had to turn out a party or a meeting, as we did back then, I would. I could argue a point, I could make *statements* . . . but I was never free.

JR: I too was insecure, and I swear I've told very few people about my childhood. But I was brought up with five sisters, five females, and when my brother was born my father took all of the att . . . attention from me. I always assumed *he* was my dad's kid and *I* was my mother's . . . My first sexual turn on was in my grandma's house. I remember sleeping and when I woke up my cousin was feeling me up.

AC-M: ¿*Tu primo*?

JR: *Prima.* A real pretty girl. And I didn't even know what getting your dick up was all about. I remember the first time coming, and when I did, it was this sensation that drove me into coming, but instead of coming, I pissed.

AC-M: Your cousin . . . how old was she?

JR: Oh, I don't know, maybe fourteen . . . fifteen . . . I was sleeping and as I got up she kinda looked at me and I just closed my eyes and went back to sleep. I think she was the first one to turn me on to jerking off, 'cause I had to figure out what was this sensation within the body that had to be released. So first I was seduced by my cousin; later I got seduced by a dog.

AC-M: By?

JR: A dog.

AC-M: A woman? An ugly woman?

JR: A dog!

AC-M: A dog?! A real dog?!

JR: Yeah, a *dog* . . .

AC-M: Why . . .?! *How* . . .?

JR: 'Cause at that time I didn't have any friends, and my dog was my best friend.

AC-M: Makes sense . . . Man's best friend . . .

JR: I used to play a lot with my dog. And I was maybe about twelve, 'cause I've always been small. And it was kinda weird 'cause I was playing with my dog, and he was always trying to sniff my butt, and I'd say, "Get the fuck outta here!" But it got to the point that his breathing got real excited . . . exciting . . . And I remember thinking that my dog wanted to fuck . . .

AC-M: He wanted to . . .

JR: Yeah! We were playing on the floor when Leo, the dog, came around and overpowered me and started to pump. And I wanted to get up but couldn't . . . 'cause his panting kinda *hypnotized* me . . . till . . . I finally remember thinking I was gonna get porked . . . by my dog!

AC-M: Oh no! And *did* you . . .?

JR: No, but he tried. And then it felt like it wasn't the dog who was doing it but demons, and I turned around and kicked him off. But oh, yeah, my dog was my best friend . . .

AC-M: But didn't you have any other . . . friends?

JR: I couldn't . . . couldn't go out and play with the boys. I had to stay at home and play with the *girls* 'cause *Mother* wouldn't let me.

AC-M: Mother?

JR: Yeah, *Mami.*

AC-M: So you were first seduced by your cousin, then by a dog . . .

JR: Yeah, but a friend of the family who was visiting tried to seduce me first.

AC-M: Your cousin, a friend of the family, the dog? What is it about you that everyone tries to seduce you?

JR: I don't know. A certain aura . . . Still to this day I could go out in my worst mood, and it's like a turn on to people. I spook the guys and the girls in my neighborhood, and I have this method when I walk toward a pretty boy. I always pretend I'm looking straight, but meanwhile I'm trying to check whether he is gonna spook me first. 'Cause if you spook him first, he'll say, "oh you faggot!" But if you let'em spook you first ('cause I don't know what it is they see when they pass me but they always end up spooking me), then you can catch'em later spooking you. *Y ellos te viran la cara*, like saying you caught me. And then when you walk away from a person who you know spooked you, you take a certain number of steps, depending on the person's look and walk, on whether he looks shy faggoty or hard core, and you turn around, and there he is . . . looking back at you.

AC-M: So first was a friend of the family, then the dog?

JR: Yeah. A friend of the family was visiting, and I didn't wanna but had to sleep with him. And he was trying to seduce me, and I was pushing him back. And I noticed his breathing, and it was like the dog's . . . or the dog's was like his . . . And yeah, I think that's what turned me on later with the dog. His breathing was something evil, something unknown. You see, I didn't know anything about my sexuality, about sex.

AC-M: So you were pushing him back . . .

JR: Yeah, I was trying to deal with it, 'cause I felt if my father came in, he'd kill this guy. And I thought if I was to say something, I'd be responsible for what happened. So I kinda let it be. And then the next day he was in my sister's bed trying to seduce her.

AC-M: How did you know?

JR: 'Cause I was there. I slept in the same room as my sister, and I could hear her saying "No, leave me alone." But she was a lot like me. She felt if she screamed, my father would come in and kill the man. So I kinda heard her say no, and him "come on! come on!," and we both ended up crying ourselves to sleep. But I never told her I knew.

AC-M: And did you ever speak to this man afterward?

JR: No, I just played it off like it never happened. I think he was air struck or something. Anyway, later I found out that his family had been known to be at war, 'cause one of his kids claimed they'd been sexually abused by his dad. He was married to this fat woman, a *santera*, and he was a born-again Christian, an *aleluya* kind of guy. I really wanted to get up and kick this guy's ass! But I was too timid . . . I was a little faggot!

AC-M: So the breathing wasn't a turn on with the family friend, but it *was* with your dog?

JR: No, I hated that guy, but my dog was my friend, and when he grabbed me I let go. But then he started pumping and tried to pork me, and I wanted to kill the dog, 'cause I knew *that* wasn't normal . . . Later me and my dog were playing in this parking lot, and I called him not realizing I was close to the edge, and he ran and jumped and fell three floors to his death. Still I couldn't figure out his breathing . . . It was demonic.

AC-M: Demonic?

JR: Yeah, it was demonic. Guys don't get fucked! And I knew I was gonna be a faggot 'cause I liked boys. I would go out and play with the guys and I'd feel like hm . . . hmm . . . hmmm . . .

AC-M: Like infatuated?

JR: Like puppy-love. And then I started watching shows like *My Three Sons*, and I'd always feature the prettiest boy. Yeah, I knew I was gonna be gay, but I couldn't figure it out. And every time *que pasaba un pato por casa tú veías a todos estos hombres pitándole y gritando,* "*Mira a ése le gusta coger por el culo,*" and I'd go, "Oh, noooo!!, that's not gonna be me. Please, God! . . ." Ha! Ha! Ha!

AC-M: And still you felt an infatuation . . . for other boys . . .

JR: Yeah, I had an infatuation with my cousin's boyfriend. And I guess he *knew* I was gonna be *un mariconcito,* 'cause I was in the fifth grade and he was in sixth, and I don't know exactly what we said, but by the time we finished our conversation, we were going to the bathroom and I knew I was gonna get fucked. All I remember is the way he came on to me, and *that* turned me on. But we were kids, you know . . . But the way he came on to me put me in a *state* that I thought this time I'd probably enjoy it. But when it happened it

wasn't all *that*, 'cause mentally I wasn't ready. And then afterward
he was kinda scared, 'cause he thought I had said something, but I
hadn't. And then there were times when he'd kinda disappear and
other times when he'd come back looking for me. And I guess I fell
in love with him . . . But the first time I *really* got into getting
clocked . . .

AC-M: Was that what you wanted—to get clocked?

JR: It wasn't what *I* wanted; it was what *they* seduced me into wanting.
I was being seduced, and all I knew was I had this feeling that came
from inside, and I couldn't control. So the first time I really got into
getting fucked was with my brother's best friend, L . . . My brother
was my dad's little boy and I was *Mami*'s, and while he had a group
of buddies he played around with, I had no friends. My father had
bought my brother a bike he used to ride around in, and I sat at
home like . . . *la nena de la casa*, and played with Barbie dolls and
did macramé. But as I sat there I'd often look out the window and
spook the boys running and having fun. And the more I looked, the
stronger my obsession to play with the boys got. Then one day my
brother was wrestling in the basement with his friends, and as they
wrestled, they started pulling each other's nuts to see who'd give in
first, when one of his friends grabbed my balls and pulled me into
the game. I had always sensed my brother's friends thought I was
gonna be gay 'cause they would give me these real long adoring
looks, and as they grabbed me, I felt *tímida como una nena*, but
pretty soon I got up my nerve, and I was grabbing their balls and
they were grabbing mine, and when I grabbed L . . . 's, my brother's
best friend's, I could sense he wanted me to grab him but not hurt
him. So I pulled his balls and stopped and held them there in my
hands, and then immediately drew back 'cause I felt his hard on
growing from the base of his dick. And that evening he told my
brother he was gonna spend the night over, and something clicked.
Boing! And as we lay there in bed, my brother facing the wall,
L . . . in the middle, and I next to the edge, I was awake for an hour,
maybe two, thinking to myself, "Should I make a pass at his crotch?
Should I see if he still has a hard on?" And finally I moved my hand
slowly, and before I knew it my hand was on top of his crotch,
y estaba dura, dura como una maceta. And I felt like "Oh, my god,
so what do I do now?!" And I started massaging his dick, and it felt
nice . . . niiice! . . . And then he said, "Let's get on the floor." And
he lay on the floor, *y me le senté ahí*—no lubrication or nothing, it
was a very natural thing. He was on the bottom, and I was just riding go lucky . . . and singing soprano, "*The Hills Are Alive with the
Sound of Music* . . ."

AC-M: But couldn't your brother hear?

JR: No, I was scared he was gonna, but he never found out—not till the
bitter end.

AC-M: Was the fact that L . . . was your brother's best friend a turn on?

JR: No, the turn on was being aware I was getting clocked by someone I liked—this cute Puerto Rican *cano*. I'd always liked L . . . 'cause he was the only one of my brother's friends who'd come to the house and talk to me. He was really the first guy I could talk to and who talked back nice, and I thought he liked me, and I kinda felt a bond with him . . .

AC-M: Did you ever talk about what happened that night?

JR: No, we just got up and acted like nothing ever happened. But I eventually found out L . . . had talked about it to his brothers, 'cause they all seemed to know. And whenever I'd run into his older brother, T . . ., in school he'd start walking down the hall *partién-dose* and doing this fag talk and grabbing his crotch like saying, "Now you can take care of me." And I'd say to myself: "You fucken *bellaquito*, I ain't taking care of your ass, 'cause I don't wanna! And 'cause you ain't got no dick!" But then his younger brother H . . . started coming around my parents' house, and he was real beautiful—long blond hair, green eyes, pretty face—and I'd play in the basement with him. And soon I started sensing that both H . . . and L . . . were vying for my attention, that they were both in battle over me. And they'd always come in separately, but then one day they got drunk and came together looking for me. I'd already moved from my parents' house, and was living in New York with my first lover N . . ., and was visiting my parents, when I heard someone knocking on my bedroom window. And wouldn't you know it, it was L . . . and H . . . ! "What the fuck do *you* want?" "Yo, man, Juan, let's go out and take a drive." "What?!" "A drive—a drive to East Rock." You remember East Rock?

AC-M: Yeah, vaguely, in a daze—the lovers' lane . . .

JR: Their other brother, T . . ., and their cousin were also in the car. And I know it was probably T . . ., who was the most *bocón*, who psyched them into *picking up Juan, taking him up to the Rock, and feeding him dick*. But I said fuck it! I mean, how often do you get all these pretty boys to come pick you up at your house to give'em blow jobs while they get high up on the Rock. And it wasn't like I was retarded or anything, no, not *anymore*, but they were so hyped up with *draaagging* me up the mountain that I thought *that* was a turn on. And, yeah, this was one of my biggest fantasies, but when it finally happened, come on!, get outta here!, it wasn't all *that*. Being dragged up the mountain felt sleazy, like I was some kinda trashy *ho*, but knowing they loved me, loved me sucking their dicks, loved *me*, that it wasn't just a wham-bam-thank-you-ma'am, that they'd later talk to me and goof around with me, *that* was the real turn on.

AC-M: So you felt they had to play this act to show their affection, their love?

JR: Yeah . . . I could tell that they liked *it* . . . they liked *me*. And as they were jerking off and drinking, and I was blowing them, I could tell it wasn't the first time they'd had this kind of camaraderie, that they'd messed around before, jerked each other off, pulled each other's nuts, but couldn't bring themselves to suck each other off. So they figured let's go get P . . . 's brother, Juan.

AC-M: And yet your brother never knew?

JR: No, he never knew—not till the end, *the bitter end*. But I always sensed he knew I was a faggot and he hated me for it. And then his relationship with L . . . and his brothers got kinda distant, and I felt they'd probably got into an argument, and in the heat of the argument, L . . ., who was a *bocón*, probably said to my brother: "You know your brother ain't nothing but a faggot, and I fucked him!" But my relationship with my brother was never great. I . . . actually used to . . . *hate* him. He was the baby *y el machito de la casa*, and my father would always spoil him. My father bought him a moped and a bike and taught him how to drive at a very early age, and he never did these things for me. I guess he just assumed my mother was doing a great job raising me. So we never had a relationship, but I always knew he loved me. But every time me and my brother would get into a fight my father would end up beating me, 'cause *yo era el mayor*. And as I got older, and started getting into art, my brother would take engines apart and bring them into the house and start them right there in the middle of my art work to provoke me. So I started staying out, and that's when I found the bars—the *gay* bars . . .

AC-M: Do you remember your first time at a gay bar?

JR: Yeah! Until then my image of gay people were these loud *locas* like M . . ., F . . ., and J . . . They'd walk down the street swishing and shaking their bangles, and if they spooked a boy, and the boy got loud with them, they'd read him and threaten to punch him out. Eventually, they all died—were killed. M . . . was found in his apartment cas . . . trated. And F . . . was killed in a bar in *Six Corners* (remember *Six Corners*?) . . . —they stuck a pipe up his butt. And J . . . died . . . —of an overdose. And then I found *The Neuter Rooster*, my first gay nightclub. It had this huge statue of *un pájaro* about to take off, and as you walked in you could hear the club's theme, "*Fly, robin, fly* . . . ," and you'd see your face reflected in all of these mirrors and all these pretty boys' faces, and I felt . . . like flying, reborn, and I flew, and flew . . . far away.

AC-M: It was then you left for New York?

JR: Yeah.

AC-M: What made you leave?

JR: Lots of things, but mostly my brother and G . . .'s wife.

AC-M: G . . ., the executive director of the antipoverty agency, J . . .?

JR: Yeah, I was still in high school, and G . . . was the young executive
director of J . . . . And though G . . . was only in his twenties, he
looked much older, and was always all dressed up like . . . well . . .
like an executive. He had this poised manner about him, *bien parao,
pero buena gente.* And I remember meeting him for the first time and
became immediately infatuated. I met him at J . . . 's new location in
Fair Haven. And I still don't know how I got there. All I know is he
knew I was a painter, and he needed some work done. And he was
extremely charming. And I said to myself what's up with this guy.
Then everyone left work, and there he is talking and goofing with
me, and all of a sudden he says, "I've got a bottle of wine if you
wanna drink . . .?" And I said, "Sure." And we kinda got drunk and
took it from there. It was a wild relationship! Weird! You see, I later
found out that G . . . 's family knew he was gonna be a faggot,
'cause he was *real* tight with this kid who was a faggot—his cousin.

AC-M: Los primos se exprimen . . .

JR: So his family fixed his marriage to his wife, R . . ., through *brujería,*
and I don't know how they did it but by the time the wedding came,
his cousin had disappeared . . . like from the face of the earth!
Nobody knew where he was. Nobody had heard from him. And
then the day I met G . . . we went out to eat, and we ran into him!
And I felt weird—like something had started the whole ball rolling.
G . . . looked visibly upset and at the same time anxious and excited.
He unbuttoned his collar, and as we talked I started to notice he had
all of these mannerisms, and by the end of the conversation there
were *plumas* flying all over the place. The very next day he took me
to his parents' house and then to his wife's. He told her I was there
to paint their house, and she stared at me with a blank face. And as
I painted the house I'd see the shadow of R . . . 's *bata* come in and
out of the room with my tray of food, and I could sense that she
knew me and her husband were having a fling. And then during one
of the séances that G . . . 's friend, a medium, was having, he told
G . . . that his parents *le habían echao un 'brujo a su casa* to make
sure that it wouldn't be sold. 'Cause once sold G . . . would be free
to go his way and so would his wife, R . . . . And the medium told
him to look under his bed where he'd find all of these ribbons tying
him to the house. And he found them and untied them. And then
one morning I got up, and I don't know why, I just couldn't stand
him. Everything positive I felt for him was totally gone that morning. And I told him I wanted to go home, and he just sat there staring at me and trying to figure it all out.

AC-M: Wow! So you went back home?

JR: Yeah. And when I got there my brother was staring at me, and there
was more hate in his face than I'd ever seen. And without saying a
word, he just got up and knocked all of my art work on the floor.
And I could tell he'd just found out, that L . . . had finally told him

I was a faggot. And for the first time in my life I got real mad and hit him. And he punched me back, and I fell to the floor. And as I was getting up, he lunged for my back with a kitchen knife. And lucky for me a friend of his jumped in and grabbed the knife as it was coming down. And as my brother's friend was desperately trying to restrain him, my sister was screaming hysterically. And when my parents came in they started yelling at me: "*Tú eres el mayor!* You should know better . . . You should . . .!" And as my father raised his hand to strike me I grabbed it in midair, and my mother started shaking and crying, and I ran out . . . Yeah, it was then I decided to run away to New York.

AC-M: Why New York?

JR: I don't know, 'cause I didn't know *nothing* about New York. I guess I was drawn to the City by some unnatural power. I had no *maletas*, all I had was ten dollars. I went to the train station with R . . ., my best friend, and as I was waiting for the train, I was crying and telling him I had to try to find myself, I had to get out. And he was asking me, "But where are you gonna go?" And I was saying, "I don't know, I don't know . . ." But by the time I got on the train I was calmer and was already laughing and saying to myself "*Free at last! . . . Free at last! . . . Thank God Almighty! I'm free at last!*" But when I got to the City I panicked—I was so overwhelmed. And all of a sudden I realized that I couldn't go back, that I no longer had a home . . . And after the second day in the City, your stomach starts talking to you, and it's like it never dawned on you that you had to eat. And so after a while you end up living like a derelict, going through garbage cans to eat. And if I had only known how to steal, it would've been different, but I didn't . . . So pretty soon I felt like a derelict, I *was* a derelict. And for about two months I slept in church benches, in alleyways, in city parks. By then, I mean, I was already a bum, *ya era una bona*. I had come down to the City in dress pants, but by then they were torn and stiff with dirt and caca— I mean, they could've walked home by themselves.

Just Telling Stories . . .

AC-M: And at no point you felt that you could go back home?

JR: I didn't know how to . . . I just didn't. I know at times I caught myself saying, "Why am I here? Why didn't I think about what I was doing?" But I was in such a daze, and then after becoming a derelict, even more. So for some unknown reason I ended up on 42nd St. And it's so weird, now that I think about it, 'cause so many of the street children who come into the City are drawn by these evil powers that live around there on 42nd St., and *that* puts them eventually in situations that force them to hustle, and they end up making a living out of it.

AC-M: But you'd never heard of the sex trade on 42nd St.?

JR: No, I just ended up there—drawn by its evil force. As a matter of fact, I remember coming into the City for the first time with R . . ., my friend. And there we where in *that* neighborhood looking for a gay bar and couldn't find one. We'd come into the City to see *The Wiz*, our graduation present to ourselves, and we'd gone to eat in a Chinese restaurant, and the waiter, *un chino*, came over to us and started talking real clear in Spanish, and I freaked out. It was like going through a time tunnel, or being in *Alice in Wonderland*, or in *The Wiz*—the *chino* didn't speak *chino* but a totally unexpected language. And I thought it was real funny, and we ordered food, and later found out there're a lot of *chinos* who speak Spanish. And then after dinner, we tried to find this one particular bar that R . . . had heard of and ended up getting stranded. So we turned to watching the people walking by and saying to ourselves: "He looks like a faggot . . . He looks not . . . He looks like a faggot . . . He looks not . . ." But soon we got scared someone was gonna punch us out, and R . . . remembered he had the address of this one friend who lived in Brooklyn. And we went all the way to Brooklyn, but couldn't get a hold of him. So we ended up coming back into the City and waiting at Grand Central for the 6:00 a.m. train. And R . . . was all pissed off and indignant, and with his nose up in the air, kept shaking his head: "I'll never come to this *traashy* City!!"

AC-M: And little did he know he'd end up living in "this *traashy* City". . .

JR: In *Queens*! So I ended up on 42nd St., and from being a derelict I became a hustler. I remember the last time I was going through the garbage cans. It was on 42nd St.—I remember it well. I was picking through the garbage when this john started flashing ten dollars at me. And I was saying to myself: "What does *he* want?!" And little did I know he wanted to play around with me. I mean, I wasn't experienced in playing around with nobody—not for money, no! So he ended up taking me home and doing all kindsa stuff to me. And at one point I was so destroyed, 'cause I didn't want to do what he wanted me to—I didn't wanna get fucked! And he was trying his damned hardest to fuck me, and I was going, "Stop, Charlie! Charlie, stop! Go to sleep, Charlie! Go to sleep!," but he kept trying all night long. And by the time he was fucking me the second time that night, I was crying, you know, and asking God to give me the strength not to turn around and kill this man, 'cause I was ready to kill him. So I was crying and praying at the same time that this be over with . . . Yeah, that was the first time . . . And after that, I kinda went back, and did it for twenty, thirty dollars, and made enough money to get an apartment and clothes.

AC-M: What kind of an apartment could you get with that kind of money?

JR: It was one of those ten-dollar jammies in those 42nd St. hotels where you just paid for the night, but I didn't stay there that long—maybe a month. Then one day I went to a club called *The Ice Palace* where I met my first lover, N . . ., and got married. *The Ice Palace* was on 57th St. and 6th Ave., and it was very old—the kind of place that had probably been there since our parents' days. It was dark and had lots of mirrors, and as I looked in one of these mirrors, I saw N . . . staring at me, and I was totally elated. And before the night was over he took me home. And as I was walking with him, I kept asking him what he did for a living, but he wouldn't really say. And when I got to his apartment on 89th and First, the walls had paneling, and everything was very old—Victorian. And I thought this man must be a prince, and this is his Manhattan townhouse apartment.

AC-M: His pied-à-terre . . . his bachelor's pad.

JR: Yeah, but he turned out to be a hustler. And after we made out on his rug by the fireplace, he sat me down and told me: "Now, I can tell you're hustling, and if you're gonna do this for a living, you have to know the *dos* and *don'ts*. You don't blow johns. You don't get fucked. You just strip and serv'em dick." And afterward I did as he told me and soon I was raking in some serious dough. Now instead of ten dollars, I was charging sixty. And as I continued hustling I found out the more domineering you were, the more *pargos* would get off on you. So that there were plenty of *pargos* all I had to do for was a real sexy strip tease act, and by the time I'd take off my clothes they'd already come. So you see, a fifteen-minute strip tease act for sixty dollars. And it was so easy to sell your dick, not your ass, that I started running ads in the papers, and went on doing it for five more years. And I never got fucked again.

AC-M: Except maybe by N . . .?

JR: Not even, for the weird part about N . . . was that the first time he took me home we were making out, and he'd given me all the booty I wanted and still hadn't come, when he said, "You wanna do something different, something kinky?" And I thought, "Oh, oh, here goes . . . *otro* space cadet!" And before I finished the thought, he ordered, "Piss on me! Piss on me!"

AC-M: No!

JR: Yeah! And I was like, "Did I hear that?" And he seemed to respond, "Yeah, piss on me! Piss on me!!" And I thought, "Oh well, why not?" And I pissed. We were by the fireplace, and there were *frisas* on the floor, and in the light N . . .'s body seemed to glow. And I thought, "This is all so bizarre," 'cause he didn't look like the type and this didn't look like the scene. But the more I was turned off, the more I was turned on, 'cause he looked so cute, like a little boy waiting to be fed. And I did.

AC-M: In the living room?

JR: No, in the bathtub, under the golden arches . . . And as the *chorro* hit his body, his dick stood at attention and he started to convulse. A real whacked out trip!

AC-M: So you always played "dominant" in this relationship?

JR: Yeah, and it was so weird, after having been seduced into being passive in Connecticut for so long, to come into the City to find myself in relationships where I was always dominant. And as I got older, I realized that most people get turned on to me as a dominant. They just seemed to take one look at me and their *patitas* went up in the air . . . looking for some place to paint . . .

AC-M: But in Connecticut you had always been "passive"?

JR: 'Cause I thought that was what was expected, but when I met my first lover, N . . ., who taught me the trade, I grew out of that. Hustling butchened me up! And it made my life a whole lot easier— *yo que soy un bellaco malo*; all I had to do was play dominant and serve dick. 'Cause *pargos*, you know, wanna be treated like faggots. I even knew some who wanted me to slap' em, put'em on a leash, and walk 'em around the house like a dog.

AC-M: Literally like a dog?

JR: Yeah. I'd walk'em around the house and pretended they were dogs. And every once in a while I'd have to pull'em back or kick'em if they stopped and raised their legs to relieve themselves. But there was this one john who insisted on tying a leather noose around his cock, and I'd have to walk him around the house leading him by the tip of his dick. And you know, sometimes the pull was painful, but he'd get off. And every time he'd stop I'd have to pull him rough and call him, "*Come, Rover! Come!*"

AC-M: How could you keep a straight face?

JR: The money kept my face straight; gave me a straight *macho* face. And it was this face they wanted me to call'em faggot with, to spit on them. Some of them wanted me to spank'em or wrestle with'em, and then pretend I'd lost.

AC-M: So you had to pretend to dominate them so they could then turn around and dominate you?

JR: That was the fantasy they were paying for. But they couldn't come out and say it; you just had to sense it. One of the last johns I was seeing was this Columbia professor, 'cause back then most of my clientele was from Columbia. And he was so *enchulao* with me that he invited me to his house out in the Hamptons. So I went thinking I'd hang out in the Hamptons and make some good money while I was at it, 'cause every time I'd see this guy I'd walked out with a week's pay. But he was not infatuated with me; he was infatuated with wrestling, and every time he'd get next to me, all the contact he wanted was wrestling. And as he'd get on top to try to pin me down, I'd be on the bottom resisting, and I'd start sweating, and he'd slide and start sniffing my armpit. And I'd try to shake him, but he was like a leach. And there were times I thought he'd attack my dick, but he'd just be there staring and sniffing at a distance . . . like a snake. And after two days of this tug of war I finally said, "Listen, I wanna go home. I'm tired of wrestling. The match is over—you won!"

AC-M: Were there other *pargos* who wanted you to dominate them so they could end up on top?

JR: Practically every *pargo* I ever dealt with wanted me to dominate him so he could end up on top. Like the Cuban designer, T . . . . Yeah, this is the story of the john who didn't really like water sports but liked *meao*.

AC-M: What's the difference?

JR: Usually water sports are played in the bathtub, which is really the place to do them if you don't wanna change your mattress all the time. I used to see this john—a real good-looking john too—and we'd have sex, and after sex he'd only get off if we'd go into the bathtub and played water sports. He'd put his crotch between his legs, and he'd squeeze his thighs and rub'em back and forth, and then at the perfect moment he'd look up, and I'd piss on him, and he'd come. But T . . . would always be sitting in the living room watching TV, and I don't know how he managed it, but he'd always have boxing on, and I'd come in and he'd call out to me, "*¡Ay, mira, Juanito, ese machito! ¡Mira esos* underarms *y esa peste! ¡Ay, hijo, mira, Juanito! ¡Mira esa pinga! ¡Ay, Juanito, yo quiero mamar pinga! ¡Juanito, yo quiero mamar! ¡Esa pinga!*" And then he'd ask me to piss in a champagne glass, and as he talked about the boxers, he'd pick up the glass and take a sip, put it back down, and continue the conversation just normal about the boxers, or the boys I was fucking, or stories I'd just make up to get him off. After all, there's just so many stories you can tell a john . . .

AC-M: What sort of stories?

JR: Stories like, "I met this girl in the street, and I took her home, and she wanted me to suck her pussy . . .," and he'd ask, "*Ay, sí, sí,* and how did you suck her pussy, *papa?*" "And how did she suck your *pinga?*" "*Pues . . ., me la mamó así, y me la echó p'atrás, y me agarró las . . . .*" And he'd just sit there staring at TV all glassy-eyed and sipping *meao*.

AC-M: And he'd get excited about you talking about girls?

JR: I was supposed to be straight, and though he knew better, in the stories he'd always want me to be fucking girls, or serving boys dick in the locker room.

AC-M: So you'd be making up stories . . .

JR: . . . and he'd be sipping his cocktail piss. And he'd play with my foreskin, suck on it, pull it, stretch it, and then ask, "*¿Puedes mear hasta llenarlo hasta el* rim, *papa?*" And I'd say, "I'll try."

AC-M: And you could?

JR: Uhm.

AC-M: Wow, that's . . .

JR: . . . an art. Just like when you deal with a john who likes to be spanked. You don't make him hurt immediately. First, you work your way up slowly, and then sometimes, if you've work your way up gradually, you can spank him till your hands get blood shot, and he'll still be begging for more. So you have to pull out a belt, a buckle, a paddle, a bat. Whamm! Whamm!

AC-M: Till they come?

JR: That's just it—they're so coked up they don't come. Besides, they don't get spanked to come—spanking *is* the fantasy. And they only stop when you tell them you've had enough. And yeah, it's easier to work with a john when you're all coked up, 'cause then you can let your imagination flow with his and go . . . *go* . . . I mean, I used to be there three, four hours, and walk out with five, six hundred bucks.

AC-M: Just telling stories . . .

JR: Just telling stories . . .

AC-M: So you'd fill your foreskin to the rim with piss and . . .

JR: T . . . would place me on top of his dining room table, take out a spoon, and start eating his *pee* soup all the while crying out, "*¡Ay, qué rico está esto! ¡Qué rico está este meao!*" And I'd be like, T . . .?!!

AC-M: *¡Qué mala!*

JR: That's what *las drogas* will do to you. T . . . was in his late forties and kind of attractive. And he'd always pick up some real good-looking guys. He had a method: he'd call for delivery, and when the delivery boy got to the apartment, there would always be some porno magazines and a few lines of coke accidentally left out on the table, and before long he'd be carrying on with the delivery boy. Or he'd wait till the subway rush hour—which he'd always time—and go out into the street butt-naked, wearing nothing but a long trench coat and a butt plug. And he'd throw himself in the middle of the crowd, and look for a guy to spook, and start giving him all these goo goo eyes. And sometimes he'd score; sometimes not. And if he did, he'd start grinding his butt against the guy's crotch, and when the guy would reach down to grab his ass he'd feel this strange object, and kinda back off in disgust, "Ughh!, nooo!, this is too kiiinky for me!"

AC-M: *¡Qué bicha!*

JR: A *mamabicho bicha!* He'd tell me that sometimes he'd go to the Penn Station bathrooms (they used to be real cruisy back then), and get on his knees, and suck off a guy who was on the toilet taking a dump. And as he was giving him head, he'd push his butt against the stall's door and fuck himself with his own butt plug.

AC-M: But he'd never come?

JR: No, that wasn't his fantasy. And, yeah, the last time I saw him he actually shit on the bed. It was one of those times you're fucking a john, and he accidentally on purpose . . . *te caga.* I mean, I like a nice ass, but I'm *not* into fucking johns. And like I said, when I used to hustle a john might say he wanted to get fucked, but most of the time he just wanted to play with my dick, roll it around his mouth, caress it, pull it, blow it, gargle with it—this nice piece of Michelangelo, this 8 1/2 inch all-purpose Puerto Rican beef! But that day I could sense he'd set me up. His white silk sheets were fresh, and I'd never fucked him in that position, you know, all spread out on his back . . . like that picture of Frida Kahlo giving birth to herself. And as I started fucking him, he began to convulse like Linda Blair in *The Exorcist.* So I tried to pull out, but it was too late. And every time I'd pull out an inch of dick, a mountain of this black greenish lava would be released. And I couldn't make up my mind whether to pull out completely or push further in. Till it finally stopped, and a yellow musty cloud passed over me. And by the time I heard it explode, my body was covered with this black-green tar oozing out of his butt. And with my nose up in the air I looked down at T . . . and saw him wallowing in it, with a satisfied smirk on his face. And I felt like, "You *fucken* . . .!" And I came real close to beating his ass, which I could sense was what he wanted. And he kept looking at me with his eyes challenging me to freak on him. And I felt he could almost taste the beating. So I walked out and wouldn't give it to him.

ONE OF THESE DAYS!

AC-M: Didn't you ever think of walking out of hustling altogether?
JR: I tried, believe me I tried. But every time I'd go out and tried to get a job, they'd hire me, and as soon as they found out I couldn't read or write . . . they'd fire me. I lost quite a few jobs that way. 'Cause my reading was the worst; even after graduating from high school, I still had difficulties reading signs.
AC-M: And they still let you graduate?
JR: Yeah, my teacher in middle school would say, "Juan, read," and I'd say, "Pass." So I'd pass. And by the time I got to the tenth grade, this reading instructor spotted my problem, and hooked me up to a computer program which would flash sentences slowly and gradually pick up speed. But the program was too simple . . . So when I got to the City I still couldn't read.
AC-M: How could you function in the City if you couldn't even read the signs?
JR: I'd always buy the paper and watch the news on TV, and I'd try to match the news stories on TV with the headlines on the paper. And as I tried to make out the headlines, I'd pick up some words. Till

eventually I found myself being able to read some stories straight through. But I still couldn't read and write good enough to get a regular job. And ever since N . . . had taught me the dos and the don'ts of the trade and how to run an ad in *The Advocate*, the money was flowing in so easy I eventually told him he could retire and live off the fat of the land, so to speak. Which he did, and got fat and domestic like a cow. But I still kept thinking of a way of making money legit. And every once in a while one of my clients would say, "You know someone who can paint my apartment?" And I'd remember how much I hated having to help my father paint our house every few years. But when I found out the money behind it, I soon turned to painting. And after painting, some of my clients would say, "Can you put up some shelves?" So I started putting up shelves, and went on from there to installing light fixtures. Till finally N . . . and me decided to advertise ourselves as a construction firm. And we were making such good money we remodeled our apartment, bought a piano, a stereo, and a car.

AC-M: So you finally quit hustling completely?

JR: For about ten years. But I didn't become a homebound virgin or a housewife popping pills—like N . . . 'Cause N . . . had a tendency to stay up till three in the morning watching TV and cleaning house. And I'd ask him, "Why don't we go out to a club? Why don't we shoot some pool, or hang out?" And he'd always answer, " 'Cause that's the way I am—I just wanna stay home!" And I'd often wonder how he'd stay up till I found myself picking up his habit and discovered he was crushing speed and putting it in the food so we'd both stay up all night long . . .

AC-M: . . . watching TV?

JR: . . . watching TV and cleaning house. And when I found out I snapped at him *so* bad I almost chewed up his face. And the relationship never recovered from that. For I realized just then that N . . . was a compulsive liar—one of those guys who lie and don't even know they're lying. And as the years went by, I discovered there were a whole lotta things he'd told me that weren't true. So I started going out on my own and socializing . . .

AC-M: Where would you socialize back then?

JR: The action then was on 53rd and Third, which was as popular as 42nd St. There, where the Lipstick Building is now, all of that, was a hustlers' neighborhood. And there were three or four hustler bars—*The Cowboys, The Haymarket, Rounds* . . . —all within four blocks. And when you walked down the street, you'd see all of these pretty hustlers smoking and sitting on the stoops and hanging out . . . Central Park was lined up with fags back then—from The Museum of National History to Strawberry Fields! Tons of them. Like garlands. You didn't even have to go inside the park—by the wall, or on the other side of it, by the ditch, there'd be all these *patitos* streeetching their wings . . . And in the Rambles, people would be sunbathing in the nude . . . Once a friend of mine was visiting New York, and he and his lover got separated, and as he walked through the Rambles, he ran into a line. And at the head of the line was this guy moaning and groaning and getting wham-banged—on both ends. And wouldn't you know it? . . . it was his lover.

AC-M: Oh, no! So what did he do?

JR: He joined the line! Yeah, I tell you, I know those paths by heart . . . And every once in a while I'd go into the park late at night, and it would be so dark it'd feel like I was sleepwalking. And then one morning in the middle of winter, as I got up to watch the sunrise, this beautiful boy appeared in a trench coat. And he was naked underneath, and he spread his coat over the snow, and we made love . . .

AC-M: And did you ever see him again?

JR: No, but that day, as I was finishing remodeling an apartment on 5th Ave. and hanging out on 53rd and Third, I met my next lover, C . . . He was this straight-looking half-Trinidadian, half-Jamaican boy, with a muscular build and full sensuous lips. And when I looked at him, his eyes sparkled, and he seemed so *enchulao* that I got off. And he said he'd just come out of the closet, and had only been with this other Spanish kid for a week. And I found out later he was a Sag, and Sag and Leo, you know, have this fire thing. And as we made love, I flipped, I just *flipped*! But he was kinda weird—an s & m child, real demonic!

AC-M: Demonic?

JR: Yeah, 'cause it was maybe the third time we'd been hanging out, and I'd been working all day renovating this brownstone, and it was maybe four in the morning, and I'd gotten this cut on my arm (which I hadn't taken care of, 'cause I was *so* determined to finish the job), when he looked at me and in a real serious, steaaady voice said, "You see that knife over there?" And I said, "Yeap." "You better pick it up! 'Cause if you don't, by the time I finish with you, you're gonna wish you did!" And I could tell he was serious, and got nervous and couldn't figure out what I'd said . . . 'Cause I'd always say something, and he'd always blow up. But I was *so* tired that day I finally said, "Look, man, if you wanna kick my ass, kick it! 'Cause I've been working all day, and I'm wasted, and have a *serious* cut. So let's go out and get it over with." And somehow by the time we got outside he'd calmed down, but he was *real* determined to kick my ass . . .

AC-M: You don't remember what set him off?

JR: No, I suppose I might've mentioned N . . ., 'cause we'd just broken up, and C . . . was still jealous. You see, N . . . had found out I was having an affair with C . . ., and then one day, as I was going out, he said, "Where are you going?" And I said, "Out!" And he could tell C . . . was waiting downstairs, and started screaming, "If you go out, don't *ever* come back!!" So I picked up my clothes and never did.

AC-M: So he was really jealous then?

JR: Yeap . . . Oh, I *really* did love C . . . But no matter how much I tried, he'd always bring up my past. We'd be walking down a street and if a dude spooked me, he'd be all up in my face, "Was that one of your johns?! Was *that* . . .?!" So we'd always end up fighting and breaking up, and when I break up, you know, *yo siempre me curo* . . . with someone else, and then he'd come back in the picture all *fresco*, as if nothing had happened, as if we'd never broken up to find me with a new piece, and that would set off the war, become the bone of contention for the next six months.

AC-M: He would set you up, I guess.

JR: Yeah, and I remember this one time assuming we'd broken up, and I hadn't seen him for a while, so I started messing around with this kid. And I don't know who told him or who opened up the door for him, but someone must have, and he caught us in bed. And before I could turn around, 'cause he was *so* demented, *me dio una galleta que caí al piso* and knocked me unconscious. And as I came to, the room was spinning, and he was yelling, "I'ma show you, mother-fucka! I'ma show you! I'ma kill *you*!!," and the poor kid was holding up a dumbbell and shaking, trying to save himself . . . And I don't remember what else happened, but three days later I got to the hospital and found out he'd broken my jaw. Ha!

AC-M: And didn't *that* make you reconsider your relationship with him?

JR: No, *that* was what made me fall in love with him . . . 'Cause it showed me someone cared, cared enough, even if the issues we fought about weren't all *that* . . . And every time I went back with him I felt good . . . 'cause I never thought I'd find someone who cared . . . cared *that* much that he'd try to beat some sense into me. But then it got to the point where it made *no* sense. The past is past! And I stopped being that little Puerto Rican *tímido* kid from Connecticut and started kicking back. And we fought everywhere, in the apartment, in the streets, in the subway, in the bars, in his mother's house, in my new car!

AC-M: And after the fights you'd make up?

JR: Yeah, and that was the *best* . . . 'cause when we'd stop and made love, it was *passionate*. And I guess we both felt sorry for each other . . . And he'd try to get me to hit him, but I couldn't, and I'd end up breaking up something, so he'd feel relieved.

AC-M: Was fighting a turn on, you think?

JR: I don't know if having someone threaten me like *that* was a turn on—but I did like him being so dominant . . . *domineering*. It wasn't like I was looking for that kinda s & m love, you know; it just appeared out of nowhere . . . Once we were having sex, and I don't know what I said, but I must've set him off, 'cause he started screaming, "You're just like your fucken johns. And you like all that *shit* you be doing to your johns. I bet you even like them *water sports*!" And before I knew it, he . . . was pissing on me.

AC-M: Pissing on you!

JR: Yeah, and I felt weird, but it also turned me on, 'cause he was degrading me—treating me like a john likes to be treated, like a faggot or a bitch . . . But after he finished, *ugh*!, *noooo*!!, I felt like shit . . .

AC-M: So you *did* like C . . . 's "s & m" treatment?

JR: No, but I learned a lot from it. And I learned a lot about females and their relationships with the men who abuse them. I'd always wondered why they stayed . . . And there I was—it was happening to me!

AC-M: So why do they? Why did you?

JR: It was an obsession, I guess. There was this real magnetism between C . . . and me. And we'd go to the baths, even as that whole era of baths was dying out in the early 1980s, just to have sex with each other and no one else, 'cause that's how much we were into each other back then. And I was such a little *tímido* kid from New Haven when I first met C . . . that, whether I'd kick him back or not, he pulled something out of me that made me feel stronger. 'Cause I'd never had anyone who cared . . . cared *that* much that he'd be willing to turn everything into a bone of contention. And he cared so much that he made *me* care and fall all over him. And he made me care so much that I eventually started fighting back . . . So you see, for what it was worth, my relationship with C . . . was a good relationship.

AC-M: So when did you start fighting back?

JR: At first he'd kick me, but I wouldn't hit back. 'Cause it reminded me of when I was a little kid being threatened like that, and it made me feel . . . feel like a rag . . . But back then I'd always have my sister to defend me, 'cause she was real butch, and *nobody was going to beat up on her little brother*! So she'd take care of all the boys who wanted to beat me up. So I'd get mad, but couldn't hit him, and I'd end up taking it out on my shit. I'd smash my stereo against the wall, or throw the TV out the window, and it got to the point where I'd go through maybe one TV a month. And all along he'd be there *cucándome* and saying, "Why don't you . . .? Why don't you *hit* me?! *Hit* me!!" But I couldn't, I couldn't . . .

AC-M: So how were you finally able to strike back?

JR: I was working at Rockefeller Center, had a 1976 Mercedes, and was doing good, *real* good. I'd run into this *pargo* I'd been dealing with some years back, and he was opening a new computer store and offered to hire me as a maintenance man. So I started working there, and the guy really liked me—thought I was a smart kid, you know. And when they hired this guy to design the space I was cleaning they called me into his office, and asked me what I thought. I told them if they laid out the space like that, I guaranteed that in a year it was gonna get cluttered with computers and things. But they went ahead, and sure enough in six months they had to close down. So they called me back and asked me how I'd redo the space, where to place the feeders and tables, the traffic flow. And at the same time the company they were buying furniture from offered to lay out the store for them for free. And when we both came back with our separate sketches, the furniture company and me, we both had the same concept! So the store managers were impressed, *real* impressed and decided to give me an office in the back and have me find locations for computer stores and figure out how to lay them out. And they eventually promoted me to the Rockefeller Center store, and I had a 1976 Mercedes, was dressing up in suits, and doing great, *real* great!

AC-M: And C . . . was he happy, happy for you?

JR: He'd cheer me on, kinda, but I could sense he was also jealous, 'cause I was doing good, supporting myself—and supporting him!

AC-M: He didn't work?

JR: No, never, he just sat there and pretended he was gonna be a successful businessman some day—and I think all that pretending just *exhausted* him . . . Then one day I'd come in and was getting ready to go out, when I put down my keys, and by the time I got outta the bathroom, the keys were gone. So I said to myself, *Oh, no, this guy's not gonna play me! Not today!* So I paid him. And by the time I came out a second time the keys were back on the table. And I was getting dressed, getting ready to leave for my meeting when he said, "I'd hate to see what happened to your car!" And I was like, *Qué* fucken trip!! And the only way I could go spook my car was to go through him. 'Cause he'd barricaded himself in the apartment—with me in it! And I was late, and getting madder, and wanted to see what had happened to my car. So I tried to pull him outta the way, but he wouldn't budge. Till I finally grabbed him, looked him straight in his *demonic* eyes and said, "*¿Qué te pasa? ¿Tú quieres que te dé?! ¿Es eso?! ¿Tú quieres que te dé?!*" And I busted his face.

AC-M: Was that . . . then a turning point in your relationship?

JR: A *serious* turning point! From then on he moved outta the way.

AC-M: And had he damaged your car?

JR: No, it was just one of his *weird* little games . . . But from then on he knew I'd fight back. And we fought so often my brother would drop by and say, "*Oh, yous playing again?!*" Ha! 'Cause there were *soo* many battles!

AC-M: Do you remember what would provoke these battles?

JR: We'd fight over *everything* . . . But one time he'd always go outta his way to *irk* me was my birthday. He couldn't afford to get me a present and picking a fight was, I guess, his way of making me remember the day. Once his mother made me a cake, and we were eating and celebrating *cuando* C . . . *se puso imprudente*, and he just kept insisting, "Let's go out! Let's go *out!*" And I kept saying, "I don't wanna! Don't wanna!" 'Cause I *knew* if we did, he'd say something to irk me *and* . . . So his mother finally said, "*Goddamn*, why don't you leave the kid alone!" And they went at it. And I said, "Let's get the fuck *out!*" 'Cause C . . . loved to argue with his mom, and I just couldn't stand seeing him disrespecting her. And I drove down to the Village, picked up my friend T . . . and his lover G . . ., and ended up in the piers smoking and drinking and chilling out. And T . . . was making out with his lover, and I was looking at C . . . like, "*You know . . . we* should be doing *that . . .*" But C . . . was funny about making out in public, so I was just sitting there and thinking the night was going *too suave*, when T . . . asked me to drive him back, and I said, "Look, I'm too fucked up, but if C . . . drives, you better hold on to your *panties . . .!*" *¡Y pa' qué fue eso!* C . . . was sitting in the driver's seat warming up his feet and he got *real* mad, 'cause *he didn't like no faggoty talk in the car*, and he looked at me and turned on the ignition and hit the gas. And you know how they used to park cars in the piers back then? Like *this* and like *that* . . . Well, he took out his first car as he was on the way out, and hit a second, which started to spin, and he panicked and couldn't get his foot off the pedal, and went straight through to the highway, and all you could see were people's faces opening and closing their mouths, and hear the breaks screeeching, and the guys in the back screaming (*shiiittt!* . . . oh, *shiiitt!* . . . *fuuuck!!*), and then *smash*, *smash!*, *smash!!* We must've gone through something like five or six cars, and he was hysterical and yelling, "What do I do?! What do I do *now?!*" So I looked up at him and said, "*Drive.*" And we dashed outta there and into the tunnel, and ended up in New Jersey overlooking Manhattan, and reported the car stolen the next day.

AC-M: Wow! Wow!! . . . So C . . . would always get into arguments? . . . with his mom?

JR: Yeah, 'cause his mom was always defending me, "Why don't you fucken leave the kid alone?! Why don't you stop picking on him?!" And he'd be screaming at her, and I'd be like, *C . . ., how can you be like that? Like that to your mom?!* And then I ended up moving next to her, and we got real close. And she could tell her son was being *abusive* . . . abusive to me, and once in the middle of an argument, *el tipo éste se desaparece, se desapareció*, and his mom came in to break up the argument, and I thought it was him, so I turned around to whack him, and I punched out his mom!

AC-M: So you got *real* close!

JR: Real close. She was like a mother to me, and she loved me—like a son. And she'd always tell me she hadn't been with a man for ten

years or twelve, 'cause the last one she'd been with was a lot like
C . . . . She couldn't talk to another man, she couldn't go out of the
house, she couldn't do *this*, couldn't do *that* . . . Till one day she
just got up, picked up a gun, and told him if he didn't go, she'd
blow his brains off! And he got *scared* and left, *y nunca más
volvió* . . . And that man . . . that man was C . . . 's dad.

AC-M: C . . . 's dad?!

JR: Yeah, and his mom couldn't figure out how C . . ., who'd hardly
known his father, 'cause they had separated when he was real young,
was so much like him.

AC-M: So C . . . grew up without his dad?

JR: Yeah, and still he turned out like him . . .

AC-M: Do you think he realized he was repeating his dad's behavior?

JR: Hell no!, he had his own reasons for kicking ass . . . and most of
them had to do with me.

AC-M: Do you think he might have resented his mom for throwing his
dad out of the house?

JR: He said he loved her, his mom . . . but every time we'd fight he'd
end up saying, "Swear your mother drop dead you didn't do that!
Swear it!!" And I'd be like, "What does my mother have to do with
this?!" And I told him, "You shouldn't be swearing on your mom,
'cause one of these days she's really gonna drop . . ." Then one day
I found out his mother hadn't visited a doctor for ten or twelve
years, 'cause she was still afraid of men after what C . . . 's father had
put her through. And I'd argue with C . . ., "You should force your
mom to visit a doctor . . ." Till she finally had a stroke, and they
rushed her to the hospital, and found out she was totally
infected . . . infected with cancer.

AC-M: Wow . . . So did that improve your relationship with C . . .?

JR: Made it worse, and we finally . . . *finally* split up. And I'd visit his
mom in the hospital, but every time I'd go, he'd be sitting there just
staring at me, like saying it was my fault she was dying, and *if she
did* . . . he was gonna kill *me*! So I stopped. But his sisters kept calling and begging me to visit his mom, "You know, she's always asking for you . . ." Till one day I found out she was being released,
'cause they could do no more for her . . . and she wanted to
die . . . die at home. And I knew it'd be maybe the last time I'd see
her, so I decided to go pick her up. And I picked her up in the limousine I was driving then, 'cause I'd lost the Rockefeller Center job,
carried her into the car, sat her down, and she was on morphine but
looked good . . . *real* good. And on the way home, C . . . started
going at it, "So who the *fuck* are you're fuckin'? Who the *fuck* . . .?!"
And his mom snapped at him real hard, "Why don't you *fucken*
leave the kid alone?!" And C . . . was in the back and his mom was
up in front, but you could still feel *el* hate *que este chamaco le tenía*.
So we finally got to his mom's, and I carried her upstairs, dropped

her off, and I remember coming down the elevator to pick up her stuff, and C . . . kept following right behind me, trying to pick on my butt, accusing me of his mom's death, and I couldn't say, couldn't say a thing, couldn't talk, 'cause I had all this . . . *tristeza* I couldn't shake off. And I took his mom's stuff to her room, laid them all out real close so she could reach them, kissed her, and left . . . And on the way down, C . . . kept bringing up all these things—how it was my fault his mom was dying . . . how I'd cheated on him . . . how he was gonna *kill me*!—and I was carrying a case of yogurt his sister had given me, and I don't know how it happened, what set it off, but before I knew it, we were on the elevator *partying*, and there was yogurt all over the place . . . And we fought on into the lobby, and people kept yelling at us to stop, till I finally punched him out and ran out and was about to take off when he came back out and started jumping *up and down* on the hood of the car . . . So I thought I'd take him . . . *take him* for a ride . . . And I swear I was dead set on smashing the hood of the car with him on it against this brick wall, so he'd *finally* quit, *finally stop*!, when a car cut me off, and I slammed on the brakes, and he *flew*, just flew and came crashing down unconscious on the wall, and me, I just kept driving . . .

AC-M: So did he, did he . . . *finally* stop?!

JR: No! And no matter where I'd go this dude had a way of tracking me down . . . of haunting me. Once we had this big blowout argument, and I ran out the apartment, got on the subway, 'cause I was gonna go *somewhere, anywhere, far from him*, when I turned around and there he was—standing right in front of me, looking at me with those big *bulging* eyes . . . And we went at it—right then and there in the middle of rush hour, kicking ass and pushing people outta the way . . . And once in this gay bar I was just *so exhausted* I came right out and told him I was seeing someone else. And I could tell he was gonna kill me, so I grabbed him first, tossed him over the bar, and tried to get away. But he was too quick, too quick with his hands, and I was almost out the door when he grabbed me *y me dio tremendo galletazo* . . . pshh . . . pshhh . . . pshhhh! And that fight lasted for like for an hour, 'cause they threw us out the bar and we kept fighting on into the street. And cops would go by and look at us, "*Mira, mira a esos dos patos peleando!*" "*Go Girl!*" And there was no way of getting this man off me, 'cause every time I'd kick him, he'd turn around and slap me, "*Mira*, you can't leave me! You can't leave *me*!" And once I thought I'd finally separated from him—I had my own apartment, far away from him—and came home to find everything I owned shattered, pulled, or broke. My clothes were all cut to pieces, the mattress was *stabbed* with a knife, *y la alfombra to'a dañá*, and he wrote all kinda wicked biblical sayings on the wall . . . like that movie where Clint Eastwood comes home and finds the woman he's had a one-night affair with has totally demolished his place . . .

AC-M: Wow . . . so how *did* you finally manage to leave?

JR: Hadda leave the City to get away from C . . . And the Mafia, which was hot on my tail.

AC-M: The Mafia?!

JR: Yeah, I'd been working in the computer store at Rockefeller Center, doing great, when the union workers there started harassing me and my crew, 'cause we weren't union . . . union men. And one night someone broke in through a window, which was underneath the security guard, and the alarm never went off, . . . no one heard a thing! And the store got ripped off . . . almost completely. So my friend, the old *pargo* who'd hired me didn't wanna . . . but had no choice than to let me go. So I left and I ran into P . . ., this old friend of mine who had two cars and was looking to start a limousine service. And he let me test drive his cars and was *real* impressed with my skills. And we went into business as *Surprise Limousines.* And we started putting on ads in the paper and in fancy magazines, and eventually increased our fleet to nine cars. And we were picking up clients from *Cartier, Orion Pictures,* big companies, you know, till we got a call from the Mafia warning us, "*You need to lay off them clients!*" And my partner, *que era cojonú,* decided to tell them, "*Fuck you!*" So they hired someone to run our cars outta business. And we ended up battling them in court, and every time we'd be in court, they'd have some excuse for not showing up. Till it finally drove my friend *crazy* . . ., and I'd say, "P . . ., let's go! Let's declare bankruptcy and go to Puerto Rico! Let's go, let's go to P. R., P . . .!" 'Cause we still had money, and had shipped one of our cars to P. R., and bought this awesome condo in a real fancy neighborhood in San Juan, with a wraparound deck and an ocean view . . . But he wouldn't, and he kept getting sicker and sicker . . . Till he finally . . . died . . .

AC-M: Died . . .?

JR: Yeah, he died . . . He was a *real* nice guy . . . and I *really* did *love* him . . .

AC-M: What did he die of?

JR: AIDS. He was HIV-positive, and the stress they put him through sent him to his grave . . .

AC-M: So you left the City to get away from the Mafia, and C . . .?

JR: Yeah, I was laying low . . .

AC-M: And did you ever see C . . . again?

JR: Once after I'd already moved to Connecticut and was coming down to the City on weekends, I was sitting in a downtown restaurant with my next lover, the artist Keith . . .

AC-M: Keith? Keith Haring? The Pop artist . . .?

JR: Right. And I looked out the window and guess who was staring at me? C . . . ! And I thought, "*¡A Dioh, carajo, ahora sí que se jodió to'!,*" but he looked at me from the other side of the window, and just waived and split, and I was glad to see him . . . to see him leave . . .

AC-M: So what became of C . . .?

JR: He died of AIDS about a year ago.

AC-M: Were you still in contact with him then?

JR: No, not really, but right before he died his sister called and asked me to go visit him. And I was shocked to see how fast he'd deteriorated—*él que era flaco* to begin with . . . He'd lost all color and was completely bedridden, but he still had that *look* and I could sense he was happy . . . happy to see me . . . And then on my last birthday his sister called to tell me they were gonna bury him the next day, and I remembered how on my birthday he'd always try to surprise me, how he'd always promised he'd take me to Puerto Rico some day, how he'd always say he was gonna buy me this and that, and how by the end of the night we'd end up battling each other again, . . . and I thought, now *that* that's very C . . .

PARADISE

AC-M: So you were laying low?

JR: I was laying low and chillin' out at my parents' house in Connecticut, and on the weekends I'd come down to hang out with my friends in the City—at the *Garage.*

AC-M: The *Garage?* The *Paradise Garage?*

JR: Yeah, it was kind of a hideout for me. You'd walk in through a garage door and up a ramp with light bulbs on either side that looked like a runway or an old-fashioned marquee, and as you heard Larry's music on top, you'd feel you were about . . . about to *take off* . . .

AC-M: Larry?

JR: Larry Levan . . . one of the original DJ divas, the *only* black Buddha, the *only one* who could send me . . . *put* me in a *state* where I'd feel *los negros santeros* dancing all around me . . . 'Cause Larry had that *gift* to take the crowd to a place where you'd feel the aura of these bodies in rhythm . . . and smelled their funk down body sweat . . . And everyone there would be on drugs, and drinking juice, and freaking out—inventing all kinda moves, freestylin', dancing by yourself and with everyone else. 'Cause you didn't have to ask nobody to dance—you'd just jump in and not get off . . .

AC-M: And would you go there to hook up?

JR: No, it wasn't that kinda place—it was a very . . . *very* spiritual . . . place . . . And everyone that came out of that environment and became famous, Grace Jones, Madonna, Boy George, George Michael, liked it, 'cause nobody there paid them no mind . . . And that's where I met my next lover Keith . . .

AC-M: Keith . . . Keith Haring . . .

JR: Right. I remember once tripping and dancing with him for like two hours, but we never made contact and went our separate ways. And later a friend of mine came over and said, "You know who that was?!" And I said, "No, not really." And he said, "That was Keith Haring! The graffiti artist . . ." And I was like, "*Okay*, Keith Haring, *whatever* . . ." And a month or so later A . . ., this friend of Keith, a *cubano*, came over and kinda nervous said to me, "I don't wanna offend you or get punched in the face, but I have a friend who's a famous artist and he wants to meet you." So I said, "Okay . . ." 'Cause, I guess, that's the kinda masculine aura I gave off back then. And he introduced me to Keith, and by the end of the night we were talking and laughing, and Keith invited us to his studio, and it was flawless . . . *flawless* . . .

AC-M: Flawless?

JR: Yeah. 'Cause Keith had this thing about buying the best pot in town—you smoked it and you were like . . . in cloud ten! So his posse eventually sneaked out, and we made love, and after we made love, he was *enchulao* . . . 'cause I was top and he was *dominant* . . .

AC-M: You were *top* and he was *dominant*?!

JR: Yeah, it was one of those Taurus-Leo relationships . . . where there was all this passion to get fucked and eat dick . . . so that's what happened. He wanted to get clocked—and so he did. And by the second day he was drawing me a picture of this cartoon character with a hippo face, and by the third he wanted me to go to Brazil . . . And I remember how I'd been putting up a carpet in my mother's house earlier that day when a friend of mine came up from the City to visit. And he'd asked me if I wanted to go down to the City, and I said, "Yes!" And I told my mother I was gonna go out for a ride, but didn't come back for about two weeks. And when I got back home my mother looked at me like saying, "Where have *you* been?!" And I said, "*Brazil* . . ."

AC-M: Wow! So that's how your relationship with Keith was from the beginning—very *impulsive* . . .?

JR: Exciting! Like living with Richie Rich. And I thought any moment now Robin Leech was gonna pop up and say, "*Now here we have Keith and Juan staying at the Beverly Hills* . . ." Ha! And Keith knew about my past—how I didn't come from no money—so he'd go outta his way to thrill me . . . And I could tell he was thrilled thrilling me . . . But I guess he did that with all his boys . . . *maybe* . . .

AC-M: So it was thrilling at first?

JR: He'd literally do things to *impress* me . . . If we stayed in a hotel in the City, it was always at the *Plaza*, and if we stayed in L.A., it was the *Mondrian* or the *Beverly Hills*. And when we traveled, he'd get tickets on the *Concord* or the *MGM* . . . And if we rode around town, he'd rent a *Mercedes* convertible or a *Ferrari*. And I'd be like,

"*This is cute . . .!*" And he got off knowing I got off . . . And we'd walk into these real fancy hotels where people were like frozen . . . in time . . . and weighed down with all their jewelry, and shit, and here would come these two homies from New York with their *Nike* sneakers, threads hanging all over the floor, and painter jeans. And they'd looked at us like, "*What the hell are* you *doing here*?!" But Keith would be *real* smooth, "*Can I have the best suite in the house*?" 'Cause Keith didn't rent no rooms; he'd rent *la cocina*, *la sala*, the whole nine yards . . . And he loved throwing his money around just to let them know, "You know, you don't have to *look* like you to *live* like you."

AC-M: So he'd always try to *impress* you in the beginning?

JR: 'Cause in the beginning you got everything . . . and in the end jack shit! And it was funny 'cause every time I'd go home I'd tell my family and friends, "*Gee*, we hung out with Madonna . . . *Gee*, we hung out with Grace . . ." And they'd be like, "*Right! Este tipo es un embustero . . .!*" So Keith decided to throw me a party to introduce me to *his* society. And he traded a $16,000 painting for it, and had it at *Mr. Chow's*, 'cause Tina, his wife, was his friend. And Yoko Ono and Beverly and Iman were there, and Mick Jagger and Bianca, and Madonna and Sean Penn, and Mike Tyson and Warhol and Grace . . . And I was totally dressed Issey Miyake from head to toe— *toditito de blanco* . . . It was my thirtieth birthday, and *I was smokin'*! And I'd invited my family and friends from Connecticut, and I knew a lotta these celebrities by then, so they'd come in and wish me a happy birthday, and my family and friends were finally . . . *finally* impressed. But then everyone started coming over, "Juan, can you get me *her* autograph?" "Juan, can you get me *his* . . .!" And I'd be like, I've *never* asked nobody for an autograph!, . . . 'cause you're either hanging out with the posse or you're not, and if you're, you don't go asking for no autographs . . . you don't go, "*Can I take a picture . . .?*" And everyone was having a great time and drinking *Cristal*, and you know how *Cristal* is so smooth you don't even know you're getting high . . . Well, people started getting *blasted*. And I remember thinking how I'd been afraid to invite certain people to the party. 'Cause I knew if I put *these* people in the same room with these *other* people, they wouldn't know how to handle it! And I was talking to some high school friends and hoping to God some of these people would just get the *fuck* outta my party, when all of a sudden R . . .

AC-M: R . . ., your best friend from New Haven, R . . .?

JR: Yeah! Well . . . she gets *real patota*! You know how she gets when she gets drunk . . .? She pushes her way through the crowd holding her drink up, and she looks me *up and down* . . . like in . . . *All about Eve*. And, you know, she's not even talking, but I can tell she's saying, "I betcha think you've made it, I betcha think you're *this* and

that . . ." And she zeroes in on my hat . . . my Issey Miyake hat, and
before I knew it, she'd pulled it off, and was rubbing the bald spot
on the back of my head. And she puts it on and walks away . . . And
everyone is looking at her like, "What the *fuck*?!" Till one of my
friends says, "Who's that *tacky* faggot?!" And I'm like, "That tacky
faggot's supposed to be my best friend . . ." And yeah, that was one
time I could've smacked him upside the head! 'Cause he put me on
the *spot*!

AC-M: Yeah, *literally*! And how did the rest of your family and friends
from Connecticut get along with all those celebrities?

JR: The girls were freaking over Mike Tyson. And the guys were asking
me for his autograph. And I was right in the middle of saying, "If
you want his autograph, you're . . .," when I turn around, and guess
who's sitting on Mike's lap?! My mom! And I thought, *Oh, no!, if
my father sees her*! 'Cause she's not like *that at all*, you know—she's
very modest . . .

AC-M: Was *that* then what attracted you to Keith—his celebrity, his
status, his lifestyle?

JR: No, I was attracted to him . . . to him as a person! I just liked the
guy . . . And I thought he was cute . . .

AC-M: Cute? *Really*?!

JR: Yeah, in a Woody-Allen dorky sort of way. And after we went to his
studio and there was all this passion brewing . . . *todo se fue a juste*!
And as I've gotten older, I've learned there are some people who
have these vibes you can pick up on . . . and Keith was one of them.
He had this *aura* . . . And with Taurus men it's always like that—
fast and furious . . . And, yeah, it was a lotta fun traveling with him
all over the world, but the best part was always coming home and
hanging out with Keith. 'Cause as soon as we landed, he'd have the
limo go to Coney Island, 'cause he liked the boys there . . . and
there were *tons* of them! And his ride was always the roller
coaster . . . But that's the one ride I just wasn't crazy about, 'cause
I'd always catch myself running out of breath . . . smack in the middle of it. And I remember once when I was little almost passing out
till my sister showed me how to psych myself for the twists and the
turns . . . But I couldn't always do it . . . couldn't always go around
the world, get off the plane, and get on the roller coaster at Coney
Island, 'cause sometimes I was too tired or too upset . . . And Keith
would always say, "Oh, come on Juan, don't be such a fag! Come
on, boy!" And I'd say, "Okay, boy, okay . . ." And I'd always end up
getting on it and *trying* to figure out when the next drop was coming . . . the next drop . . .

AC-M: So it was stressful then to have a relationship with Keith?

JR: No, not at first. *He* was the one who wanted it. And he kinda threw
it at me, "Why don't you come and move in and we'll try this
out . . .?'" So I moved into his studio, 'cause he was still living with

Juan Dubose, this black kid who eventually died of AIDS . . . And
when they finally broke up, he wanted to move into a new apartment. So I found one, built it, painted it. And I worked in the
house, kept it together, cleaned it, and cooked. And I drove the
limo, did some construction, stretched out his canvases, even helped
him paint . . . *You know that mural in Paris* . . .?

AC-M: . . . the one for the children's hospital?

JR: Yeah, he'd draw the outlines with these real cool colors, and I'd fill
them in . . . So I eventually fell in love with the guy . . . 'cause he
was good to me . . . But there was a couple of times I almost walked
out. 'Cause I wasn't gonna have it! *Wasn't!* But he'd always make it
sound like, "Juan, don't worry! I'm always gonna take care of you.
That's just the way I am . . ." So I said, Okay . . . But I always knew
there would eventually be someone else . . . And in time . . . I
guess . . . that's what happened . . .

AC-M: What would upset you enough to make you want to walk out
on Keith?

JR: That he'd always have to have boys around him—to keep his creative juices *flowing* . . .

AC-M: And did he need a lot of boys to keep his creative juices *flowing?*

JR: Lots. He used to hang out at these outlaw parties which people
would throw in places like abandoned buildings or vacant schools.
And there would always be rap music, and graffiti art, and lotsa pot,
and people would be selling brownies spiked with weed and shit.
And somehow Keith would always know where the latest outlaw
party was, which was mostly in Loisaida, in the Puerto Rican neighborhood, in the Lower East Side. And all of these homies would
come outta nowhere to hang. And whenever he saw a cutie at one of
these parties his tail would start *wagging como un perro sato* . . . and
lose control . . . And when he'd do his street art it'd be just like
that—he'd have rap music, and lotsa pot. And the boys would come
outta the woodwork to watch . . . *a master at work*, and get high.
And if he saw a cutie, he'd zero in on this kid . . . till he'd finally
invite him to his studio . . .

AC-M: . . . like he invited you?

JR: Yeah . . . but by then I was living with him . . . And it got to the
point where I just *hated* having to go to the studio to see *who* the latest piece in his Polaroid collection was . . .

AC-M: He kept a Polaroid collection of boys?

JR: Yeah, 'cause it was all about boys . . . boys . . . *boys* . . . And I knew
that was part of his creative energy—what made his energy flow—
'cause there would always be a bunch of kids hanging out at his
studio watching him paint, and he'd always have great music, food
from *Balducci's*, and the *best* pot. And it was cool, *real* cool watching him paint . . . but *damn*!!

AC-M: Do you remember your first time watching him paint?

JR: I remember the first time . . . I was familiar with his subway art, but didn't think it was all *that*. 'Cause I thought any caveman could've done it . . . But when I saw him paint . . . *Wow!* The way he moved around the room without a sketch! And the *size* of it! Like in Detroit where he took this *huge* room which was square, and by the time he'd finished, it was round! And he painted quickly! Sometimes preparing the scaffold would take longer than painting, like when he painted *The Ten Commandments*, which took only three days . . .

AC-M: *The Ten Commandments?* The mural? That's my favorite!

JR: Me too. And the way he portrayed the Commandments . . . I mean, I'm not very religious, so I didn't really recall all my Commandments, but when you looked at these images you knew, you just *knew*, "Oh, Thou shall not take the Lord's name in vain". . . "Oh, Thou shall not lie". . . 'Cause they were *so* . . . modern, and some *so* . . . pornographic . . . "Thou shall not lie" had two home-boys sucking off the cross, and "Thou shall not steal," a homeboy walking around with a hard-on . . . hoarding things . . . And most of them were about boys . . . boys . . . *boys* . . .

AC-M: So Keith needed all this boy sexual energy for his work?

JR: Yeah. And I could understand . . . but *damn*! A lotta times it was just nerve-wracking having to compete . . . And people would always go outta their way to introduce him to some new kid. So I finally decided to let him . . . let him be—what he did or *who* he did in his studio was his world! And I know I let him have his cake and eat it too, but, *fuck it!*, I thought, I could have my cake and eat it too . . .

AC-M: And *did* you . . . have your cake and ate it too?

JR: No, not really, not till the last year when I had an affair with D . . ., this stacked-up white girl Keith nicknamed D . . . Dick. But by then he was too busy with Gil to notice. But my ideal has always been a steady relationship—it just hasn't happened yet, I guess . . .

AC-M: So Keith was having relationships with all these kids who visited his studio?

JR: No, not all . . . but *most* . . .

AC-M: So the kids were gay?

JR: They were gay, . . . they were straight . . . They were these artsy-farty seventeen-to-eighteen-year-olds who were into the arts and the *happening* scene. And when you hung out with Keith, you'd be hanging out with Grace, Iman, Brooke, Beverly, Madonna . . . So you *knew* scenes were gonna be happening. And the kids *liked it*. So they were impressed . . . *real* impressed . . . 'Cause it was a totally *cool* environment . . .

AC-M: *Scenes?* What kinds of scenes?

JR: Most of the time wherever Keith hung out was the scene. He'd show up with his posse of kids at an event. And the event could be a show by Clemente, a party for Jean-Michel Basquiat, or the opening of Keith's latest work, *whatever*, a party for someone famous (or almost famous) given by someone rich. 'Cause the people around him were *loaded* . . . *stupid* rich. And Keith would bring in the posse, and the music, and the *ultimate* pot. And he'd carry a b-box, decorated with cartoon figures by Kenny Scharf. And people would gather around him—graffiti artists, street kids, the hoods, and the rich—listening to music, and smoking pot . . .

AC-M: . . . at museums and galleries?

JR: At the Whitney. I remember once everyone smoking pot at the Whitney—*hasta las viejitas.* Keith had Larry Levan's music on, and everyone was drinking *Cristal*, 'cause that was his drink, when all of a sudden Keith lights up, and people start gathering around the smell of weed. And all of these rich *viejitas* hanging out at the Museum and trying to find a *boyfriend* start shoving each other, "Let me get in there! Let me get in . . .!" Ha! I mean, it was *cool* to have *that* kinda power to go somewhere and create a *scene*. And most people loved it . . . loved the *flava* Keith was bringing to these places. Except maybe Kenny Scharf . . ., 'cause *he* was *so* bitter . . . And Jean-Michel . . .

AC-M: Jean-Michel? Was he jealous of Keith?

JR: No, but Keith loved the crowd; Jean-Michel *hated* it. And he'd walk around, "*Juan*, let's get away from these *fucken* white people . . .!" 'Cause he had no time for these *trashy* white people who thought his work was all *that*. And he couldn't understand why they were so *obsessed* with him. I mean, he'd probably do drugs, and freak out, and throw up on canvas whatever messages he was getting from up beyond, and all of these white people would be there—just eating it up! And there were times Jean-Michel would lock himself in the bathroom, and Keith would have to go spook him out, and he'd be like, "*This* party, man, and *these* people—they are just *not* my style . . ." I mean, if he'd had his way he probably would have spit on them, but then again they probably would have been like, "Oooh, *gosh*, could you do *that* again?!"

AC-M: So many of Keith's *scenes* were like an "outlaw party" or a night at the *Garage*—except with rich people and *Cristal*?

JR: Right. 'Cause there was a certain crowd who knew each other from the *Garage*—Iman, Beverly, Madonna, Grace . . . —and they'd been hanging out since like the late 1970s. And as their careers flourished—as models, singers, and artists—they kept hanging out. So they'd go to each other's events . . . but they were like a *wild* and dysfunctional family . . .

AC-M: How wild?

JR: *Wild*, and the wildest was Grace. She had a restaurant, 'cause a lotta celebrities were opening restaurants then, and we'd go there to eat and hang out. And most of the time she'd be playing her own music, getting high, and talking about how she *should've been a man* . . . instead. And once I was helping Keith with this huge skirt he'd painted for her, 'cause she was gonna be wearing it at *Roseland*, and I was supposed to be underneath the skirt holding her up on a scaffold while Keith painted her. And as I was holding her up, she started *sweating . . . y se prendió Grace . . . se prendió*, and the whole skirt started *smelling . . . a toto*! And Grace was on top singing and calling me out in her deep *deep* voice, "*Juan, don't my pussy smell sweet . . .? Juan, don't my pussy . . .?!*" Ha! Ha!!

AC-M: Ha!! . . . But wouldn't Keith get jealous?

JR: No. Not with Grace. But he did have this rivalry thing . . . with Madonna. And it was all about *boys* . . .

AC-M: Boys? What kind of boys?

JR: Street-looking Latino boys . . . 'Cause they both liked the *same* boys. And when I first met Madonna I remember being warned by Keith if I even came close . . . that would be *it* for me. 'Cause Keith had had this big falling out with Madonna over this Puerto Rican kid named B . . . M . . . You see, Keith had been going out with B . . . M . . ., and one day he'd taken him to Madonna's birthday party and said kinda jokingly and *boasting*, "Madonna, here, your birthday present . . . ." And Madonna, wouldn't you know it? *took him* . . . took him at his word, and wasted no time in snatching up the kid. And ever since then Madonna and Keith hadn't really been talking. So when I first met Madonna she was sitting with her man Sean on one side of the table, and me and Keith were on the opposite end, and all the way across the table she'd give me these *long* lusting looks like *ummmm* . . . ! And meanwhile I was spooking her man! Ha! 'Cause Sean was cute—and had *mucho* attitude!

AC-M: But didn't you ever feel *used*?

JR: Used?!

AC-M: Yeah. Didn't you ever feel that you and the posse of kids were being used by Keith and his crowd to add *flava* to their events?

JR: That was what was cool about it—*the mix*! And I was having a good time—and so were the kids.

AC-M: So you felt everyone in K . . . 's crowd was accepting of you and the kids?

JR: Not all, but *most* . . . And a lotta times the person standing next to Keith when we'd hang out with his artsy friends was me, and I'd stand there and listen or help . . . But then when we'd go to a party and all these celebrities would be chillin', I'd show up and everyone would be *Juan! Juan!* So that made me feel welcome . . . And yeah, there were people who I always *knew* felt that these *lowlife Puerto Rican* kids were bringing down Keith. But that's 'cause they wanted his fame, or his money, or his boys, or wanted him for themselves . . . But if anything, we were . . .

AC-M: . . . you were?

JR: . . . his inspiration, I guess, what motivated him . . .

AC-M: But don't you think he also took a lot from these kids and the street, hip-hop culture they came from and used it to promote his art . . . and himself?

JR: A lotta people would say *that* . . . 'Cause the aborigines had used the same images and Keith had just *swiped* them! But it wasn't a matter of swiping—Keith knew how to continue the conversation. And he knew how to continue the line with the street artists.

AC-M: But don't you think he *used* graffiti artists to promote his work?

JR: He *collaborated* with them. And some graffiti artists, like L.A., he helped a *lot*. But the problem with L.A. was fame hit him too hard. And by the time I met him, yeah, Keith was up and over with him. He was a pretty young boy but kinda *tímido*, you know, *un jíbarito*, when Keith first met him. And Keith took him under his wings, and traveled through Europe with him. And when I first went to Europe I was surprised to see how much juice L.A. had there, 'cause a lot of people knew him and thought he was *totally* cool. But L.A. never followed up on *that*. And he eventually got fat, and would get high and act real loud like he was Mr. Big. But by then he wasn't doing *nothing*, 'cause graffiti art was no longer all *that*.

AC-M: So Keith kind of outgrew him?

JR: Yeah, 'cause L.A. . . . stayed small . . .

AC-M: . . . *local*?

JR: Yeah, 'cause Keith traveled a *lot*, and his images were known all over the world, and people would be constantly calling him from everywhere—galleries, museums, major businesses . . . Once we were staying in the South of France, and they called him from a cosmetics company to paint this model's body for a new line of sunscreen. And Keith thought it was *cool* and agreed to do it, and they were paying him *mucho* bucks. And we were staying with these people who were kinda playboyish, Yves, the very handsome, debonair son of the famous painter Arman, and Debby, his wife, this rich Texas girl who was *totally* sexy. And they were wild and crazy people, and every day with them was some sort of *event*. Yves was a free-lance photographer for *Penthouse*, and he was constantly spooking young girls. And Debby was like hanging out and *trying* to figure out if she was gonna get upset. And then finally the day came when the project was supposed to start, and this gorgeous woman, taller than Keith, shows up. *Y esa mujer era bella*, I mean, *bella!, pero laaarga . . . como el cielo*. And real sexy. And Yves's tail started wagging, and Debby was looking at him all pissed off, 'cause Yves was on top of the woman, "Would you like *this*? Would you like *that*?" And Debby was like, "You fucken faggot!" So Keith decided to hire her and started painting her right then and there in Yves's living room facing the water and Princess Grace Ave. And as Keith was painting her with his fingers in bright colors and African style, as he'd done with Grace, Yves was going cuckoo, 'cause the woman was naked except for her . . . *panties* . . . And when Keith finished she was *flawless*—like a fucken walking piece of art! And we had to take her through the streets naked to this legendary hotel in Monaco where a lotta movies had been shot. And it was rush hour and cars were honking and breaks squeaking, and this woman was strutting, just strutting down, carrying on with the photographer, playing to the camera, till about five police cars come swooping down and . . . *wee*!! "Why is this woman *naked*?! What the hell do you think *you* are doing?! It's causing all these traffic jams!" And Yves was trying to explain, "It's an art project . . . No, I don't have no permit . . . But my father is Arman . . ." And the cops were getting angrier, and people kept gathering while the woman kept posing—*to the right, to the left, a lo loco* . . . Till the cops finally warned us *if this woman doesn't put on something . . ., you're all gonna get busted*! So Keith brought out a canvas and opened it in front of the cops, and before the cops could finish asking, "*What the fuck*?!!" in French, of course, she'd thrown herself on the canvas and started rolling up and down and making a print of herself. And Keith and me were rubbing her against the canvas, and the cops were freaking out. Till they finally escorted us back to the house . . . in front of the camera and to the applause of the crowds, and they made some phone calls . . . but decided to press no charges . . .

AC-M: Wow! That was some *scene*! So every day was some sort of event like that?

JR: Yeah, constantly. 'Cause we'd always hang out with some real big time people in Europe. If we went to the races, the *Grand Prix*, we'd be hanging out with the winner of the race. And if we went to a club, we'd be hanging out with Princess Stephanie and Caroline. And once Debby asked me to cook dinner for Princess Caroline. And I was like, "Princess Caroline? That would be an honor!" 'Cause I cook pretty good, you know, when it comes down to it. But it's usually something *criollo* or something pretty quick. And Debby knew my cooking 'cause she'd been to our apartment in New York *con el hijo de Pablo Picasso*, Claude. They wanted to see this real cool apartment people had been talking about we lived in, and they came over, and I cooked. 'Cause I'd always cook for Keith and keep house—it wasn't like I was living off him! And they loved it . . . *loved* my cooking.

AC-M: So what were you gonna be cooking for Princess Caroline?

JR: *Algo boricua*, you know, *arroz blanco, habichuelas colorás, ensalada de aguacate, pollo frito*—what I'd always cook for Keith. But that's the best! 'Cause Keith *loved* my cooking, and it was always an honor seeing him *ohhhing* and *ahhhing* my food. So the day came, and before Princess Caroline got there, the Palace security guards checked out Debby's place. And as I was getting ready to cook my dinner, Debby stepped into the kitchen and handed me this pot of

beans—with the pods and everything! And I was like, "What's *that*?!"
And she, "The beans! The beans you're gonna cook for Princess
Caroline." And I was like, "I'm not cooking with *that*! Don't you
have a can? A can of beans—*Goya* beans?!" And she was like, "No!,"
and kept insisting I cook with her beans. So I went into my bag, got
a can of beans I'd brought with me from New York, opened it, and
seasoned them, and made my beans. So the beans were done, and
the rice was done, and I was right in the middle of frying some
chicken when Debby walked back in, "Juan, that's not gonna be
enough!" And I was like, "Well, if it's *royalty* that's coming, one
piece's enough—they're not gonna *chow* down two or three pieces
like we Puerto Ricans do!" But she kept insisting . . . And I knew
she liked my cooking, but *damn*! So I decided to take a shower, and
get cleaned before I continued frying more chicken, and I told the
maid to put on the fire real low to make sure the food stayed warm.
And here I am taking a shower and feeling *flawless*, 'cause everything is turning out just *great*, when I started smelling . . . *burned
rice*! So I rushed out the shower, put on my dress pants, got back in
the kitchen with no shirt, no shoes, and my feet all wet. And the rice
wasn't totally burned, *pero olía a quemao* . . . And here I was trying
to save the rice, remembering my mother's advice to air it out
and put onions on it, when in came Yves with Princess Caroline
and said, "And here we have Chef Juan Rivera, preparing tonight's
delicious . . ." And there I was *en la cocina tó mojao*, 'cause I'd
rushed outta the bathroom, no shirt, no shoes on, being introduced
to the princess of Monaco, and feeling like the *only pendejo* . . .

AC-M: Ha! Ha! . . . And did they eat your food?

JR: Yeah! And *loved* it! Princess Caroline ate the rice and beans, which
were burned too, with *Cristal*! And she thought it was *flawless*! And
I couldn't speak to her that evening, 'cause she wasn't speaking in
English—only in French. But I got friendly with the woman who
was hanging out with her, and she spoke Spanish and said to me,
"You know, these beans have kinda smokey flavor." And I said,
"Well, they are *smoked* Puerto Rican beans." And after I told her
what had happened we both ended up drinking *Cristal* and
laughing . . . hysterically.

AC-M: So some big time people in Europe would constantly want to
hang out with you and Keith?

JR: Yeah, and sometimes they liked us so much it was scary!

AC-M: Scary?

JR: Yeah, and weird! We'd run into all these couples who liked us so
much they wanted to get laid by the both of us in the worst sorta
way. And they'd come on to us, "We'll send the kids to bed, and
we'll go and smoke some *pot*. *Okay*?!" 'Cause *pot* for them was the
ultimate. And they'd smoke and get high, *y querían chichar . . . a la
mala*! Once in Venice we were dealing with this big time businessman

who was a supplier of weapons to some foreign country and art dealer on the side. And Keith and him were negotiating over dinner, and I was talking to his wife when I started noticing she was giving me these *goo-goo* eyes. So I looked at Keith, and we tried to excuse ourselves and told them we were gonna go get high on *E*, and they got real excited and wanted to try some, so we ended up splitting our *Ecstasy* with them. And we were on *Ecstasy* when the gondola shows up to pick us up and take us back to their place. And there we were riding the waters in the middle of this darkness and this . . . *stench* . . . And Keith was up in front talking with the guy, and me and his wife were riding in the back in this compartment. And you could tell she was getting giddy and *girly*, sticking out her tongue, and opening her legs, *y la mujer se estaba calentando*, and getting ready to attack. And I was like, *Oh, no!, nooo!!* And she had a good body, but her *face*—man, the Wicked Witch of the West was like Lady Di next to her! So I tried to pay her no mind, and decided to move up in front. But in the meantime her husband up in front kept telling Keith how fed up he was with his wife, how he wanted to just . . . *murder* her! And Keith was looking at me like, "This guy's *tripping*!" So we got off, walked around those deserted alleys in Venice and went back to the house to sleep. And there we were back in the house trying to sleep when this guy starts knocking on our door. And we open, and he was standing there *butt naked*. Hah!! So we told him, "*Thanks*, but no thanks." And he was like, "What about my wife? Would you take my wife?" And he was already calling her when we shut the door and went back to bed. But we could sense they were standing there just waiting. And I guess we were in *their* home and we were *their* guests, so they probably figured we owed it to them—to clock'em! And one of them would probably end up getting hurt, and we'd be chased all over Venice . . . for murder!

AC-M: So they were *obsessed* . . .

JR: *Obsessed*! And they wanted a piece of us, literally. Or to be us, like in Japan.

AC-M: . . . in Japan?

JR: Yeah, 'cause they loved Keith there and there were all these tacky images of his work—all over the place. And when we got there people would be trying to impress us by taking us to these Japanese homeboy clubs where they'd be playing New York City music, and kids would be hanging out and showing off their latest moves . . . And they were all very modern and keeping up with our styles, but I thought it was *weird*, 'cause they'd be wearing our styles to the fullest—like at a costume ball. So the second time we went there Keith took a nice posse of New York City kids and paid all their way. But after they walked through Shibuya and looked at the neon signs there, they got bored with Tokyo and just *hated* it. And, yeah, my first time in Tokyo was *cute*, but after a while you just wanna get away from perfection, 'cause everything there's *perfect*, and you start craving some dirt.

AC-M: And how did Keith feel about seeing all these images of his work?

JR: He thought it was *cool*. But then he started bugging out, 'cause he couldn't tell if they were connecting with him or with those hyped-up tacky images of his work. And the New York kids were all dissing Tokyo, so he started getting frantic . . . and *pissed*. And I was like in the middle—between him and the kids. And it got to the point where he started picking on me. I couldn't open my mouth without him snapping at me. And once we went to this restaurant, and me and the kids were on one side of the table, and Keith and his artsy friends were on the opposite end, and the waiter screwed up my order, and I went to say something when Keith blew up, and started yelling at me. And everyone could tell he was *not* in the mood and was taking it out on me. And I don't know what was going on with him—if he was already sick, or seeing Gil . . . But I had had it, and wasn't gonna stick around and be humiliated like this! So I went back to the room, got up the next morning, took my passport and ticket and flew back to New York. And when I got to Customs they couldn't understand how I'd flown around the world without a fucken *maleta*. So they took me into this room, put me through this machine, felt me up, and had me take off my shoes. And they kept asking me what the bubble in the sole of my sneakers was, and I kept saying, "They're *Air Jordans*! *Nike Air Jordans*!" But they kept messing with my shoes, and I was about to tell them not to pull off my odor-eater patch, 'cause if they did they were gonna get some *serious* whiff . . . when the room started *stinking* . . . And they hadda . . . hadda let me go . . .

AC-M: So you split up with Keith then?

JR: No, I just wanted him to think things over . . . 'Cause the first time we'd gone to Japan he'd been so *enchulao* he'd gotten us wedding bands and we'd painted the town red. But now he'd gotten so obnoxious . . . and *cold* . . . that there was nothing I could do that wasn't *wrong*. And I guess he must've already been dating Gil . . . And after Japan he went on to Europe, and by the time he got back, he had all these KS spots . . . all over him . . .

AC-M: Kaposi's sarcoma lesions . . . ?

JR: Yeah.

AC-M: Did you know he had AIDS?

JR: No, he never told me. And when he finally did, all he said was, "You better get yourself checked!"

AC-M: And did you—get yourself checked?

JR: Yeah. And I found out I had ARC—not AIDS.

AC-M: And how did you *feel* . . . about *that*?

JR: I wasn't struck by it—not at all. And I swear to God, it didn't bother me. And if the doctor had said I had AIDS, I would've accepted that too. Like saying you're pregnant. *Wow*, like I didn't know *that*!

AC-M: So you weren't surprised?

JR: No. And when the doctor told me, I was like, "What does *that* mean?" And he made it sound like I had three years. So I said, "Three years . . ." And I was a little *struck* by that, but I said, "Wow, that's good." And when I went to another doctor he gave me two years—if I didn't get on AZT . . . And ever since then every doctor I've seen is like, "Haven't you heard your prognosis?" But when it comes down to it, I've been experiencing the thrush, the fungus on the feet, and the cold sweats ever since like the late 1970s. So, no, I wasn't surprised . . . 'Cause I'd come to the City to try to be a successful and *good* person, and believing I was a person of good, and all of a sudden there's this epidemic, and those of us who have to use the streets to survive have to be so *damn* aware that most of us are dead.

AC-M: Did you ever talk to Keith about his illness?

JR: No. And *that* really bothered me. 'Cause he'd come home and act like I didn't exist. And if he got horny, he'd just shut the door, watch his videos, *y se acabó*. And, yeah, there were times I'd go to his side and try to be *amable con él*, but he was so *fucken* cold—it wasn't funny. And I knew he was dying, but I couldn't do a thing! 'Cause he'd always be in a state of anger, and most of the time he'd take that anger out on me.

AC-M: Didn't you think he might have wanted you out? Out of the apartment?

JR: No, but *maybe* . . . And in this relationship had I stayed on *a la mala*, had I been more *cojonú*, had I battled with him . . . 'Cause with Taurus men, you know, you have to wave that red cape and hit 'em upside the head to keep 'em interested! And maybe I was *too* nice . . . 'Cause I know he wrote me a couple of times saying how nice I was and how I *deserved* better . . . But being nice, *where* did it get me?! 'Cause I could always sense the more *cojonú* I was the more he'd desire me . . . 'Cause Keith was always like *that*—he always wanted what he couldn't have, or be. Like Gil . . .

AC-M: So was Gil his ideal, his fantasy boy—what he couldn't have . . . or be?

JR: Gil was this street-looking young Puerto Rican boy, straight, supposedly, and with a girlfriend. And they were supposedly *buddies*—not lovers. But if you've got an obsession like *that*, I guess you gotta call it something . . . *Y él hasta le hizo un libro a ese chamaco*, and dedicated it to him: Gil Vazquez . . .

AC-M: How did you find out about Gil?

JR: Well, Keith was never very discrete about his flings. At some point he'd slip or leave a Polaroid picture of his latest piece on his desk. So I think I might've seen Gil's picture there, and I found out he worked at *ACU Joe's* on Astor Place. And I remember Keith deciding to go to Europe by himself. And I'd usually travel with him, 'cause I was Keith's lover, travel companion, and friend. And something told me to check *ACU Joe's*, and when I got there they told me Gil had gone to Puerto Rico for two weeks. And somehow I knew he hadn't gone to Puerto Rico, but had gone to Europe instead. So I waited for Keith to get back to New York and decided to go meet him at the airport. And when I got there I spooked him out at a distance, and there was Gil, standing by his side. So I said, Okay, that's *cool*, and left.

AC-M: So you finally split up with Keith?

JR: Yeah, separated . . . I just got up one morning, and I couldn't understand why I'd been so totally rejected by Keith. And I was feeling bad . . . *real* bad . . . and thinking how here I was in this relationship with a man who was dying, and I couldn't do a thing. 'Cause he didn't—didn't want *me*. And I thought real hard, and decided it'd be selfish of me to wait around till he hadda get a new apartment. So I stepped aside, and let him enjoy the little bit of time he'd left in his own apartment.

AC-M: Did you hear from Keith after that?

JR: He called me once from Europe while he was traveling with Gil, 'cause Yves, our friend in Monaco, had just passed away in a traffic accident. And Keith was so devastated he would have preferred me being there instead of Gil. And I remembered all the times we'd hung out with these two crazy people, Yves and Debby. And how there were times Yves would drive so fast Keith and me would stick our heads out the window and the wind would deform our face. And sometimes Grace would be in the car, and she'd be screaming at the top of her lungs, "*Sácale el pie al pedal ése. Sácale el pie!!*" Till Yves would pull over and let her walk home. And Yves would drive so close to the edge of those cliffs in Monaco that you'd feel you were about to drop . . . off. But Keith and me didn't mind really, and figured, if it happened, let's just enjoy the ride down and hope it's not too long.

AC-M: And did you ever see Keith again?

JR: Right before he died he called me. And I was spooked, 'cause here he was calling me right before he passed away. And I was already seeing J . . . C . . ., and he was going through changes, 'cause he thought I was gonna leave him, but I told him, "This man *needs* me, and I wanna be there for him." So I went to visit him, and stayed with him three days. And during those three days I was being affectionate to him, and he was being affectionate back to me. And I remembered he'd once asked me to sign a palimony agreement to make sure I wouldn't take him to court some day. And I'd said, "Sure, give me the papers. I'll sign them!" 'Cause he felt everyone always wanted something from him, and I wanted to let him know that it wasn't like that with me. And when he saw my reaction he backed off. So when he called me to his side those last three days I felt that he'd finally realized, he'd finally understood, that if anyone *loved* him for who he was . . . it was me.

AC-M: So did you sign the papers?

JR: No, never did.

AC-M: And did he put you in the will?

JR: No. And I remember those last three days we spent together he went on a mission to sell this picture of a cartoon character with a hippo face he'd drawn for me. 'Cause, I guess, he knew he was gonna be leaving me hanging. So he figured he hadda accomplish that much . . .

AC-M: And did he—sell the piece?

JR: Yeah, for $70,000, and he left that to me.

AC-M: But didn't you get any money from his estate—the estate he built during those three years he was with you?

JR: No.

AC-M: Who did?

JR: I heard Gil ended up with some of Keith's pieces, a little recording studio, and a BMW that was supposed to be mine. And I suppose his family must've gotten some. But most of Keith's money went to the Foundation.

AC-M: The Foundation . . .?

JR: The Keith Haring Foundation to promote his art and to support organizations working with AIDS and kids. Especially homeless and runaway kids.

AC-M: How ironic . . .

JR: Right . . . 'Cause some time after that I developed AIDS, and went to the Foundation to ask for some money, so I could go visit a doctor and buy vitamins. And Julia Gruen, Keith's old assistant who I'd known for years, was now directing the Foundation, and she wrote me back that I needed to get a job and go for counseling at GMHC! And she said the Foundation didn't give away money to people, *even* Keith's lovers, 'cause they *knew* what they'd do with it.

AC-M: And what would you have done with it?

JR: Buy food, vitamins, some decent clothes, go to a dentist, get a *fucken* phone, visit my family . . . Live—just live.

AC-M: So how did you end up making a living?

JR: Hadda go back to hustling . . . 'Cause my finances were *the worst*! And I couldn't get a job, had AIDS, and needed to take care of myself. So I put an ad on an escort service line. And it was the day before Father's Day, and I had no money and needed a trick, so I could go visit my dad, when I got a call on the numbers line. And the guy on the other side of the line asked me to meet him at a restaurant in the Upper West Side. And when I got there, all these people were hanging around him. And as soon as I showed up he snapped his fingers, and everyone just got up and left. And I was like, *Who the fuck is this girl?*! And he sat me down, flashed all these magazines covers with his picture on them, and kept telling me how *famous* she was . . .

AC-M: And *who* was he?

JR: David Hampton . . .

AC-M: The guy they based that play and film on, *Six Degrees . . .?*!

JR: Yeap. And we spent the night together, and I told him I was HIV-positive, but he didn't care, didn't wanna play it safe. And he thought I was very *special*. And he was a Taurus—like Keith. And the next morning I was waiting to get paid, so I could go borrow a friend's car and visit my dad when he insisted I had to take his car instead. And he insisted so much I finally said, Okay! So we walked through the park talking, and laughing, and goofing all the way. But when we got to the West Side he wanted to have lunch first. So we went to a restaurant, and he ordered all this food, and in the middle of lunch he got up to make a call and let his people know we were on our way. And I waited and waited, and an hour went by, and I started eating slower and slower, but he never showed up. And there I was in this fancy restaurant—*no* money and all this food! So I finally told the waitress I'd leave her my driver's license and my watch while I went to an ATM to get some cash. And I ended up walking home. And never made it to Connecticut for Father's Day.

AC-M: And did he ever contact you again?

JR: Three days later he called me back and told me he'd been in an accident. And I said, "Sure, *that* explains *that*." And I told him how I had to leave my driver's license and my watch at the restaurant. And he said, "Don't worry, I know—I've got them. Just come by my house." *Pero ese perro ya me había mordío*, so I went back to the restaurant instead. And sure enough, they still had my driver's license and my watch. And they let me pay for my part of the meal, and I called him back, "*Fuck it*! The game's over! I've got my driver's license and my watch!" But *still* . . . I stayed in touch with him . . .

AC-M: Why?!

JR: 'Cause he was legendary for being like that . . . Once he called me to tell me the Keith Haring Foundation was having a party, and *was I invited?* And he knew how the Foundation had treated me, and he was *pissed*. 'Cause he felt Keith owed it . . . owed it to me—to leave me in the will after he passed away. And I said, "No." And he was like, "This *fucken* white people . . . Ain't it just like them!" And he took it upon himself to get me invited, and wanted me to give him

Julia Gruen's home number, but I wouldn't. So he said, "Watch me! And stay on the line, so you can see how crafty I can be." And he called the Hamptons, 'cause he knew Julia had a house there, and he made it sound like he was from the press, and sure enough, he got Julia's home number in New York. And he called her, and got an invitation and a press packet, and ended up going to her apartment dressed as a delivery boy to pick it up. And he came back to my apartment with his booty—the "*authorized*" biography of Keith by John Gruen, Julia's dad. And the party was a celebration of Keith's life in Kutztown, his birthplace. And it was weird 'cause when Keith had died the funeral had been there, but almost none of his friends from New York had been invited. People like G . . . or A . . . who'd been his right-hand assistant and closest friend, and none of the posse from Lower East Side or the *Paradise Garage*. And Julia, who'd arrange the service, was holding on to Keith's ashes like they were her . . . baby. And, yeah, it was nice, 'cause we spread Keith's ashes on top of a hill in a corn field where Keith used to play, and as we spread them, the sun went down, and the sky turned red, and a flock of *pájaros* flew overhead. And I couldn't help it and broke down and ran down the hill crying. And when the service was finished Julia came over, "*Well, it seems that you always have to have the last word!*"

AC-M: And did you—have the last word?

JR: Didn't mean to . . . But David kept insisting that I hadda go to the Foundation's party! So he read me portions of John Gruen's book—how me and *these Puerto Rican gay hustlers* had brought down Keith, according to Kenny Scharf–and he read the Foundation's letter to me. And he took me to this lady at a restaurant, who turned out to be the celebrity columnist, Florence Alexander, and she had the letter printed in *The Post*—on *Page Six*.

AC-M: Wow! And how did people react to *that*?

JR: It was a *scandal!* The headline read "*AIDS Fund Stiffs Founder's Pal.*" So the Foundation finally decided to fork over some money—a small living stipend. But soon after that they stopped making payments, 'cause Julia kept insisting I wasn't in the will. So a year or so later I was back to square one, and David, who'd helped me, had *fled*. And every once in a while he'd call me to tell me he couldn't make it down to the City, 'cause *she* was in *Paris* . . . So I assumed *Paris* was jail. And there I was penniless, without a job, with full-blown AIDS, and *depressed*. And I got myself into such a depression that I started *wasting*.

AC-M: Wasting?

JR: Yeah, I developed wasting syndrome—*yo que siempre he sido flaco pero duro*–was looking gaunt and spent. 'Cause I'd put myself in a state of mind . . . *que no, que no queda más na'* . . . *y uno esperando la muerte*... And I'd try to snap out of it, but there was really nothing going on for me, and mentally and spiritually you just get *tired*... And I was thinking: Here I'm thirty-seven, just living, barely trying to keep myself above water, so I don't have to go home... go home to my parents. And I'd come to the City to try to outgrow poverty and help my parents, and somehow it seemed that every time I'd done well for myself, something would snatch it right back, and I'd always end up finding myself sliding back into *that*...

AC-M: That?

JR: Hustling. And I figured it was like a destiny. And I was thinking I was cursed. 'Cause they say when we die we go to hell, but I was thinking—*here I've been living a hell.* And I kept thinking, *¿Dios mío, por qué me tienes aquí metío en este* hell? And I had this real ugly aura hovering over my head. Till I just got up one morning, it was a perfectly beautiful morning, and I decided to call it quits. And I started cleaning up my apartment, getting rid of all the bad things. 'Cause I figured if I committed suicide no one was gonna find a thing... a thing...

AC-M: What kinds of things?

JR: Magazines, porno flicks, sex toys, weed—I just threw it all away... And I took some sleeping pills and angel dust and went out, and ended up in the Cathedral of St. John the Divine. And I don't know how I got there, but when I got there I felt all this peace. And as I walked into church the first statue I saw was this sculpture of a man who was really in pain. And his eyes were looking out and his hands were outstretched like begging someone to give him strength. So I figured that would be the spot where I'd chill out, but every time I'd get ready to take the sleeping pills and the dust, I'd hear someone walk up and stop right in front of me. And every time I'd open my eyes thinking I was gonna meet my Maker, I'd meet the flash of a camera instead. 'Cause every time I'd open my eyes there would be this Japanese person taking pictures of me by the statue...

AC-M: ... committing suicide ...

JR: ... committing suicide. So after a while I decided it just wasn't gonna happen, and I walked outta the church. And as I was walking outta the church, a cab pulled up, and there was a priest inside, and I walked over to him, 'cause I was very much in need of something spiritual, of some answer, of help. But he looked at me and acted like I was gonna mug him, and ran to the back of the church—like *he* was being chased. So I followed him to the back of the church and ran into another priest, dressed in a sky-blue outfit, who took one look at me and pointed to some doors. "Son, the help you need is through those doors," he said. So I said, *Okay.* But as I was gonna go through the doors, a guard came up behind me and said, "You can't go in!" So I asked him why, and he said, "'*Cause nobody's in.*" So I sat there looking at those doors and thinking how the help I needed was behind those doors but I couldn't get to it, how no matter how much I tried to figure it all out it was always over there, on the other side of me, when my body started shaking, and a voice I couldn't recognize at first was crying and out of breath. And the world around me looked like I was looking at it through *una pecera*, and the guard was talking, but I couldn't hear him—like in a silent film. Till I finally started making out some words, and I got up, dusted myself off, and left.

AC-M: And you went home?

JR: Yeah, finally . . .

"I'm Juanito Xtravaganza": An Epilogue

AC-M: So you went home?

JR: I went home . . . and when I got there there were all these legendary faggots from the *House of Xtravaganza* I used to hang out with at the Sound Factory inviting me to go to a ball . . .

AC-M: A ball?

JR: A *ball* . . . a drag queen ball . . . You see they'd always wanted me to walk *banjee*, or street hoodlum, with *face* at a ball, 'cause they thought I'd no face problems and would just look *flawless* walking up the runway . . . with the fresh sneakers . . . the beads . . . the bangles . . . the *cara de palo* . . . the *yo!-yo!-whatsup?!* But at the time I was married to Haring, and he'd just founded a house, so I ended up becoming a member of the *House of Haring*, and never walked. And though I'd never walked, I'd always thought of myself as a child of the *House of Xtravaganza*, 'cause I'd been there with the legendary children of *Xtravaganza* when the houses were being formed. And then when Keith died I came back here to live in El Barrio, and I was invited to a ball . . . the *Tiffany Ball* . . .

AC-M: Tiffany . . .?

JR: Yeah, *Tiffany* . . . The ballroom was done up in Tiffany blue with white ribbons and little bottles of perfume dangling from the boughs. And during the Grand March when they were introducing the legendary children of the *House of Xtravaganza*, I heard my name being called: *Juanitooooo!!! Xtravaganza!!!!* I had a nice purple suit on, which I'd bought on 42nd St. for $90, and a fuzzy *Kangol*. 'Cause I'd always figured it wasn't *who* or *what* you were wearing, but *how* you walked . . . And I don't remember walking . . . not really, but when I finally got up, I could see a lotta the street kids I'd known throughout the years . . . in the audience. Kids who had come to my house when they were expecting their HIV-test results. Kids who knew I was HIV-positive and were curious to know . . . just how I'd managed it all. 'Cause they were hustling and they knew that I too had been on that other side of the hustle, the side of kids who are forced to hustle 'cause they've

Figure 2.1 Courtesy Juan Rivera.

got no other choice . . . And they were shouting and calling me,
Tío . . . Tío . . .
AC-M: And you? Were you shouting back?
JR: Yeah . . . *Bendición . . . Bendición . . . Bendición . . .*

Juan Rivera, a.k.a. Juanito Xtravaganza, continues to live in El Barrio
where he struggles to keep his HIV-positive status in check and works,
as often as he can, renovating homes. He dabbles in photography. In
1997, an exhibit of his photos, titled *Besos Dulces: My Three Years with
Keith Haring,* was shown at *A Different Light Bookstore* in Chelsea,
New York City (see figure 2.1). More recently, in fall 2003, his photos were shown at the group exhibit *Leisure,* curated by Troy Bent and
Randal Wilcox for The Black Market Group, and on-line at Roulette
Fine Art.

CHAPTER 3

A Radiated Radiant Baby
KEITH HARING and an
Aesthetics of Identification

One of the most popular and beloved American artists of the twentieth century, Keith Haring would be catapulted to international fame by the mass media. From his arrival in New York City in 1978 at age twenty to his death at age thirty-one, his images would acquire, in the short span of twelve years, that instant popular recognition garnered only by images of the modern masters: Picasso, Dali, and especially Warhol, whom he considered his greatest influence and his immediate predecessor. Indeed his iconic images of a crawling "radiant baby," his identificatory graffiti writer's tag, the barking dog with a rectangular muzzle, the chains of silhouetted urban homeboys breakdancing would became so immediately available to the public imagination that, one might say, they would disappear into the general consciousness of the times where they would be reappropriated by the mass media and the market—a phenomenon that Haring would increasingly bemoan toward the end of his life in his posthumously published *Journals*.

And yet it was this popular fame that Haring deeply desired and considered the proper ambition of a late-modern artist in a globalized, media-oriented age that would also keep him from being acknowledged by the art establishment. During his lifetime few museums would collect his works and few critics would write about them. And even as he was dying, he would never see a retrospective of his vast, frenetically produced, multimedia output in a major American museum, and only posthumously, in 1997, would the Whitney Museum of American Art devote an exhibit to him in order to "rectify" the "skewed" vision of his work as merely a product of marketing and of 1980s celebrity culture (Sussman 8, 24).

Beginning with the End

Perhaps because of this critical dismissal of Haring's work as an international market and media phenomenon, as overexposed, most sympathetic accounts of his art begin by turning back to the conservative Pennsylvania Dutch country towns of his childhood, Kutztown, and of his birth, Reading. Returning him thus symbolically to his hometown in death, these accounts hope to distance Haring from associations with commercialism, the media, and the New York street cultures from which he emerged and to shelter him from their putatively harmful, self-dissipating effects. They also seem to suggest that what would later become the internationally recognizable Haring style was somehow always already there in the genius that was Haring, as in a seed, prior to his encounter with New York City, its underground art scene, its urban youth movements, such as hip hop, and the lesbian and gay subcultures of the black and Latino, especially Puerto Rican, youth of the Paradise Garage discotheque, and his desire for them.

Typical of these accounts is John Gruen's influential biography of Haring, *Keith Haring: The Authorized Biography*, which begins with Haring on his deathbed: It's February 12, 1990, and Haring is agitated. He asks for a pad and a pen. Haltingly, he draws what would be his last image, the symbol that had launched his career ten years earlier, his graffiti "tag," the Radiant Baby. A few days later, on February 16, Haring would die, according to Gruen, peacefully of AIDS complications (Gruen 1991 ix–x).

From this account of Haring on his deathbed Gruen turns then, through the connecting figure of the Radiant Baby, to Haring's birth in Reading, PA, and to his early childhood experience in Kutztown of learning how to draw his cartoon-like characters from his father's hand: "My dad," Haring explains, "made cartoon characters for me, and they were similar to the way I started to draw—with one line and a cartoon outline" (Gruen 1991 9). Haring's graffiti-inflected art, Gruen would thus seem to suggest, through narrative crosscutting can be traced back to these sessions with his father from whence his style emerged out of a familial and personal history.

Similarly, in a star-studded tribute to Haring at the Cathedral of St. John the Divine on May 4, 1990, the artist's birthday, Kay, Haring's sister, would recall her brother the artist as essentially the same person as the child she grew up with. In a moving portrait, with which Gruen significantly closes his text, Kay would affirm that "the brother that I grew up with is the same brother that all of you [in New York] know" (Gruen 1991 220). "Only the neighborhood get-togethers [of our childhood] became the Manhattan club scene; the art projects with kids [of our childhood] grew to include thousands and thousands of youths; . . . and the canvas on which he drew became the whole world" (220).

ART IS LIFE

But in Haring's own versions of becoming an artist in his posthumously published *Journals*, it is not so much growing up in Kuztown, though he would acknowledge this as both formative and deforming (". . . my parents weren't part of the sixties cultural revolution at all. They were on the other side of it—the redneck side of it," he would recall; Gruen 1991 10), as migrating from there that would define his particular style and approach as an artist. Climbing atop a tree like a Mark Twain character about to set off on an adventure, Haring gazes at the river below as he readies himself to leave. And as he reflects, the message that comes from the changing river below, which opens his *Journals* and sets him off on an artistic path, is clear: Forget all your "preconceptions" and "misconceptions" and "just live!" (Haring 1997 2).

It would be a message that Haring would take to heart, developing it into a sort of method. Life, by which he meant change, mutation, the spontaneous and unscripted, the unprocessable and unquantifiable, the unrepeatable and ephemeral, chance, as well as all that and those who could not be represented because it was or they were considered disposable, expendable, "other," even demonic, in short, trash, had to be his guiding force, dictate his artistic path. Art, or "[p]ure art," that is, unvarnished and unconventional, raw, *brut*, he would insist, "exists only on the level of instant response to pure life" (Haring 1997 11).

Looking back at his career from this vantage point, rather than from either his deathbed scene or childhood in Kutztown, one could say that his passion for leaving the fixed familial safe ground and crossing over onto the uncharted territory of otherness would become for him an eros and an art. It would also be what made him a specifically gay artist, as he acknowledges in his *Journals*, in the tradition of Burroughs, Gysin, and Genet, artists for whom homosexual desire was an access to difference, theirs and others', rather than an affirmation of identity or sameness.

Marked as an X, or as a Christian +, crossing over into otherness, going a-cross, is symbolized in Haring's works as sacrifice and banishment but also as sex. It is entering a site both of violence and embrace, where bodies are violated, penetrated, and zapped but where social banishment can also be turned, through the most intimate of encounters, the encounter with "life" and sex, into an unending chain of joyously interlocking bodies that constitute a sort of tribal, utopian community, as is repeatedly seen in his work (see, for instance, *The Marriage of Heaven and Hell*, 1984; *St. Sebastian*, 1984; *The Tree of Life*, 1985; *Untitled*, 1984; *Untitled (Palladium Backdrop)*, 1985; *The Great White Way*, 1988; *Once Upon a Time*, 1989; *The Last Rainforest*, 1989; and *Gil's Dream*, 1989).

In *Gil's Dream*, a drawing completed in 1989, shortly before his death, and dedicated to Gil Vazquez, Haring's last companion, a black outlined cross with a black outlined Christ figure is filled in with Haring's interlocking design of breakdancing homeboys and iconic barking dogs (see figure 3.1). Filled in with the same design as the

Figure 3.1 *Gil's Dream*, 1989. Acrylic on canvas, 61 × 91 cm. Private collection; courtesy The Estate of Keith Haring.

cross's, the Christ figure would seem to meld into the cross (or the cross into the figure), the foregrounded subject into the generalized background, the content into the frame, as if to suggest that sacrifice and martyrdom are merely the obverse side of the joyously erotic affirmation of communal life, which is here represented by an interlocking, apparently endless chain of breakdancing homeboys.

An Energy Called Hip-Hop

Like countless other gay youth, including Juan Rivera, who would become his lover and partner in 1986, Haring would arrive in New York City in 1978, escaping the conservative turn of suburban and small-town America against the values of liberation and personal freedom emblematized by the 1960s, chief among them sexual self-expression. New York was then a polarized city. It had emerged out of a fiscal crisis that had pushed it to the brink of bankruptcy in 1975 (captured by the legendary *Daily News* headline of the times, "Ford to New York: Drop Dead!") to become a global, postindustrial capital of real estate, insurance, and finance. Yet many of its inner-city neighborhoods remained a devastated war zone of abandoned and burned-out buildings and vacant lots, overrun by the drug trade and patrolled by an unsympathetic police that identified the impoverished, working-class residents of these neighborhoods, mostly Latino and black, as the cause, rather than the victims, of their neighborhoods' decline.

Abandoned by the manufacturing industries, the federal and state governments' diminishing social welfare programs, disinvesting landlords, and a fleeing suburbanizing white middle-class, these residents, many of whom had been relocated from other areas in the city where "slums" had been cleared for "urban renewal," had struggled to curb further deterioration and displacement and maintain a sense of community in places such as Harlem, El Barrio/East Harlem, the South Bronx, Coney Island, and the Lower East Side (Loisaida). And amidst the ruins and rubble a vibrant youth culture had developed, built by the mostly second-generation children of these often immigrant Puerto Rican/Latino, West Indian, and African American residents (see Flores 2000 115–39; Rivera; and Rose).

Bereft of institutional resources and support, uprooted from their traditional family networks, and trained for vocations that had become increasingly obsolete in the global postindustrial job market, these inner-city youths would retool their technical skills in order to create out of the urban detritus around them a subculture that provided them with name recognition, a sense of belonging or place, alternative familial networks, and some income, as Tricia Rose has so eloquently and incisively explained (34–35). Modeling themselves after gangs, these youths would organize in crews or posses to battle each other. But the battles they would wage would be over style in breakdancing, graffiti writing, deejaying, and rapping for name recognition and turf in a world that denied them both. And the name and territory they claimed, based as they were on their ability to unpack and master someone else's intricate, intentionally difficult, or coded style (or as graffiti writer and hip-hop entrepreneur Fab 5 Freddy has called it, a "style nobody can deal with"; qtd. in Rose 38), were more diffuse than those of traditional gangs. Instead of claiming their immediate blocks around them, these youths would extend their names and their neighborhoods' or 'hoods' by marking and reappropriating the established networks that mapped official city space with their graffiti, their dance moves, and their sounds. "Riding" these established networks and layering them with these alternative languages, moves, and sounds, they would build atop the officially established city other alternative cities, which though visible, and stridently so, were not so readily accessible or legible to the uninitiated.

Arriving in a New York thus crisscrossed by these alternative languages, movements, and sounds, Haring would feel, more than a fascination with their possible (alternative) meaning, the pull and provocation of their implicit conversation, of their intense dialogue, what one might call their energy, or vibe. "There was this incredibly raw energy in the air," he would recall, "and the energy was called Hip-Hop" (Gruen 1991 90).

He would settle in the Village first, moving soon to the East Village across from the legendary gay bathhouse, the Club Baths, and enrolling in the School of Visual Arts (SVA), where he would study graphic art and painting, as well as performance and video art, avant-garde film, and semiotics, a discipline that considered visual images as a language or system of signs whose ability to communicate specific (political) meanings depended on their order or syntax. But it was on the streets, as he traveled to museums and galleries, or in the subways, as he fantasized over the dark boys around him (with their "dark eyes, dark hair and gorgeous bodies, [and] penetrating gaze"; Haring 1997 70), that he would complete his education by studying the graffiti art he encountered. And it was this other education that would excite him and incite him, inducing him to participate, to engage, to commune, and to communicate.

A RADIATED RADIANT BABY

CLONES GO HOME!

Haring would arrive in New York late in the summer of 1978, settling first at the YMCA on 23rd St. in Chelsea, by then a well-known gay cruising haunt, as the gay disco group *The Village People*'s hit that year, *YMCA*, which topped the charts, would proclaim: "It's fun to stay at the Y-M-C-A! They have everything for you, men, to enjoy. You can hang out with all the boys!" But he would not stay there long, as he would soon discover on his first exploratory tour of the Village Christopher St.: "It was like landing in a candy store, or better, a gay Disneyland!," Haring recalls (35). He would walk west from there onto the Hudson River piers where he would encounter lots of people cruising and hanging out, and he would be both mesmerized— and shocked (Gruen 1991 35). He would almost immediately move in with someone he met at the piers, settling in the heart of the developing gay district, on Bleecker and W. 10th streets. And during the next year, while he studied at the SVA, he would explore the gay nightlife of the Village, with its bars, discos, and after-hours clubs that featured backrooms where people could have casual, anonymous sex. And the art that he would produce at the SVA would begin to reflect this experience of discovering what he would call his "single strongest impulse" ("more than art?," he would wonder), his "sexual energy" (Haring 1997 70). In a typical piece of this period, he would draw tiny, white-chalk outlined penises in multiple witty poses (erect, recumbent, arched), creating a seemingly inexhaustible pattern of abstracted, calligraphic forms.

It was the late 1970s and love was in the air, as John Paul Young's disco hit that year affirmed. And what to some seemed then—perhaps disparagingly—the dance of gay liberation was nowhere near its end. After so many centuries of silence, a decade or two of celebration, one might quip, seemed hardly excessive. But the centrality of dance and club culture for the development of a gay community and a gay communal identity in the 1970s can neither be demonized nor trivialized.

For so many of the youths coming into the Village then to experience gay liberation for the first time, young men from suburban or small-town America like Haring, or Juan, dance and disco were not merely a fashion, or as they would later become, an emblem of the times. They were the very instrument and trope through which their communal belonging was being imagined and built. A community built on love—on love's unattainable utopia of finding one's equal, one's own (ever-receding) image through romance and sex, as the mirror ball on the disco dance floor seemed both to promise and defer. For so many of these youths this new, never-before-seen identity, based on likeness, was a validation, a way of giving themselves value, of attaining self-worth. It was also a way of exorcizing older, shame-bound models of gay identification that shunned reciprocity, where gay men were supposed to play the "faggot" or "pervert" to someone else's straight-identified "trade."

Simplified, this model of identification would become personified by the "clone," the new muscle-bound, virile gay man, whose sartorial style, so popular throughout the 1970s and on to the 1980s, would include most often a uniformed attire of a flannel shirt, tight button-fly jeans, and an impeccably groomed mustache. Promoted by the gay media, pornography, and the arts, as Martin P. Levine has discussed, this model would be universalized as the symbol of a new liberated, post-Stonewall homosexuality. And like all utopian models universalized, this model would also engender or breed its own area of repudiation, its own repressed underside, which included all of those things associated with (hierarchical) difference and shame: male femininity, transvestism, and transexuality, to be sure, but also to different degrees, ethnicity and race.

In a sense, one could say, this utopian universalization would set the terms for the commodification and packaging of the new developing gay Village by real estate interests and the market, leading to the increased gentrification, homogenization, and mainstreaming of a community whose roots had been anti-assimilationist and anti-normative, that is, countercultural, and some of whose founding figures, such as Stonewall veteran Sylvia Rivera, had been drag queens (see Duberman; on gay gentrification, see Castells; Lauria and Knopp). And although the gay Village would never be fully homogenized and gentrified throughout the 1970s and 1980s—its symbolic center, Christopher St. itself, with its spaces where black and Latino gay and transgender youth would cruise and congregate, remaining a bulwark of difference throughout the period and on to this day—by the end of the decade, it is true, the general tenor of the community, especially as compared to what was then coming to be known as the East Village (see chapter five, "Loisaida"), seemed dominated by a normalizing trend (Marotta 326–28). And Haring, like so many other disaffected youths escaping suburban and small-town America, would find his way to the East Village, settling on First Ave., between 1st and 2nd streets, across from the Club Baths (see chapter five, "Bathhouses"), which was literally, in his words, "twenty steps" away (Gruen 1991 42).

Compared to the Village, the East Village seemed then, if not a harmonious, a more multicultural, multiethnic, multiracial, and multiclass space, not yet dominated by the West Village's homogenizing trend. While undergoing an intense process of abandonment and disinvestment, as a preamble to reinvestment and gentrification, it was also home to a cultural movement that sought to curb displacement by reconstructing the neighborhood's public spaces and its residents' sense of commitment to place (see chapter five, "Loisaida"), as well as to a long-standing tradition of countercultural politics, performance, and art, whose latest incarnation was the punk rock scene.

In the East Village, Haring would join a group of brilliantly creative artists, most of them "arty-farty misfits" who had fled middle America for New York, as the performance artist Ann Magnuson, herself one of these youths, would ironically describe them (Magnuson 128), and who would gather at a "hole in the wall" located in the basement of an old Polish church on Saint Mark's Place, Club 57. Frequented by fellow SVA students Kenny Scharf and John Sex, and later photographer Tseng Kwong Chi, and Ann Magnuson herself, who was then club manager, Club 57 would become, along with the Mudd Club, which though located in TriBeCa, was very much a part of the East Village scene, a leading promoter of the early 1980s East Village "underground" art movement.

Under Magnuson's direction, Club 57 would offer an eclectic mix of entertainment, ranging from live music to poetry readings, video performances, art shows, and movie theme nights, which featured such themes as the worst monster films ever and campy sci-fi flicks. It would encourage artists to experiment by mixing media and venturing into each others' fields (John Sex recalls, for instance, organizing shows where painters would be asked to tap dance and poets to sing; Gruen 1991 51). And indeed one of the club's most enduring legacies would be a zany, gay, genre- and gender-bending cabaret from which would emerge the likes of legendary female impersonator Lipsynka (Cameron 58).

Using Club 57 as a platform for experimentation, Haring would set out during the next couple of years on what he considered the single most important search for a contemporary artist, the search for artistic forms that could disrupt established means of communication or established media in order to provoke new dialogues between artists and audiences, new communicative networks (Gruen 1991 56; Haring 1997 28). Drawing from his studies of semiotics at SVA, which posited that all images were signs whose meaning depended not on fixed definitions or values but on the way they were organized, and from the gay avant-garde writers William Burroughs's and Brion Gysin's "cut-up" technique, which consisted of cutting up sections of printed material and randomly pasting them (Gruen 1991 55; Sussman 12), Haring would mix video, poetry, performance, and art, seeking to disrupt established forms of communication and to effect a new dialogue. In one of his performances, for instance, during the summer of 1980 at Club 57's performance art series *Acts of Life*, he would recite an hour-long poem based on seemingly endless rearrangements of the same randomly chosen words while holding up a junked, hollow TV frame around his face. It was as if somehow he had taken over the media and recycled it for some other, enigmatic sort of communication (Blinderman 15).

From these language-based experimentations Haring would move on to forms that engaged broader audiences. Inspired by Jenny Holzer's street signs (provocative statements printed on cheap paper and posted on city walls that forced the viewer to face his/her political assumptions), and Jean-Michel Basquiat's (ironic aphorisms scrawled on buildings and streets, written in collaboration with subway graffiti writer Al Diaz and signed SAMO [or, as Basquiat would later explain, "the SAMe Old shit"; Hoban 25]), and the graffiti writers' appropriation of urban space with their elaborate subway pieces and tags, Haring would begin to post Xerox copies of collages that ironically recycled established forms of public address (such as newspaper headlines) in order to provoke a reaction in the viewer and make him/her think about his/her political situatedness and context (Aletti 96–97).

Seeking to establish communication with a broad audience, Haring would end up joining what seemed then the predominant artistic movement of the times, as artists moved out of the galleries and into the streets in order to engage viewers and to contribute through art to the creation of alternative spaces and communities (Sussman 12). (Two of the most influential artists' collectives of the times, CoLab in the Lower East Side and Fashion Moda in the South Bronx, would focus primarily, for instance, on artwork that involved artists and communities in joint projects to transform urban space; Cameron 44–45, 49.)

Haring's first street intervention would be telling—it would combine his newfound sense of liberated gay sexual self-expression with a cultural politics of place that asserted diversity and difference against the encroaching market-driven homogenization and gentrification of neighborhoods. With the aid of a stencil, he would spray-paint in capital roman letters a warning from the humorously apocryphal militant gay organization FAFH, or Fags Against Facial Hair, in the border between the Village and the East Village that read: CLONES GO HOME (Gruen 1991 57; Magnuson 128) (see figure 3.2). It was a critique of

Figure 3.2 *Clones Go Home*, 1980. Powdered pigment and graphite on paper stencil, 51 × 66 cm. New York, The Estate of Keith Haring.

the increasing homogenization of the gay community and of gay culture to be sure, but it was a provocation as well—a call of sorts to reclaim the ethnically and racially diverse experimental and avant-garde roots of urban gay culture, which would remain for Haring a primary source of inspiration until his death.

A Radiated Radiant Baby

In his desire to communicate with a broader audience, Haring would turn away from drawing and painting, which he considered personal and abstract, toward a more direct, social, language-based, street art. But as he posted his provocative signs and Xerox collages around town (*REAGAN SLAIN BY HERO COP*, read one), he would wonder whether drawing and painting could not also be used to communicate socially, and inspired by the graffiti writers' application of a marked, "hard-edged," black, graphic line (Gruen 1991 44), he would pick up spray paint and sumi ink and produce the first iconic drawings for which he would henceforth be known.

A hybrid of sorts between his early drawings and paintings of abstract, calligraphic designs and his later language-based art, these iconic drawings—outlined, silhouetted figures of flying saucers, animals that seemed to resemble cows, sheep, or dogs with angular muzzles, crawling babies and breakdancing boys, dolphins, nuclear reactors, computers, and pyramids—were more like indexes or symbols than actual depictions of subjects, and depended for their meaning, like all linguistic signs or symbols, on the combinations, associations, juxtapositions, and substitutions interlocutors or viewers could make of them.

Often presented in panels, like comic-book stories, these hieroglyphic signs called for deciphering, for interpretation. And although most of the icons seemed easily recognizable, or accessible, the stories they narrated seemed more polyvalent (often perversely so), creating thus a sense both of familiarity and uncanniness. As a matter of fact, the icon from which all others derived, the first icon in Haring's new series of pictograms, the ur-icon, as it were, which kept reappearing in all other panels as if it were somehow prior to the series or outside of it, its point zero, though familiar, seemed itself drawn from the recesses of America's pop-culture unconscious: it was a 1950s iconic image of a flying saucer, which looked like, in Haring's words (Gruen 1991 57), a Mexican *sombrero*, and which went about radiating or zapping humans, animals, and things with its ominous beam of energy.

In one of the original series of panels Haring would produce (see figure 3.3), this iconic flying saucer would zap a dog with a rectangular muzzle, which would then pass on the beam of energy to an outlined male human figure through anal sex, setting off a chain reaction in which anyone or anything contaminated with, and penetrated by, the alien ray would be transformed and glow. The chain of mutations, set off by the flying saucer's ray and transmitted most often through anal sex, would be reinforced by a frieze at the bottom of the drawing where iconic images of the dog and the silhouetted male human figure, now crawling, or in a pose reminiscent of the dog's, would alternate.

Playing on the multiple associations of dog in contemporary popular, and especially hip-hop, culture, where "dog" refers not only to the animal but also to a male member of a hip-hop crew or posse, or to a homeboy, as well as to the act of having anal intercourse, or "doggy style" sex, Haring would build a homoerotic street vocabulary whose central trope or metaphor was sex among (home)boys as a way of incorporating and passing on creative energy and whose cipher would

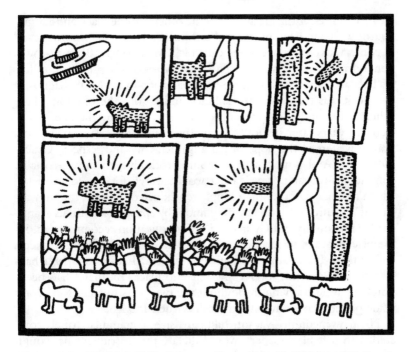

Figure 3.3 *Untitled*, 1981. Ink on vellum, 43 × 48 (109.2 × 121.9 cm). Private collection; courtesy The Estate of Keith Haring.

be the crawling male figure, or what would later become Haring's most famous (and beloved) tag or street trademark, his crawling radiated "radiant baby."

Haring's iconic image of a 1950s radiating flying saucer had been taken, he would recall (Aletti 100), from those campy sci-fi flicks about aliens and monsters featured at Club 57. But unlike these films, which traded on popular fears of the alien and its invasive, body-snatching capabilities, as in the 1956 classic film *Invasion of the Body Snatchers*, in Haring's drawings the invasive force of the alien was not destructive—it was procreative. It set off the possibly endless chain of mutations through (anal) sex, which was for him artistic creation, as if somehow art were itself a call to be invaded, or penetrated, by an ominous alien other in order to become an-other, in order to create, to glow.

In retrospect, it seems almost prescient that as early as 1980, years before AIDS would become a crisis, Haring had already placed his art under the sign of a body-invading otherness. And yet it was this creative desire for the racial and ethnic other, for the black and Latino youths who had been proscribed to him as a young man growing up in conservative ("redneck," he called it; Gruen 1991 10) small-town Pennsylvania, which would, in a sense, symbolically prepare him for his later acceptance and creative transformation of his AIDS diagnosis. And it was this desire to embrace and absorb the ominous alien other that would also lead him to want "to continue the line," as it were, as years later his lover Juan Rivera would explain, begun by graffiti writers in the hope of gaining their love and respect (Gruen 1991 70). And armed with a (homo)erotically generative, socially communicative language, Haring would search for a medium from which to engage, rather than simply reproduce or imitate, the subway writers' gesture and art. He would find it by chance, as both his avant-garde (Burroughs and Gysin) and street education recommended, in the black, vacant ad spaces on the subway stations' walls. "As I kept seeing these black subway panels everywhere, I realized what I had discovered. Suddenly, everything fell into place. All that I had been watching and observing throughout the two years I was in New York made perfect sense," he would recall (Gruen 1991 68).

His new medium—vacant, billboard-size, rectangular panels covered with soft black paper—would dictate the instrument he would use as well as the form of his drawings: they had to be "quick and simple," Haring would remark, "not only for easy readability but also to avoid getting arrested," as they were still "technically . . . graffiti" (Haring 1984). And they had to stand out, or "shine," and yet underscore the tenuous, human fragility of his pared-down graphic line "in the middle of all th[e] power[,] tension[,] and violence" that he thought was the daily experience of poor and working-class people in the subway lines (Sheff). Common white chalk, with its sharp, grainy trace on paper, would reveal itself as the ideal, and most portable, vehicle for Haring's iconic drawings. He would run to the closest stationery above ground to buy some chalk, and for the next four years he would produce hundreds of drawings along many of the city's subway lines, especially the #6, which connected the South Bronx with the Lower East Side.

Positioned next to the subway's commercial ads (actually substituting for them, or illegally taking their place) and facing the moving trains, Haring's drawings seemed to mediate between these two—the mass-media ads and the graffiti writers' moving subway art. Indeed the theme of most of Haring's iconic drawings would revolve around the epic struggle of his constantly moving crew of outlined homeboy figures with the lethal powers of a mass media and technology transmogrified into gigantic serpents, caterpillars, and robotic monsters with TV and computer screen heads (see figure 3.4).

Unlike the monsters, the homeboy figures seemed to represent a highly charged, "primitive" libidinal force whose strength appeared to derive from their natural ability to evade technology's deadly powers by contorting their bodies, constructing multidirectional, interlocking, corporal structures, or using each other's bodies as escape routes, literally as "manholes." Transforming thus, like the Brazilian martial art of *capoeira*—one of the common sources of breakdancing and of Haring's art—negative, empty space and vulnerability into an advantage, Haring's homeboy figures seemed to suggest the possibility of surviving, of traversing, like his crawling radiated radiant baby, his famous tag, a hostile urban environment unscathed and unharmed. They also seemed to propose the possibility of redemption, of turning technology's deadly assault into an opportunity for rising, like batwinged angels, over the hell of modernity's dehumanizing, robotic urbanscape.

Haring's premodern vision of an epic struggle between the body and technology, sacrifice and redemption, heaven and hell, whose

Figure 3.4 *Untitled*, 1985. Chalk on paper mounted on board, 117 × 153 cm. New York, The Estate of Keith Haring.

protagonists were urban hip-hop boys would endear him to graffiti artists, garnering their respect and admiration, and indeed their love. But a simple, even cursory look at the graffiti art that covered the exteriors and interiors of New York subway cars during this period would confirm that Haring's primitivist drawings had little to do with the intention and spirit of the graffiti writers' art.

For though writers liked to think of themselves as transgressive, as "nasty," as "outlaws," they certainly did not perceive themselves as "natural," or as "primitives" locked in a struggle with technology's evil and dehumanizing force. If anything, graffiti writers claimed their right, and the right of the communities they came from, communities that had been deprived of resources during the city's painful transition to a non-manufacturing, global service economy, to dispose freely of technology. Closer to modernists, as Kirk Varnedoe and Adam Gopnik have argued in the catalogue to their Museum of Modern Art (MOMA) exhibit, *High and Low: Modern Art, Popular Culture*, graffiti writers had by the late 1970s "absorbed" what had by then become "the commonplaces of modernism . . . —the faith in the glory of individual innovation, the insistence on a fiercely competitive battle of new styles, the sense that the entire history of art, high and low, should be ransacked and recycled and made one's own signature style" (Varnedoe and Gopnik 376).

Graffiti writers were then decidedly not antimodern. On the contrary, they were first and foremost riders; they wrote the trains, and rode them. With their increasingly dense, interlocking, Alhambra-like, calligraphic "wild style," they sought to capture and overtake the movement and speed of the trains. As their names became illegible under an abstract, almost Pollock-like barrage of crumbling letters and exploding colors, their signature style was no longer defined by, or contained in, the letters of their tags; it was their writing's very movement that was their style (see figure 3.5).

Figure 3.5 *Style Wars* by Noc, 1981. Composite photograph by Henry Chalfant. Courtesy Henry Chalfant (Cooper and Chalfant 1984).

By contrast, Haring's subway drawings were static and, like all conventional primitivisms, flat. And though they were about movement, movement was always signaled in them by gigantic comic-book marks; that is to say, in Haring's subway drawings movement was not so much captured as quoted. Rather than a prolongation of the speed of the graffiti artist's line, Haring's subway drawings were a sobering parenthesis, a commentary: they did not so much continue the writers' line as commented on the culture that produced it.

Coming at a time when the city was waging an all-out war against subway graffiti as a sign of the "urban crisis" it had just experienced (Austin 147–66), and galleries sought to revitalize a sagging art market by infusing it with the "outlaw" energy and excitement of the streets, Haring's more distant, mediated subway graffiti must have seemed a welcome relief, and politically and financially more expedient.

True enough, for a brief period, 1981–1984, as the city engaged in a massive multimillion-dollar destruction of the top-to-bottom pieces (graffiti pieces that covered entire cars) that had made graffiti famous, the East Village galleries first and then more established downtown venues would pick up the graffiti artists' work, exhibiting it on canvas (Patti Astor's Fun Gallery in the East Village would show A-ONE, LADY PINK, RAMMELLZEE, CRASH, SEEN, and NOC, among others, and Lee Quiñones, Fab 5 Freddy, CRASH and DAZE, and Futura 2000 would see solo exhibits in the more established Barbara Gladstone, Holly Solomon, Sidney Janis, and Tony Shafrazi galleries, respectively; Austin 191–92; Cameron 51). But soon the art world would lose interest in graffiti.

In the absence of "any systematic critical or curatorial attempts to establish [aesthetic] standards" by which to judge its production (Cameron 51), graffiti would end up being marketed for its sociological significance. And once graffiti had been transposed on to canvas as its illegal subway version was being effaced by the Metropolitan Transit Authority (MTA), this authenticity would come increasingly into question. To be taken seriously as art graffiti would have had to develop then in short time a cadre of connoisseurs who could translate (if that were possible) its very rigorous street standards into art-market aesthetic criteria, as Cameron has argued (51), or assume a Pop-like, ironic distance from its street origins, which militated against the very way it was being sold as genuine and immediate. In the end, it would be Haring's more distant, not primitive but primitivist take on graffiti that would be propelled to international fame, enjoying wide acceptance in galleries, and even among some city officials (in 1984, the city's former Commissioner for Cultural Affairs, the art critic and curator Henry Geldzahler, would pen a glowing introduction to Tseng Kwong Chi's book of photos of Haring's subway drawings, *Art in Transit*).

We know from Haring's *Journals* that he was intensely aware that his almost immediate public acceptance derived from his connection to the "primitive," a term he was loathe to use but that nonetheless captured the simple, "carved" line that he thought he shared with graffiti writers (Gruen 1991 44; Haring 1997 101), and his role as mediator for peoples and cultures that he believed were being imperiled in a dehumanizing technological age. And that awareness produced in him a sense of responsibility, and perhaps guilt:

> The social responsibility that I find in my work is found in the LINE itself. The acceptance of my LINE is responsible for my acceptance as a public figure. The connection to the "primitive" (I hate that word) culture is the key to understanding how and why my art became completely acceptable and quite natural in an age that finds itself technologically and ideologically very far removed from these so-called "primitive" cultures. (Haring 1997 96)

During the next five years, as he continued to draw on the subway, he would become more intimately connected with the graffiti art world. With graffiti writers Fab 5 Freddy (Fred Brathwaite) and Futura 2000, he would organize in the spring of 1981 the first comprehensive exhibit of "graffiti-based, -rooted, [and] -inspired works," titled *Beyond Words*, at the Mudd Club (Cameron 44). And for weeks thereafter the home of elite downtown club culture would become a community center of sorts for graffiti artists from all over New York, to the discomfort of its purportedly hip, underground owner Steve Maas (Gruen 1991 73–74). And he would take long walks with Fab 5 Freddy into what was then, according to Brathwaite, a "scary" neighborhood, overrun by crime and drugs, "Alphabet City—avenues A, B, C, and D, the real Lower East Side," to look at writers' tags and imbibe its local ambience (Gruen 1991 66).

One day during one of these strolls they would spot a group of boys spray-painting or "piecing" the courtyard of a local junior high school, P.S. 22, and Haring, "in ecstasy," according to Brathwaite (Gruen 1991 67), would join in and end up meeting ("discovering" would be his term; 80) the graffiti writer who would become his major collaborator and an important influence: L.A. II, a New York Puerto Rican Loisaida writer whose tags, LA II and LA ROCK, Haring had long admired, as he wandered through the neighborhood, for their beauty and perfection (80). And to his amazement, LA II, "the veritable graffiti king of the Lower East Side" would turn out to be Angel Ortiz, Little Angel, a fourteen-year-old (82)! With their winding and swerving loops and rapid-fire change of direction, LA II's signature tags were, Haring felt, "as close as the Western World ha[d] [come] to a stylized form of writing similar to Eastern calligraphy" (Haring 1997 86). For the next five years Haring and LA II would collaborate in hundreds of works, becoming especially noted for their sculptures and vases, faux archaeological artifacts and classical statues painted in bright Day-Glo colors on which Haring would draw his iconic subway figures, LA II filling in the negative, empty space with his swerving, interlocking, multidirectional, calligraphic tags.

Initially Haring would ask LA II to tag a junked taxicab hood he had found, adding later his homeboy, barking dog, and crawling radiant baby figures to LA II's scrawls. But after he had finished combining both their marks, LA II would insist that they fill in all of the remaining negative, empty space. "I like it when everything's covered," he would explain (Dieckmann 115). And it would be this dense, all-over pattern, with its tension between Haring's simple, outlined figures and LA II's aggressively swerving calligraphic tags, as if somehow the erotically charged dialogue between Haring's more static drawings and the subway writers' moving marks had been displaced from the subway station onto their collaborative work, that would end up dynamizing Haring's art and propelling it to wider recognition and appeal, as has been argued by critics (Dieckmann; Moynihan), most recently and notably by Ricardo Montez.

In collaborative pieces such as a their fiberglass Day-Glo bust of Western art's homoerotic icon par excellence, Michelangelo's *David*, this erotic charge, which drove Haring's production and his reception as well, serving thus as a trope for cross-cultural, cross-racial consumption and exchange, would be singularly evident (see figure 3.6). Thoroughly covering *David*'s bust, except for its fluorescent green curls and sensuous red lips, LA II's aggressively swerving scrawls appeared to surround Haring's dancing homeboys and crawling babies, prodding them on, zapping them, and energizing them. But around the mouth and spanning the length of *David*'s neck, Haring's homeboys seemed to have mutated or morphed into walking or winged phallic figures that now contained LA II's tags, as if they had somehow swallowed or absorbed them, incorporating them.

Haring's aesthetics of embracing and incorporating the energy of the purportedly dangerous, menacing other would now be rewarded with a major solo exhibit at one of SoHo's premier galleries, Tony

Figure 3.6 *Untitled*, 1983. Day-Glo enamel and felt-tip pen on fiberglass bust, 34 × 16.5 × 13 (86.4 × 41.9 × 33 cm). Collection of Lia Rumma; courtesy The Estate of Keith Haring.

Shafrazi's, catapulting him to fame. The opening, which would be covered by *CBS Evening News* with Dan Rather, would be a star-studded affair with established artists Roy Lichtenstein, Robert Rauschenberg, Sol LeWitt, Richard Serra, and Francesco Clemente in attendance as well as family, friends, lovers, and graffiti writers.

For the show, Haring would cover the walls of the gallery with motifs from his subway drawings, now in color ink on paper and vinyl silk-screening ink on multicolor tarpaulins, and he would frame his pieces with friezes of crawling babies and tumbling homeboys. Prominent on one of the walls was a black-and-red drawing of two homeboy figures reaching out to an immense, glowing red heart while an image of Mickey Mouse masturbated next to them, and a shirtless Héctor "Macho" Camacho, the Puerto Rican boxer, then world champion, smiled from above (see figure 3.7). The entire basement of the gallery would also be covered and devoted to a black-light installation whose stunning centerpiece was a fluorescent, Day-Glo statue of Venus, the goddess of love, emerging, as it were, as its title humorously suggested, from "the half shell." And on this recycled icon of Western heterosexual love LA II and Haring would inscribe their tensely contrasting and combining black-ink outlined figures and swerving scrawls.

But perhaps nothing would confirm Haring's rise to stardom as a Spectacolor billboard in the then blighted Times Square's Times Tower. Sponsored by the New York City Public Art Fund, this electronic billboard would show every twenty minutes a thirty-second animation of Haring's iconic, crawling, radiated radiant baby (see figure 3.8). At a time when the city was preparing to rid itself of the "scourge" of subway graffiti, as a sign of the economic and social crisis it had just (supposedly) overcome, this installation of Haring's

Figure 3.7 "Keith Haring" exhibition at the Tony Shafrazi Gallery, New York, October 1982. Courtesy The Estate of Keith Haring.

Figure 3.8 Spectacolor Billboard, Times Square, New York City, 1982. Courtesy The Estate of Keith Haring.

homoerotic cipher of cross-cultural incorporation through (doggy-style) homeboy love over the city's devastated core would seem—retrospectively—either a sly triumph of the popular through a gay aesthetics and politics of love, or a more-than-innocent sign of the gentrification to come. Or both.

A Love Interlude: The Paradise Garage

Strolling through the streets of the West Village with his friend Fred Brathwaite late one night, Haring would encounter the place that would become his home away from home, his sanctuary and refuge, the place he would consistently return to after exhibiting and traveling all over the world, and where he would find a racially and culturally mixed, extended alternative family, and love: the legendary under-ground disco the Paradise Garage. He had been walking on Seventh Ave., South of Houston, when he came upon a club tucked away on a side street, in the periphery between the Village and TriBeCa, on King St., and as he walked up a ramp and onto an immense dance floor on an actual, abandoned garage where up to two thousand swirled, sweated, and stomped, he would be, in his words, "mesmerized" (Gruen 1991 88–89). "I [would] never be the same since I walked into Paradise Garage!" he would later exclaim (Gruen 1991 88).

For the Garage, as it was known to its underground denizens, was a disco—a gay disco at a time (homo)phobic attacks from rock critics and fans had been furiously—if prematurely—declaring that disco was dead (Lawrence 363–94)—but "it was nothing like other gay discos" Haring had known (Gruen 1991 89). Unlike the gay discos he knew, which by 1981 had become increasingly racially and cultur-ally homogeneous and middle-class, if not high-brow, in tone, the Garage was not merely racially and culturally mixed. It was also frequented primarily by young men of color, "tough street kids," as Haring would call them (89), the kind of kids he had until then asso-ciated mostly with black and Latino inner-city neighborhoods and the hip-hop scene (89).

Some critics have likened this encounter with the Paradise Garage to Gaugin arriving in Tahiti (Sischy). And certainly walking into the Paradise Garage Haring must have felt as if the subject of so many of his drawings and paintings, those utopian homoerotic chains of homeboys dancing, had somehow come alive and was inviting him to participate.

But a more apposite analogy to Haring's encounter with the Paradise Garage might well be his discovery of a gay avant-garde two years earlier at the Nova Convention in the East Village, where he would become acquainted with the work of artists such as Burroughs and Gysin, who would later become, along with Warhol, his most important queer predecessors. For the Garage, which had been officially launched in 1977 as the brain child of Michael Brody and Mel Cheren, two Jewish young men who had been inspired to open a club while dancing at Italian American DJ David Mancuso's legendary, racially mixed, underground parties in his apartment on Broadway, North of Houston, known simply as the Loft (Cheren 107), was more than a primitivist's Nirvana.

It was certainly a sanctuary of sorts for some of the people whom Tim Lawrence, in his learnedly anecdotal account of disco, *Love Saves the Day*, has called America's "grown-up orphans" (Lawrence 27), that is, New York's disenfranchised and increasingly impoverished youth, especially queer Latino and black inner-city kids who were then "coming out" and looking for an alternative sense of community and belonging, as is repeatedly affirmed in Josell Ramos's recent documentary on New York dance music culture, *Maestro* (2005). But it was also a place of intersection for a culturally and racially diverse constituency, where community was not simply a matter of arriving at a given, predetermined, "primitive" state of undiluted identity; it was also produced through fiercely competitive dancing and creative experimentation. No wonder the dance floor mantra of a place like the Garage was, like that at the black and Latino competitive drag balls, "Work it!" And no more demanding task master than its reigning DJ diva, Larry Levan, a member or "child" of the drag House of Wong.

By 1981 the gay disco scene, which had begun as a countercultural opening of the traditional dance floor by bringing together a racially, ethnically, sexually, and socially heterogeneous group of dancers under the polymorphously perverse seductive umbrella of an all abiding beat or rhythm (Lawrence 25–27), had become increasingly segregated. In clubs such as the Flamingo, and the ultimate gay male disco, the Saint, which had opened in 1980 in the East Village, at Second Ave. and St. Mark's Place, the heart of what was then the city's alternative, multicultural neighborhood, the patrons were almost exclusively white and male, and the environment seemed thoroughly engineered to produce a sense of communal belonging through the isolation and exaltation of their patrons' visual commonality. In fact, it was this visual commonality that, according to the testimony of some patrons (424), would produce an almost spiritual, out-of-body sense of tribal community. As writer Edmund White notes of his experience dancing at the Flamingo, "We were packed in so tightly we were forced to slither across each other's wet bodies and arms . . . . Freed of my shirt and touchiness, I surrendered myself to the idea that I was just like everyone else. A body among bodies" (424–25). A body among other visually similar bodies, that is: uniformly toned, homogeneously muscular, and overwhelmingly white.

Concurrently, as gay nightlife became segregated, hip-hop cultural forms, which had developed in tandem with disco's DJ art of remixing and other analogous queer arts forms, such as vogueing (Brown; Lawrence 45–46, 384), would become increasingly understood and promoted as authentic, hard-core, masculine, and street vernacular black cultural forms in opposition (and resistance) to the purportedly artificial, market-driven, white, gay, and fey art of disco. As argued then by African American cultural critic Houston A. Baker, among others, hip-hop forms had emerged in opposition to an "enemy" that was "a dully constructed, other-side-of-town discomania that made South and West Bronx hip hoppers ill" (Lawrence 383). "[C]lub DJs were often gay," he would claim, and "Hey," he would conclude with a measure of braggadocio and disdain, "some resentment of disco culture and a reassertion of black manhood rights(rites) . . . was a natural thing" (383).

It is in this broader context of segregation and polarization of cultural forms that had developed in tandem, that is, as a result of a prolonged and intense dialogue, that the Garage's particular racial, ethnic, social, and sexual mix—from freestyling homeboys to vogueing drag queens, straight-identified banjee boys to recently "out" gays, up-and-coming media celebrities to East Village underground experimental artists, and music industry insiders to homeless and thrown-away kids—could be seen, as Haring would see it, as "mesmerizing" and mind-altering.

Like the Nova Convention two years earlier, the Garage would represent for him a link with an alternative gay counterculture that continued to stress racial, cultural, and sexual difference. It was also proof positive that community, even a sense of "family," as many of the Garage's patrons would describe it (see Ramos's *Maestro*), could be achieved without forfeiting radical difference and experimentation. As recounted by Cheren, cofounder of the Garage and disco music promoter, there was no dance floor like the Garage's, "in part because of its size, [but primarily] because the people on it were so different from those at every other major disco at the time. For one thing, they were without question the city's most serious dancers. There was no attitude here, no cliques defined by their muscles, no fashion victims, no A-list. These people were dancers" (Cheren 198). "Or perhaps you might say," he would correct himself, "dancing was their posing. Artists vogueing into new realms of realness, macho men competing furiously with 'Miss Things' for attention—the intensity of the disco pyrotechnics was unlike anywhere else" (198).

A crucially determining factor of these "pyrotechnics," of the Garage's patrons' radical expressivity, of their ability, that is, to turn "dancing into declaration," as Sischy would aptly put it, was without a doubt the style of its reigning DJ diva, as Rivera would call him, Larry Levan. A "child" of the House of Wong, his best friend and "Godfather of House" music, Frankie Knuckles, who had met him while beading a gown for a black boy named Duchess, queen mother of the House of Wong (Cheren 103), would remember him as a decorator of sorts. He was, Knuckles would claim, someone who was into creating a total disco environment long before this was the norm (Ramos). And in fact Levan, who had indeed begun his career as a decorator for DJ Nicky Siano's racially and sexually mixed disco, the Gallery, was meticulous and demanding about his environment to a fault.

He had learned the craft of spinning records by watching Nicky Siano and attending David Mancuso's legendary Loft parties, and had gone on to become DJ at the Continental Baths's first all-male gay disco, where Bette Middler would also launch her career as an exquisitely campy torch-song chanteuse. He had risen from outer-borough boy to respected underground personality and admired award-winning DJ at a time when there were almost no black DJs at discos, and the Garage would be *his* house, the culmination of his career—literally his home: he would meticulously see to every detail of the construction, décor, and audiophile acoustics of the reconverted second-floor garage, and he would build himself a bedroom right behind the DJ booth where he would live during the week and retire to between sets (Cheren 201).

Although there are multiple appraisals of Levan's art as a DJ, both admirers and detractors seem to agree that he would become in no time the absolute, undisputed master of what is known in the dance music business as "peaking." Based on the ritual progression of the African American or black religious service, peaking is the art of leading a diverse group of people to a point of communion where everyone feels a sense of spiritual transcendence or "presence" simultaneously (Fikentscher 102), yet expresses it or testifies to it in a highly individual, personalized way. Like the African American preacher, the disco DJ would create through his particular remixing of music and words a sense of anticipation that would encourage people to "reach out" for something beyond music and meaning, beyond themselves, and it is this reaching out, this stretching the body beyond its limits, this "working it," as disco dancers exclaim, that would be the very proof of transcendence, of the presence of some otherworldliness.

Like all discos, gay and straight, the Garage reached for transcendence, for Paradise, but unlike them, the Garage would challenge its patrons to produce it through what some of Levan's detractors would call his jaggedly uneven, "erratic" style, a style others would simply characterize in racial and class-inflected terms: "He was a great technician and delivered wonderful performances," they would say. "But his music didn't attract the white gay crowd because he wasn't into that sensual, sexual music that they liked. He was into R&B, and you can only take so much of Evelyn 'Champagne' King" (Lawrence 425), adding with a knowing wink: "[The Garage] was NOCD: not our club, dearie" (427).

Instead of installing its patrons in a seamlessly sensual flow of music under the validating gaze of the stars, confirming thus their status as the chosen, the select, as the all-gay-male disco the Saint, for instance, did so well, Levan's style, which might be seen to derive from his experience as a member of the drag House of Wong, would teach, as he would insist, through "attitude" (Lawrence 358).

Like a walker at a drag ball Levan would seduce his audience while actively engaging it by summoning it and demanding from it a unique, personalized response through that studied distance and artful display of disdain that in ball culture is called *attitude*. As Toni Morrison has said of African American music, he would both rebuff and embrace: "[African American music] never really gives you the whole number." "[It] makes you hunger for more of it . . . It slaps and it embraces, it slaps and it embraces" (Morrison 1989).

In fact Levan, who was both infamous and renowned for his unpredictability and volatility, would tease his audience into reaching out for transcendence by stopping the music in midstream. "'He would stop the music in the middle of the night, and he would put on a little a capella,'" one of Lawrence's informants for *Love Saves the Day* recalls (358). And the crowd would begin to scream and he would stop: "I'm not saying ten seconds. He [would stop for] five minutes until the entire room [was] stomping on their feet, and you [could] feel the entire building vibrate" (358). Then he would put on another short number, and the crowd would scream more wildly still. And "he [would take] it off, and . . . just [wait]" (358). Until finally, "a couple of minutes later," he would put on a new record—the record he had been playing five times that night to the indifference of the crowd, which had been calling for its favorites—and "the entire room [would] *just [explode]*—a thousand people all trying to grab the ceiling at the same time" (Lawrence 358).

No wonder Haring would claim that ever since he had walked into the Paradise Garage he would never be the same (Gruen 1991 89)! He wouldn't. From up in his booth, Levan, "like a god," would summon him with his demanding, imperious style, as Haring recalls (89), and Haring would answer him by reaching out, stretching out, and incorporating otherness. He would immediately cover the club's walls with an installation of black and white sumi ink drawings of homeboy figures ascending to heaven like breakdancing and freestyling angels. He would integrate Levan's music into his exhibits and work routine. And he would share in the experience of forming a community in difference while dancing with his first lover the African American DJ Juan Dubose and his next lover Juan Rivera, whom he would meet there, in 1986, as Rivera tried to escape a dangerously abusive relationship and the desultory, disintegrating effects of the streets.

In the succeeding years, while Haring exhibited and traveled all over the world, and as his images became more internationalized and abstracted from the street context from which they had emerged, he would yearn for the queer community in difference that was represented by the Paradise Garage. On Saturdays evenings, no matter where he was around the world, Haring would try to return to the periphery of the Village, on King St., where a queer sort of family of thrownaway kids, urban orphans, and music industry insiders awaited to start the trek toward a land unknown that was the product of their outstretched bodies and of their very sweat.

Pop and the Limits of Universalism: Shibuya, Japan

Following his first SoHo exhibit at Shafrazi's and his Spectacolor animated billboard on Times Square, the "Crossroads of the World," Haring would be propelled to international fame. During the next few years, he would work at such a frenetic pace, exhibiting all over Europe, Latin America, and Asia, especially Japan, where he would be treated with all the media fanfare of a rock star, that nothing or close to nothing would be recorded in his *Journals*. It was as if somehow he knew long before he had been diagnosed with AIDS that his life would be cut short.

He would also play hard, attending openings and concerts, going out to private parties, restaurants, and clubs with other media celebrities

(Madonna, Brook Shields, Grace Jones), getting to know his idols, the legendary artists of his time (Burroughs, Gysin, and especially Warhol, whom he considered his immediate predecessor, the artist who had made him possible; Haring 1997 117), and just living, as Juan would say, the "life of the rich and famous": the best restaurants, the best hotels, the first-class planes, the limos, the clothes, the quality drugs. And he would enjoy his relationship with Juan.

They had met at the Paradise Garage one night while dancing, and Haring had become instantly smitten by his looks: "One night, at the beginning of 1986, I go to the Paradise Garage, and I see this incredibly beautiful boy," he would recall. "I look at him and see that he's the man of my dreams. I convince myself that should he look at me . . . then *that's* going to be *it*! I will have found my new love" (Gruen 1991 138–39). And indeed Juan seemed then, as pictured in the photos of the period that appear in Gruen's "authorized biography" and Haring's *Journals*, perfectly made for this moment in Haring's rapidly ascending international career—not only "street" or urban New York and handsomely photogenic, but of a certain equivocal, Puerto Rican cast and hue that would make him appear paradoxically internationally indigenous or local, as Haring, barely disguising his envy, would remark, "Juan, forever handsome with a chameleon face that adapts to every place we go, making him look Brazilian, Moroccan, or . . . Japanese" (Haring 1997 211–12).

Haring's increasing international profile would make up however for his lack of ability to pass, which he deeply desired, and he would begin to enjoy the attention (he had previously unsuccessfully sought) from beautiful boys all over the world who felt a kinship with his young, urban male-identified, (homo)erotically charged art. During the next years he would be asked to exhibit in some of the world's major galleries: Tony Shafrazi's (with LA II) in 1982, and 1983; Tony Shafrazi's (solo) in 1985, 1987, and 1988; Leo Castelli's, New York, in 1985; Galerie Watari, Tokyo (with LA II), in 1983; Robert Fraser's, London (with LA II), in 1983; Salvatore Ala's, Milan (with LA II), in 1984; Paul Maenz's, Cologne, in 1984; Museum of Contemporary Art, Bordeaux, in 1985; Stedelijk Museum, Amsterdam, in 1986; Hans Mayer's, Düsseldorf, in 1988; and Gallery 121, Antwerp, in 1987 and 1989.

He would also be invited to participate in renowned national and international group exhibitions: *Documenta 82*, Kassel, Germany; *Whitney Biennial*, New York City, 1983; *Bienal de São Paulo*, 1983; *Venice Biennale*, 1984; *Bienal de La Habana*, 1986; *Vienna Biennial*, 1986; and group shows at the Centre George Pompidou, Paris, 1987;

Institute of Contemporary Art, London, 1987; and the Centro Cultural de Arte Contemporáneo, Mexico City, 1987.

And he would often be asked, or request, to do some on-site artwork, an installation or a mural on a public building, concurrent with his gallery exhibit, his public work serving not simply as promotion for his gallery exhibits, as some have cynically proposed (Haring 1997 158), but as a concrete image or metaphor for his aesthetic project and improvisational artistic style.

In these on-site works, Haring would paint without a sketch using the specificities of the given location to his advantage, as he did for instance at the Museum of Contemporary Art in Bordeaux where he would transform the building's immense arches into tablets for his awe-inspiring series, *The Ten Commandments* (Gruen 1991 136–37), and incorporating any accidents that may arise into his overall design while he listened to hip-hop and underground dance music, often Larry Levan's, and an audience, often boys or urban young men, hung out and watched.

It was painting not as the production of objects but as a performance or process, or what one might call, considering his body paintings of choreographer Bill T. Jones and disco music diva Grace Jones, painting as dance, whose goal was to transform a given public space and the spectators' relationship to it, not unlike the way graffiti writers transformed public space. At its best, Haring's performed painting sought to inform the public's perception of his gallery art, infusing it with the streets' transgressive, cutting-edge life, while his gallery exhibits would conversely give high-cultural credibility to his public work. But as his painting performances played increasingly to the cameras, they would become an appendage to the gallery, a simulacrum or a mass-media event, contributing to the eventual disappearance of the "street" as a space of transgression and social critique.

Haring however had infinite faith in his capacity to incorporate otherness, whether that otherness was the media or the street, and to remain both cutting-edge and "himself." A certain hubris sustained this faith, but hubris was not the largest part of it. He felt that he had been born to a new generation of artists of the "Space Age," for whom a certain ironic distance from the mass media was no longer possible. Comparing his situation to that of earlier Pop artists, he would stress: "The artists who were doing it 20 years ago were calling attention to the new cultural things from [a] somewhat . . . objective stance. I was born in 1958, one of the first babies of the space age. I grew up on TV. I feel more that I am a product of Pop, rather than a person who is calling attention to it" (Blinderman 18).

Warhol, whom he recognized as his predecessor and the artist without whose work his would have been impossible, could still aspire to incorporate the media from a certain ironic stance, that stance constituting his unique vision and his art. But contemporary artists like Haring, so he felt, had no space outside the media from which to launch such an independent artistic vision. And as his images began to be internationally imitated and reproduced by the media, Haring would become increasingly concerned and engaged, as his *Journals* show (Gruen 1991 128; Haring 1997 218), with the problem of "restraining" and channeling such commercialization toward art and toward "himself" as an individual artist and author. His Pop Shop, which some have seen as a sign of his capitulation to commercialism, would be, on the contrary, born out of this concern for the specificity of art and of individual artistic vision, and Japan, where he would open his only Pop Shop outside New York, would be the limit case of such engagement with commerce.

For some time Haring had been noticing imitations of his work everywhere he went, and both proud and amused, he would stop to tag the fakes, humorously inscribing on them: "Not a Keith Haring!!" (Kolossa 19–20). But the imitations he would encounter in Japan would be more unsettling: For one, Tokyo seemed awash in them: "It's hard to find a store that *doesn't* have some fake KH . . . or KH-inspired things," Haring would exasperatedly note (Haring 1997 218). "[A]nd this time, they [were] really well done. They look[ed] like the real thing," he would add in distress (Gruen 1991 181).

And indeed these Japanese imitations were perfectly wrought reproductions, but they were so accurately and flawlessly "redrawn" that they lacked the "gesture" or "spirit" of his primitivist "carved" line, effacing thus the signature or stamp of individual expression that he felt was the "very essence of [his] work" (Haring 1997 220). Instead of the masculine expressiveness Haring intended his images to convey, these imitations were "cute," or as they were called in Japanese popular culture *kawaii* (meaning both lovely and kitsch, and associated with the concept of *shojo* or girliness; Yamagiwa).

Devoid of a deep identification with Haring's aesthetic project or with the culture from which it had emerged, devoid indeed of identi-fication *tout court*, these flat, purely plastic reproductions could circu-late, as so many other Japanese imitations of the West did, as sheer expenditure or excess, participating thus in a contemporary Japanese youth subculture whose goal was to resist the traditional aesthetics of *iki* or restraint, and the social conformity promoted by it, through a market-friendly consumerist aesthetics of waste (Yamagiwa).

Seeing his work (and the name associated with it, *his*) so over-whelmed and "overshadowed" by these "cute" fakes, Haring would begin to question his "naïve confidence" in the Japanese understanding of his work (Haring 1997 220), and his faith in his ability to incorporate the other (the market, the culturally different, the street) while remaining both cutting-edge and himself would be intensely shaken (218). For Japan was not just another market for Haring. It had a special meaning for him—it was, in a sense, a metaphor for what sustained his belief in his work.

He had until then thought that if any place understood his aesthetics, had an immediate, deeply embedded connection with it, it was Japan. (He had even imagined himself as a Japanese painter in a previous life; Haring 1997 193.) And that immediate, deeply embedded connection with his work was based on a shared reverence for (and a deep abiding faith in) the indestructible, unco-optable human spirit expressed in the trace of an individual's line, which traditional Japanese arts, such as calligraphy, cultivated.

As long as one had that trace, he believed, one could incorporate anything (the market, the foreign other, the street) and remain singularly personal, individual, unique. Japan, so he thought, was proof positive that one could thoroughly absorb (and be absorbed by) the market, even expand upon it, while retaining one's irreducible, personal difference. And it is this belief that begins to falter as Haring sees his images circulating eviscerated, flattened, and dissociated from him, and starts to question his idea of a deeply embedded, unmediated, cross-cultural connection between Japan and his work.

For in the end though Haring's aesthetics, unlike the gay culture of sameness he had previously critiqued, was one of difference, it was nonetheless an aesthetics of identification. And what Japan, as well as Juan's relationship, would put simultaneously to the test, as he prepared to open his Pop Shop in Tokyo, in 1988, was this cross-cultural identification on which his promotion of radical difference and resistance to market commodification was based.

And this critical questioning could not have come at a worst time. Haring had just discovered his first clear symptoms of AIDS, and was much in need of reassurance about the survival of his artistic legacy, the immortality of his work. But instead of reassurance, within the next few weeks most of the important relationships that sustained his work—his symbolic relationship with Japan, his sexual-romantic relationship with Juan, and his affective relationship with New York's urban youth culture—would begin to come undone.

For some time now Juan had been making demands of Haring, asking him to clarify his relationship with him, to commit, and typical of Haring, he had opted to answer him by inviting him to Tokyo, along with a posse of New York City kids, to help him celebrate the opening of his new Pop Shop (Haring 1997 191, 211–16). He had paid everyone's way there as well as their stay, and had hoped they would all connect with Tokyo's youth culture, but the New York posse, far from seeing what Haring claimed to see there, had actually hated it. They had taken the typical neon-sign tour of Shibuya, the shopping district, had played the *pachinko* slot machines, had stopped in Harajuku to gawk at the Japanese kids dressed up as hip-hopsters, and rather offhandedly and obnoxiously, had dismissed it all. It was all a costume ball, they felt, they couldn't relate to it, and by the way, they wanted hamburgers—not raw fish.

Haring had felt the rumblings, but busy with the promotion of his new Pop Shop had been unable to address them, and meanwhile, unbeknown to him, an actual rift between the kids and him had been developing and growing until it would finally burst out in the open at the most inopportune time. They had all been sitting for dinner at an Italian restaurant (as a concession to the kids) with Haring, his secretary Julia Gruen, his photographer and assistant Tseng Kwong Chi, and his Japanese agents Fran and Kaz Kuzui at one end of the table and the New York City posse mostly on the opposite end, when Juan, uneasy with his position in the middle, had decided to get up and move away, in Haring's recollection, from the "intellectual" end (Haring 1997 214). "I think I'll move to the other side of the table–away from the *intellectual* end," he might have said, inadvertently exposing, and naming, the unspoken rift. And Haring, according to Juan (he didn't know why), had just blown up and proceeded to humiliate and belittle him. He would go back to his room that night and would leave for New York the next morning silently, without speaking a word to Haring or taking any money, clothes, or keys. And Haring, visibly shaken, would desperately try to reach him during the next few days. He would finally get a hold of him at a friend's apartment, and they would reunite some time later in New York, but it would never be the same.

"The *intellectual* end," such a simple phrase, and yet it would be this phrase that would disarticulate Haring, laying bare many of the contradictions in his work, serving as a substitute or metonymy for all those things he had tried so hard—and perhaps unsuccessfully—to bridge: the New York City street culture and the established art world;

the mass-media market and the fine art gallery; the racial and cultural other and the white middle-class avant-garde; the poor and destitute and the nouveau riche.

During the next year Juan and Haring's relationship would deteriorate. They would continue to live together in New York, but Haring would become increasingly incommunicative and cold, according to Juan, not even sitting down to discuss his AIDS diagnosis after he had arrived from Japan with Kaposi's sarcoma lesions on his body ("You should get yourself checked," was all he said, Juan claimed). And though Juan would remain to the end Haring's lover ("I love Juan very much and . . . I d[o]n't want to jeopardize my relationship with [him]" reads the next-to-the-last entry of his *Journals*, dated Wednesday, September 21, 1989; Haring 1997 272), Haring would search elsewhere in an attempt to recover that initial look of identification across differences that had sustained his work.

He would find it in the figure of a strikingly handsome, straight-identified, eighteen-year-old Puerto Rican boy from Loisaida, whom he had met outside his studio after they had both locked eyes: "It's funny, because we met on the street in front of my studio and we just looked at each other and instinctively said 'Hello,'" Haring recalled (Gruen 1991 188). He would proceed to invite Vazquez to travel with him throughout Europe to serve as an "intellectual companion" for him (Haring 1997 273), because he needed a new, "fresh outlook" that Juan, his lover, could not provide (272). But he would torture himself because Vazquez was "still incredibly beautiful and almost the exact image of what I always thought I wanted in a partner" (250). And he would put himself through the rigors of attempting to turn eros into pedagogy, homoerotic desire into platonic, disembodied friendship and immortality. But the pedagogy he imparted was always about his work and the ultimate effect of his teaching was always the other's production of his own image. And in the end, it was this image reflected back to him that would justify spending the precious little time he had left with Vazquez: "He is a good company and a good way to reflect my self to myself," he would tell a virtual reader and himself (250).

Juan had also been once one of those special people who reflected Haring's image back to him. He had had once what Haring called "the gift of life," that life force which fueled his work silently bonding him with other people (like children, like Juan) who instantaneously recognized and understood him (Haring 1997 123). But now Juan had become too problematic, too demanding, too weighed down, too bound up with the complications of daily living, of HIV-AIDS. Like

Japan, like the street kids, like the mass-media market, like life itself, Juan had turned into a "wall," become opaque (241). And Haring needed so desperately some reassurance then, to see his image once again on the reflecting mirror of other people's gaze, to feel that it would be passed on, that his work would survive.

Because of concern for his legacy he would put Vazquez in his will, not Juan: "I've gone ahead . . . and [written] him into the will . . . 'cause I think I'm sort of teaching him (or trying to) to understand how I feel about everything so he can be my voice in the future," he would explain (Haring 1997 240). And he would establish the Keith Haring Foundation to promote the continued appreciation of his art. But in the end nothing would confirm his legacy more, the immortality of his work, than that last fleeting look which the beautiful youthful image of Vazquez, like the vanishing figure of Tadzio in Thomas Mann's *Death in Venice*, a text that would haunt Haring's *Journals'* pages to the end (147), would return to a dying and agitated Haring so that he could once again see himself. On February 16, 1990, at 4:40 in the morning Haring would pass away, surrounded by family and friends, especially Vazquez, who was rarely seen leaving his side, it was said (Gruen 1991 218). And before the day was over a not-so-shocked art world would learn of Haring's passing and a brief art-market boom would ensue for the next few years over the then calculated $25-million Haring estate (Sischy).

CHAPTER 4

Listening Speaks (II)

Testimonio, Queer Latino Representation, and Shame

Listening, your heart is in your throat.

—Wayne Koestenbaum, *The Queen's Throat*

For more than 10 years I would agonize about the retelling of Juan's tale, yet I couldn't let it go. And I'd begin to record some of our conversations, not really knowing where they'd lead. And as I transcribed them, in search of *the* story, I kept getting tales, concatenated, variegated tales that would force me to follow Juan's lead, to jumpcut to an earlier or later moment in our conversation, to wait in anticipation for *the word*, or better yet, the silence, the nuance, the detour, the stress that would signal, rather than an interruption, a continuation of his story elsewhere and on a different track.

I thus found myself literally following Juan's t(r)ail, and the transcription of his tales began to transform to reflect this experience of listening. I'd stress a word, delete a phrase, change the order of a sentence or a paragraph, splice two sections that were far removed, reorganize paragraphs and sections around emerging clusters of meaning, figures, tropes in order to be faithful to Juan's involved, convoluted storytelling.

It was a hard lesson in listening for elusive meanings and emerging significations, for Juan's convoluted storytelling placed before me the task of interpretation, obligated me to listen for *another* voice. Not a voice that expressed fullness of meaning or presence, as Derrideans would say, but a voice that manifested itself in absence, in elision, in detours, such as those minimal, yet heroic, deviations in singing that make up, according to Wayne Koestenbaum, an opera diva's personal style, that render it rife with anticipation and "unspeakable complexities" (Koestenbaum 1993 21).

As a matter of fact, in my attempt to be faithful to this other voice, I'd so inductively followed Juan's storytelling trying to bring out its own inner logic, its own inner structure and semantic nodes, that when I'd finally finished and decided to turn to the editors' introductions of well-known Latin American *testimonios* for a possible, if retrospective, justificatory model, I was hard pressed to keep from crying at the realization of how I'd gotten it all wrong.

Had I only imposed some outside structure from the beginning, some guiding questions from the start, as both *testimonio* editors, Miguel Barnet and Elisabeth Burgos-Debray, recommended in *The Autobiography of a Runaway Slave* (Montejo) and *I, Rigoberta Menchú: An Indian Woman in Guatemala* (Menchú), respectively, I would have saved myself much time—and heartache. Instead, I'd put myself through a practice of listening that required me to follow the trail of Juan's voice, to judge my retelling not only by its fidelity to the events in Juan's life, but by its fidelity to the traces that living had left in his voice—by all that ambivalent under- and over-living that marked his and other people's lives, preventing them from being reduced to mere living, to mere usable circumstance.

For—I must admit—I always figured Juan's voice as a literary voice. And even while I represented the urgency and significance of his story to others, as I searched to give it form, in terms of reference, I never stopped conceiving it to myself in terms of art. And it was this voice that kept me going, prodding me, urging me on—for ten years.

So for ten years I wouldn't feel adequate to the task of retelling Juan's story, but I couldn't give it up. And I'd read fragments of my edited interviews to colleagues and friends, secretly hoping that someone would relieve me of this task—but I got no takers. And whereas my writer friends were unanimously enthusiastic about Juan's tale, my academic friends, affectionately yet firmly, advised me caution.

What if I was secretly feeding a prurient interest—mine as well as others'—for Latino lives under duress? What if I was aestheticizing—and thereby neutralizing—sheer wretchedness? What if I was turning into palatable, tasty entertainment truncated lives? What if I was assuaging someone's guilt, my own included, about living, just living or going about one's daily life while entire populations were being reconnoitered and targeted? Or even worse: what if I was providing someone with a walk on the wild side so that that someone, me included, could finally feel, could *com-probar*, could both confirm and taste that joyous sigh of relief, that jolt that may be experienced at reliving "lesser" lives at a distance, safely sconced at home, in one's comfortable armchair, with one's ubiquitous cup of coffee by one's side, as is thematized in Cortázar's short story "Continuity of Parks"? "He could taste the almost perverse pleasure of disengaging himself . . . from his surroundings," of immersing himself in the "sordid" scene that the novel he was reading was recounting, says Cortázar's narrator of his protagonist's adventure in reading. And yet: "[H]e could feel at the same time that his head was resting comfortably on the velvet of his armchair's high back, that his cigarettes remained within easy reach of his hand" (11).

Coming in the wake of the 1980s Latin American boom in testimonial writing and of American critics' promotion of *testimonio* at universities, it was only natural—and necessary—that such questions about *use* should be raised. Critics had so invested in *testimonio*'s counterhegemonic discourse as a means of intervening in the university's culture wars that when, by the mid-1990s, *testimonio* had become canonical and institutionalized at American universities, they began to wonder about the value, and the ethics, of reducing subaltern discourses to internal, American university struggles over cultural politics. And a generalized sense of guilt, a collective *mea culpa*, began to pervade academic writing.

Such contextualization helped to shed light on the caution my academic friends were advising, but it gave me no relief. Quite the contrary, a feeling I can only retrospectively name overpowered me—shame. And for about ten years the transcription of Juan's interviews lay there in my study, dormant and partially edited, sleeping, as one would say in Puerto Rican Spanish, *el sueño de los justos*, the righteous' uninterrupted, otherworldly sleep. And in the meantime, as in a Latin American *Boom* novel, the original tapes were lost.

A RETICENT GENRE

Latin American cultural critic Doris Sommer has reflected on the reticence of *testimonio* subjects, such as the Guatemalan Indian activist Rigoberta Menchú, to give full account. And she has persuasively argued in her book, *Proceed with Caution, When Engaged by Minority Writing in the Americas*, that such reticence needs to be considered the testimonial subject's artful response to more powerful subjects', the editors' or the readers', appropriating, prying moves. And though such a belief in art or in the artfulness of the testimonial subject's voice would eventually help me overcome my own reticence in editing

Juan's interviews, I must admit, Menchú's partial silence struck me as also deriving from another more subjective, more intensely personal source.

Faced with the urgent command to tell her people's story in order to preserve their lives, as a genocidal campaign against the indigenous population of her country raged on, Menchú would pause to reflect:

> In my community's terms, I was already a grown woman, and I was very *ashamed* at being so confused, when so many of my village understood so much better than I. But their ideas were very pure because they had never been outside their community. (Menchú 121; my italics)

What made Menchú pause here on her way to telling her community's story, first to other Guatemalans, then to Elisabeth Burgos-Debray, the Venezuelan anthropologist who would turn her testimony into a book, *I, Rigoberta Menchú, An Indian Woman in Guatemala*, and, through her, to the rest of the world, was not only, I felt, her awareness of the possible appropriating moves of more powerful others but her own sense of inadequacy to tell her tale. What made her pause here and turn self-reflexive, that is, turn her gaze on herself in shame, was, I thought, the sudden paralyzing realization that though she was inadequate to the task of telling, she was the one who had been chosen, commanded even, by her community to tell the tale.

In a historically assailed community such as the Indian community of Guatemala, literally under siege, secrets may not only be strategically necessary, they may also be socially constitutive, foundational: "My father used to say: 'There are many secrets we must not tell. We must keep our secrets,'" Menchú would explain. And she would conclude: "If we don't protect our ancestors' secrets, we'll be responsible for killing them" (188). And yet the community's command before her was just *that*: to tell her community's secrets, to betray her ancestors, to put them at risk, as it were, in order to save them—to stray in order to be faithful, in order to return. And it was the enormity of this paradoxical command that would make her pause, that would almost make her want to dissolve in shame.

Like all transculturated subjects, Menchú stands on the brink, between contradictory loyalties, facing a paradoxical command. And like all transculturated subjects, she must construct a new subject out of the very substance of shame. For shame is the price that is exacted by her community for moving forward, for fulfilling the command on which its very survival rests.

For shame makes one pause, I would come to know, but it does not make one stop, frustratingly. It creates a barrier, as psychologist Silvan Tomkins has concretely proposed, but it also makes one conscious, hyperconscious, of the irreducibility of one's engagement with the extra-communal other, of one's investment, even of one's love (157). And it forces one to search, as such, for new paths, new ways to reconnect.

Like the figure of the paradox in Gilles Deleuze's *The Logic of Sense*, the trope for the simultaneous affirmation of two mutually exclusive *senses* (both meaning and direction), shame forces the subject to take seriously two contradictory commands, to walk in two opposite directions at once, toward the community and away from it. Shame made Menchú pause and reflect, but it would not make her rush back in repentance or retreat. On the contrary, it would urge her forward and backward in a mutually reinforcing counterpoint: the more she wandered out of her community telling its secrets, the more she would insist on holding on to her Indian heritage, to her cultural and racial otherness.

Foreign in a Domestic Sense

I am certainly no Rigoberta Menchú and U.S. Puerto Ricans, though the children of a forced, government-sponsored migration that "relieved" the Island of a third of its working-class population, underwriting its process of industrialization, are no Guatemalan Indians running from an overtly genocidal campaign. (Instead, Puerto Rican migrants have been said to have transformed, as the writer Luis Rafael Sánchez has proposed, the imposed, one-way route of emigration into a more wieldy, two-way travel in a figurative "air bus"; Sánchez 1994). Yet the shame that paralyzed me and kept me from editing Juan's *testimonio* for ten years, I felt, was not unrelated to Menchú's shame.

I had arrived in New York from Puerto Rico in—of all years— 1969. I was then fourteen. And I can still remember the heaviness in the air that summer in which, significantly, both Nuyoricans and gays rose to political visibility in New York, leaving behind, in Allen Ginsberg's memorable words, that "wounded look that fags all had 10 years ago" (Duberman 208). For the summer of 1969 was both the summer of the Stonewall rebellion and the founding of the first militant New York Puerto Rican political party in El Barrio/East Harlem, The Young Lords. And I recall walking around New York that summer and feeling the weight, the markedness even, of being labeled "Puerto Rican" for the first time. Because one didn't have to say "spic," or qualify "Puerto Rican" back then; it was itself an insult—it interpellated you in order to shut you up. And people, practically anyone, U.S. citizens as well as aspirants to, could wield this word with impunity and authority. For people *knew* Puerto Ricans, intimately. People who couldn't locate the Caribbean Sea on the map, much less Puerto Rico, could tell you *what* you were and *who* you were. How could they know Puerto Ricans so intimately, I wondered. How could one account for such familiarity with a people whose history one didn't know, or didn't care enough to know, or simply, refused to know, because it disturbed one's notions about the anticolonial cast of American republicanism?

"Foreign in a domestic sense" had been the term the U.S. Supreme Court had finally adopted in 1900, after much debate (Cabranes 43), two years after the U.S. acquisition of Puerto Rico (along with Guam and the Philippines) in the Spanish-American-Cuban War, to account for the Island's anomalous status in the Constitution of a nation whose very foundations were anticolonial. And spurred by a generalized feeling that Puerto Ricans—the first air mass migrants to the city since U.S. immigration law had halted the influx of Europeans in the late 1920s—were invading New York, propagating themselves inexplicably ("like roaches"), swelling the ranks of its poor, and jamming its social services, a whole cottage industry of social science research had developed to render this paradoxical "domestic foreignness" of Puerto Ricans fully knowable (Briggs 2002a 80–82).

No two other texts made Puerto Ricans then, or have made them since, more available to wide academic and popular knowledge than Oscar Lewis's 1965 National-Book-Award-winning, bestselling ethnography, *La Vida: A Puerto Rican Family in the Culture of Poverty—San Juan and New York* and Robert Wise and Jerome Robbins's 1961 film version of the musical *West Side Story*, which would catapult the image of Puerto Ricans around the world.

In her incisive and elegant study, *Reproducing Empire: Race, Sex, Science, and U.S. Imperialism in Puerto Rico*, Laura Briggs has argued that social science research during the decade of the 1960s in New York created a discourse of Puerto Rican difference by translating race into culture and grounding this culture, specifically a "culture of poverty" shared both by the Puerto Rican poor in the Island and New York, in notions of gender and sexual difference. There was a secret at the heart of Puerto Rican culture, this research seemed to suggest, and that dirty secret was, one might say, using a Foucauldian turn of phrase, sexuality—an unbridled female sexuality, whose logical counterpart was an impotent masculinity and an excessive, compensatory, irrational machismo. And indeed both *La Vida* and *West Side Story* trafficked in these representations.

LA VIDA, OR THE RETURN OF THE PRIMITIVE

La Vida was the multigenerational portrait of a Puerto Rican "slum family," the fictionally named Ríos, as told by its members in their own life histories or rhetorically constructed first-person accounts, selected and edited by Lewis from extensive interviews conducted and translated from the Spanish by his mostly Puerto Rican research assistants. As introduced by Lewis in a long theoretical essay, these first-person narratives, which tell the seemingly unmediated story of the prostitute Fernanda and her four children in the slums of San Juan and New York, were so dominated by the Ríos's "present-time orientation" and "short-range hedonism" (li–ii) that "the line between the routine life and the 'gay life,'" between social responsibility and pleasure blurred and disappeared (xxxi). Indeed, as asserted by Lewis in a broad cross-cultural comparison in which one may still read his shock, "[t]he Ríos family [was] closer to the expression of an unbridled id than any other people I have studied" (xxvi). And this absorption of social responsibility by an unbridled, out-of-control sexuality or id was nowhere more evident than in the very title of Lewis's book, *La Vida*, in which the Spanish word for "life" and the metonymic expression *estar en la vida*, or to be in the life—of prostitution, that is—assimilated and fused.

In Lewis's analysis, the story of the Puerto Rican "culture of poverty," which his edited first-person accounts served as evidence for, became the tale of a mostly female, disordered sexuality whose "pathological" results (free unions, unstable marriages, high rates of illegitimacy, and matrifocal households) were perpetuated culturally through deficient child rearing or bad mothering. "Once [this culture of poverty] comes into existence," Lewis would warn,

> it tends to perpetuate itself from generation to generation because of its effect on the children. By the time slum children are age six or seven they have usually absorbed the basic values and attitudes of their subculture and are not psychologically geared to take full advantage of changing conditions or increased opportunities which may occur in their lifetime. (xlv)

Caught in this self-perpetuating cycle of poverty, Lewis's Puerto Rican informants (he called them "characters") appeared, despite his attribution of first-person subjectivity to them, as the cast of some turn-of-the-century naturalist novel, tossed about by forces that, though of their own making, remained beyond their control.

Indeed, Lewis's characters, for all their ethnographic realism, may be more accurately construed as figures or tropes of an earlier scientific and medical discourse whose focus on the sexuality and reproductive practices of Puerto Rican women had served, as Briggs has proposed (2002b), to launch the social policies of U.S. colonial administrations in Puerto Rico. In this discourse, later exported to the United States as Lewis's "culture of poverty" and to the rest of the Third World as U.S. "development" policy, Briggs claims, knowledge, management, and regulation of the bodies of women of color was deemed of paramount importance in order to eradicate poverty and foment modernization.

For the "poor" the Ríos as a figure represented in Lewis's text were not just the Puerto Rican poor but a much broader class: they were the poor of "under-development," and their "culture of poverty" was only the most extreme, the limit case, of Lewis's theories of cultural adaptation among the poor in societies with colonial legacies that were then undergoing Western-style modernization, Puerto Rico certainly, but also Mexico, India, and Cuba, societies that Lewis studied intensely. Compared with the Mexican, Indian, and Cuban "slum dwellers" whom he had studied, the Puerto Rican poor, Lewis would insist, were more thoroughly deracinated, more ignorant of, and detached from, a local national tradition (xvii). And it was this cultural deracination of Puerto Ricans—and not merely their economic condition—that made them, he would suggest, the purest example of the "culture of poverty." The Indian lower castes or the Jews of Eastern Europe may be poor, according to him. Yet they did not share in the Puerto Rican slum dweller's "psychopathological" traits, for a complex system of clan leadership in the case of one, and an ancient religious book culture in that of the other, prevented them from free-falling into the disorganized present-oriented state that characterized the "culture of poverty" (xlix).

Given the celebratory tenor of most social science research conducted on post–World War II industrial development in what was then called the Third World, including most literature on Puerto Rico's industrialization program, known in Spanish as *Manos a la Obra* and in English as "Operation Bootstrap," Lewis's research focus on populations that had been marginalized or "left behind" by the process of modernization would seem to stand out then as a critical, even progressive, corrective. And it was thus that Lewis's ethnographic accounts would enter the socially conscious canon of Latin American literature as forerunners of *testimonio*. Yet what his friend and colleague Margaret Mead would call, in a sympathetic evocation of Lewis (Lewis 1975 viii), his "ardent faith" in the ultimately salutary powers of modern technology would seem however to predispose him to look elsewhere for signs of the root causes of poverty—to look, that is, not at the economic politics of development but at the "psychology" of those marginalized Third World populations as expressed in their familial bonds and in their sexual and reproductive behavior.

Writing at a time when cultural relativism, as represented by Mead and her Columbia professors, Franz Boas and Ruth Benedict, had long triumphed in the American academy, Lewis would appear to return then, by psychology's circuitous route, to anthropology's founding gaze. And his study of Third World poor families would in the end turn into a study of the return of the "primitive," now defamiliarized, rendered strange, even grotesque, as in Freud's concept of the "uncanny," by being out of context, by being, that is, in the midst of what he would call "our highly complex, specialized, organized" modern world. At a time when anthropology had already affirmed the complex social structure of so-called "primitive cultures," Lewis would recover, in his view of the menacing, disordered otherness of the Ríos, a Puerto Rican transnational "slum family," a glimpse of anthropology's founding gaze, now anachronistically—and shockingly—lodged at the heart of the world's most technologically advanced society:

> When we look at the culture of poverty on the local community level, we find poor housing conditions, crowding, gregariousness, but above all a minimum of organization beyond the level of the nuclear and extended family. . . . Indeed, it is the low-level of organization which gives the culture of poverty its marginal and anachronistic quality in our highly complex, specialized, organized society. Most primitive peoples have achieved a higher level of socio-cultural organization than our modern urban slum dwellers. (xlvii)

"But These P.R.s Are Different—They Multiply!"

It is here, in Lewis's recovery of the anthropologist's primal gaze, in the uncanny return of the primitive in the midst of America's highly specialized, technologically advanced society, where *La Vida* meets *West Side Story*. For *West Side Story*, like *La Vida*, is the story of an anachronistic, modern primitive-ness, also represented here in highly sexualized terms, and of the misplaced, misguided, liberal attempt to transform or redeem that primitive-ness, to recuperate it for society, as it were, by channeling it through—what else?—the powers of (heterosexual) love and romance.

The Puerto Rican cultural critic, Alberto Sandoval-Sánchez, has suggested that in *West Side Story* Puerto Ricans are identified with nature and "barbarism," as evinced in the Puerto Rican gang's name, the Sharks, with its historic associations with a purportedly Caribbean cannibalism (169). And he concludes that in identifying Puerto Ricans as such, the film "others" or marginalizes them, driving a wedge between what is acceptable and what is not, what is valuable and what is not, Anglo-American and Latino cultures, the United States and Puerto Rico, the mythically upper-class East Side and the then immigrant West (168).

Yet if it is true that the film more emphatically, though not exclusively, casts Puerto Ricans in the role of modern barbarians, it is also true that the film's main concern is not with marginalization and distancing but, as Frances Negrón-Muntaner has astutely noted, with incorporation: "Ultimately, the film's main and long-lasting effect is not that it divides," she contends, but that it "incorporates [in a queer way] the specter of Puerto Ricans into American culture" (62–63). And if initially this central concern of the film with incorporation—with all of its menacingly cannibalistic associations—is projected onto Puerto Ricans, in the end it is the film itself, not Puerto Ricans, which is the most ruthless and effective agent of incorporation.

As the film opens, the camera shows the white "American" ethnic gang, the Jets, reveling in its absolute command of the neighborhood's social spaces (the streets, the playground, the candy store, the gym) by dancing through the streets with soaring plane-like movements, allusive of its name. But time and again the "Puerto Rican" rival gang, the Sharks, pop up unexpectedly to interrupt the Jets' soaring movements with their own more grounded, jaggedly defensive moves, taunting them with (to them) incomprehensible Spanish words (*Mira, mira ... Andale, ándale ... Por aquí ...*), and luring them into the neighborhood's shadowy back alleys in order to ambush them. Once in these back alleys the Jets (and the viewers) come shockingly face to face with a gigantic graffiti image of a shark, whose menacing, teeth-wielding open jaws seem poised to devour them.

From the perspective of the Jets (and of the viewers), Puerto Ricans are clearly like this iconic representation: furtive, shadowy, devouring. And later, as the Jets meet to devise a plan to deal with what they perceive as the "Puerto Rican threat," the Puerto Rican encroachment on "their turf," Riff, the gang's leader, attempts to rally his men by reminding them, "We fought hard for this turf and we ain't just gonna give it up. When the Emeralds claimed it, we shut them out. The Hearts, remember, they tried to take it away, and we knocked them down the cellar." But immediately the other gang members express reservations, protest: "But these P.R.s are different," they claim, "they multiply!" "They're cockroaches! Close the windows! Close the doors! They are eating all the food! . . . all the air!," they urge.

Yes, Puerto Ricans are different—for the Jets. They are not like earlier white ethnic immigrant groups; theirs is not the universally told story of immigration, where each new incoming group must literally fight its way through the native's rejection and scorn in order to gain acceptance and turf. No, Puerto Ricans are different: "Close the windows! Close the doors!" Their reproduction threatens to overwhelm all public and private space, all turf, even the very divide on which turf itself is based.

Like the discourse of Puerto Rican difference identified by Briggs, Puerto Rican racial difference in *West Side Story* may be traced to colonialist notions about the relationship between the Island's disordered, "tropical" reproduction and underdevelopment. As Anita, the most thoroughly sexualized character in the film, Bernardo's lover and foil to his sister, ingénue Maria, exclaims in one of the film's signature musical numbers, *America*, "I like to live in America" because . . . in Puerto Rico, "my heart's devotion," she ironically adds, the "hurricanes" are always "blowing," and the "population growing," and the "money owing," and the "sunlight streaming," and the "natives steaming . . ." "I like the isle of Manhattan," she concludes. "Smoke on your pipe and put that in!"

Anita would like to escape, to leave behind this Puerto Rican tropical world where sexuality and underdevelopment are caught up in an endlessly self-perpetuating natural cycle, and represents her assimilation into American society as a Manhattan girl as an act of forgetting, of burying the past: "Puerto Rico . . . My heart's devotion . . . / Let it sink back in the ocean." And yet, ironically, it is here, in "America," where that past will not go away, for throughout the film, Anita, played by Rita Moreno, whom Hollywood nicknamed "the Puerto Rican Firecracker," is relentlessly sexualized, her sexuality even serving as a metonymy, or a standing in, for the gang's turf war itself.

In what is clearly the film's climax, the main characters' intentions are juxtaposed through crosscutting or parallel montage as they sing their own versions of the musical number *Tonight*. As the sequence opens, the Jets are shown marching down the crumbling back alley of an inner-city neighborhood and singing to a martial beat: "The Jets are gonna have their way tonight . . . The Puerto Ricans crumble, fair fight, but if they start to rumble, we'll rumble them right." The camera then crosscuts to a rooftop scene where the Sharks are rallying and singing to the same driving beat: "We're gonna cut them down to size tonight. We said okay no rumpus, no tricks, but just in case they jump us, we're ready to mix." The parallel montage continues as Anita, wearing a dark sheer slip and sitting in bed, raises a leg to the camera to put on a stocking, as in a classic pin-up shot, and sings of her upcoming meeting with her lover Bernardo in the third person and to the same bellicose beat: "Anita is gonna get her kicks tonight. We'll have our private little mix tonight." But then the music shifts tempo, picking up a lyrical, soaring, waltz-like momentum, as first Tony, then Maria reprise their earlier version of *Tonight* in which, like a modern-day, inner-city Romeo and Juliet, they vowed eternal love on the fire escape: Tony: "Tonight, tonight I'll see my love tonight and for us stars will stop where they are." Maria: "Oh, moon, grow bright and make this endless day endless night."

Marked by this change in tempo, crosscutting from the gangs' version to Tony and Maria's would seem to contrast the characters' opposite intentions: to either reestablish boundaries by utterly crushing the racial other (or as the Jets put it, "to stop them once and for all") or to unite and fuse with the racially different in an endless utopian night of love. Crosscutting from the gangs' version to Anita's would on the other hand seem to foreground instead the continuity between the gangs' intentions and Anita's anticipated night of lovemaking, as both their versions share not only the same tempo but the same warlike language ("Anita is gonna get her kicks tonight. We'll have our private little *mix* tonight"). Whereas crosscutting to Tony and Maria's rendition would seem to ask the viewer to choose between the phobic destruction of the racial turf war and its opposite—the potentially productive unity of love—crosscutting to Anita's version would appear to invite instead a metonymic link in which Anita's sexuality would be asked to substitute for the gangs' racial turf war, even to fuel it.

Earlier in the film, Maria had asked Anita, "Why must they [the Sharks] always fight?" To which Anita had answered: "You saw how they dance? Like they gotta get rid of something quick—that's how they fight." "Get rid of what?" Maria had insisted. To which Anita had offered: "Too much feeling. And they do get rid of it. Boy, after a fight that brother of yours is so healthy! Definitely Black Orchid!"

And later, as Anita tries to deliver a message to Tony and ends up being assaulted and almost raped by the Jets, she is accosted upon entering Doc's candy store by a tellingly metonymic insult: the Jets whistle *La cucaracha* as she comes in.

Either way, then, whether Anita's sexuality is fueled by the rumble, as in the former example, or whether it substitutes for the fear of—and desire for—the presumed uncontrollable reproduction of Puerto Ricans that fuels it, as in the latter case, Anita's sexuality in *West Side Story* is too caught up in the racial turf war, too intimately imbricated with it, to be transformative or liberating, as she, in Rita Moreno's impassioned performance in *America*, combatively affirms: "Girls here are free to have fun," she exclaims as she leads into the show-stopping, sensuously self-creating performance that would win her a legendary status in Hollywood and an Academy Award.

How to transcend then the unending cycle of the turf war? How to transform and neutralize the threat (or the fear) of Puerto Rican racial difference which seems to fuel the turf war? If Puerto Rican racial difference is discursively constituted as a form of disordered sexuality—if race and sexuality, that is, are mutually constitutive, as recent queer and postcolonial scholars contend (Somerville and Stoler, for instance)—then, *West Side Story* would seem to suggest, Puerto Rican racial difference can be transcended and redeemed through a poetics and politics of love. It can be normalized or mainstreamed, that is, not because "love," so the platitude goes, "conquers all," but because "love" can also be a disciplining tool—one that channels improper sexualities into proper, modern, heterosexual unions through romance and marriage.

Disordered heterosexual desire however is not the only libidinal force that fuels the turf war—so is homosocial desire, that is, desire among men. Critics had long remarked that all of the creators of *West Side Story* were Jewish and gay: its choreographer, Jerome Robbins, its composer, Leonard Bernstein, its lyricist, Stephen Sondheim, and its librettist, Arthur Laurents. But not until recently had a critic offered a reading that would account for the charged intersection of homoeroticism and race in the film. Contextualizing *West Side Story*, the Puerto Rican critic, Frances Negrón-Muntaner has proposed that for a certain proto-gay audience of the late 1950s and early 1960s, an audience with whom its creators may be said to have shared a communal gaze, both the film and the play might have been read as "a spectacle of desire for [straight-identified] working-class, gentile, 'rough' ethnic men," for what in gay parlance is known, that is, as "trade" (71).

Puerto Ricans in *West Side Story* may be stigmatized and degraded, she claims, but they are also desirable and seductively stylized. And true enough, there is considerable evidence to suggest that by the 1950s Puerto Rican migrants had become a visible object of queer desire, "electrifying," as an earlier Italian immigration in the 1920s had done, the local New York gay scene, as queer historian George Chauncey has proposed (Negrón-Muntaner 107). Indeed, *West Side Story* seems not only to have been influenced by the desire for ethnic "trade"; it also appears to have influenced in return gay hustler fashion in Times Square, so that, uncannily, the stylized "rough" ethnic types represented by *West Side Story* on film and stage could also be had as one walked out of the theater for pay (Friedman 1986 120).

This racialized homoerotic charge of *West Side Story* may also be read into the very plot of the film and play. Like such classics as *Huckleberry Finn* and *Moby Dick*, *West Side Story* belongs to a long tradition of American writing where the idealized, "innocent" homoerotic bonding of a young white male with a racially different or "primitive" male other in nature or the wilderness is offered up as a socially critical way to resist the domesticating or deadening effects of the "civilized" world, identified with heterosexual romance and marriage, as Leslie Fiedler, in *Love and Death in the American Novel*, famously proposed around the same time *West Side Story* was first being performed, in 1960. Indeed much of the tragic end of *West Side Story* may be seen to devolve from that initial scene where Tony, now integrated into work, into the labor force, tells his best friend and fellow gang member, Riff, that he is no longer interested in the gang, that the "kicks" he used to get from being a gang member he now gets from, as he sings, "Something [that]'s Coming," and that something that's coming will of course turn out to be heterosexual romance and union in the form of a Puerto Rican girl named Maria, played by Natalie Wood. Riff, however, can't "dig it" and refuses to give up his "kicks," managing to drag his friend Tony back into the turf war, where he is caught up in its escalating violence to tragic ends. And neither can the Sharks give up theirs. Though they may be sworn enemies, as far as their "kicks" are concerned, they are complicit. As long as the turf war lasts, their homosocial attachments will remain unabated.

If "innocent" homosocial attachments had once been idealized in American writing as a form of social critique, by the 1950s they had become suspect and were being demonized as a sign of a new youth culture that had opted out of middle-class American values and refused to integrate into what was seen then as the conventional or "civilized" world. In films such as *Blackboard Jungle* (1955), *Rebel Without a Cause* (1955), and *The Young Savages* (1961), these homosocial attachments would be both condemned as well as sympathetically explored as compensatory formations for what was becoming then the standard explanation for the crisis of juvenile delinquency gripping the nation, family dysfunction, usually represented in the form of a weak or absent father or father figure, as has been discussed by James Gilbert in *Cycle of Outrage*.

But what's particularly significant about *West Side Story* is that it parodies all of the liberal, well-meaning psycho-sociological explanations about juvenile delinquency and youth culture that circulated then. In a memorable musical number symbolically addressed to authority figure police officer Krupke, the Jets mockingly sing of their being "psychologically disturbed" and "sociologically sick" because: "Our mothers all are junkies. Our fathers all are drunks. Golly, Moses, naturally we're punks . . ." Dismissing thus all psycho-sociological explanations that would account for their behavior through parody, the characters in *West Side Story* would seem to unapologetically affirm, as befits a dance musical, the one explanation that their erotically charged performances repeatedly put on display—their kicks.

How to gather and channel then, how to "recathect," as Freud would say, that excessive, disordered libidinal force, represented by Anita's "tropical" sexuality, on the one hand, and the gangs' intense homosocial attachments, on the other, which fuels the turf war, toward proper, socially constructive relationships? Heterosexual marriage and romance have their seductions, chief among them, their being posited in the film as universalisms beyond the tribal enmities of ethnicity and race. Yet in the end, the film's violent incorporation of these "modern primitive" libidinal energies into a "civilized" order occurs not through heterosexual romance and marriage but through the disciplining powers of death and mourning.

As the film comes to a close, members of both gangs lift Tony's dead body aloft and Maria, donning the black shawl of mourning, follows them, as in a ritualized funeral cortege, while the soundtrack plays musical phrases from one of the couple's signature love songs, *Somewhere*: "There's a place for us. Somewhere a place and time for us . . ." Ironically, there's no place. And yet it is this utopian "somewhere," this etymological no-place, that materializes right in front of us in that final image of a community bonded in mourning, a community whose be-longing is not founded on and secured by the attainment of mixed-race heterosexual union but by melancholy, or the endless mourning for it.

That Senseless Sense of Shame

Given this (shall we call it "colonial"?) history where Puerto Ricans' every act and word were always already intimately known, always already referred to and retrofitted into a predetermined sexualized discourse that left them so denuded and exposed, so in need of (state) intervention and rescue, to tell Juan's tale—a tale in which sexuality and, dare I say, love occupied center stage—provoked in me no small measure of anxiety and a deep, unrelenting sense of shame. Shame for potentially betraying, for collaborating with those who would damage and disable Puerto Ricans' lives and choice, for lending my voice—and Juan's—as so much fodder to fuel the seemingly endless needs of that disciplining discourse.

It brought back an old feeling—that silencing knot in your throat Puerto Ricans call simply *sentimiento*. "*Le dio sentimiento*," they say when a child is confronted with an act that does not necessarily hurt him or her but damages his or her community instead—an act whose consequences might jeopardize the familial bond, betray the loyalty of those whom he or she loves most. The child is then flooded with such *sentimiento* or emotion that he or she literally breaks down—can't utter a word. For just the thought, the mere thought, that one could damage, that one could betray, is enough to make one want to dissolve—in shame. Yes, "*le dio sentimiento*," they say. It's *sentimiento* all right, confirms the discerning parental gaze.

And it made me pause on the edge of that feeling the Puerto Rican writer Luis Rafael Sánchez has called "*el sentimiento insensato de la culpa*" (1979 119), that senseless or un-sensible sense of guilt, or rather shame, he claims haunts all of Puerto Rican writing, surveys our every word, lest we risk harming our communal ties, lest we supply the terms—and the weapons—for our own demise, lest we feed that machine, that greedy, human-eating machine with our very own blood—all the worse because it's not ours, but the blood of those whom we love most.

In a recent book, *Boricua Pop: Puerto Ricans and the Latinization of American Culture*, Frances Negrón-Muntaner has claimed that modern Puerto Rican identity both in the Island and the States has been primarily constructed, that is, narrated and performed, in response to the shame-producing condition of being considered a colonial and/or a devalued, racialized, and feminized ethnic subject. Faced with the mark of invisibility imposed by the stigma of colonialism, and ethnic racialization and feminization, Puerto Ricans have tried, she contends, to make themselves "pretty," or socially presentable, as

Maria in *West Side Story* would sing, in order to appear in public as valued and valuable subjects. And whereas the Island's cultural elite has by and large chosen to counter this tainting mark of invisibility with pseudo-epic nationalist cultural displays that attempt to disavow feelings of "disgrace" and shame at being identified with the lowly racialized, feminized colonial other (33–45), the Puerto Rican popular classes, particularly those in the diaspora, Negrón-Muntaner affirms, have tended to assume and recycle the toxic colonial, racial/gender slur as a way of gaining visibility and intervening in public space (xiii–xiv). Thus Warhol "superstar," Puerto Rican drag performer Hollywood Woodlawn's poetics of recycling devalued subjects or "trash" (101–14), Rita Moreno's refashioning of the Hollywood Latina stereotype through her creation of the satiric character of "Googie Gómez" in Terence McNally's *The Ritz* (80–84), and Jennifer Lopez's embrace and joyous deployment of her stigmatized butt (233–46) acquire in Negrón-Muntaner's analysis all their (well-deserved) pride of place.

If one can see how the cultured elite's response, shot through as it is with a measure of complicity or the adoption of the dominant Other's gaze, a characteristic that at least since Sartre has come to define the conflicted, double vision of shame (Sartre 255), could qualify as an instance of (disavowing) shame; the popular reaction, in its refusal to assume, or identify with, the dominant Other's gaze, if not its actual products or effects, one would have to admit, would come closer to insolence than shame, or as contemporary queer Latino scholars, such as Lawrence LaFountain-Stokes, have called it, *sinvergüencería*, or shamelessness.

Yet my particular sense of paralyzing shame, I felt, had neither to do with insolence nor the disavowal of personal disgrace. It was certainly conflicted and risked being complicit with the Other's gaze, but it was also closer to what the theologian Carl D. Schneider had described as "discretion-shame," that sense of shame that comes as a result of transgressing or breaching a community or personally sanctioned secret, mystery, or veil that proscribes indiscriminate access and sets limits to one's and others' invasive gaze (Schneider 18–28). My sense of shame, I felt, had to do with wanting to live up to that impossibly simultaneous command at the heart of Rigoberta Menchú's *testimonio* both to shelter and expose, to divulge and protect, to heed the communal injunction and follow the allure of Juan's intimate, personally charged tale, refusing perhaps un-sensibly, and even childishly, to give up one love for the other, to move on.

For shame, the psychologists Silvan Tomkins and Michael Franz Basch had explained, was a rupture in the continuity of mirror-like identificatory looks between a self and an other, caused by that other's failure or refusal to recognize the self, or by the other's unexpected strangeness or estrangement from the self (Basch 765; Tomkins 135). But it was a very ambivalent rupture—one in which the self did not completely break with the other, in which the self's "investment of positive affect in the other" was never "completely surrender[ed]" or "reduced" by the other's estrangement or contempt (Tomkins 157). Like Freud's early version of melancholia (Butler 1997 133; Freud 16), Tomkins claimed (138), shame refused to give up its love objects. Yet unlike classical melancholia, we might add, it recognized loss; it lived in loss. And it was this ambivalent rupture that characterized shame that made it productive and possibly mobile, always tending, always on the verge.

And it was this ambivalent rupture that would keep me straining and force me eventually to look for forms to reconnect, making my coming out of paralyzing silence contingent on my ability to listen to Juan's tale and to find there that soundboard, expansive chamber, or context in which his hesitations, detours, and displacements would acquire weight, resonate. My ability to come out of shameful silence was thus predicated on my ability to listen for forms that not only placed limits on my desiring, denuding gaze but also offered ground for dialogue, for engagement; my ability to speak on *his* ability to have his conditions of speech restored, finally.

IDENTIFICATION AND QUEER SHAME: THE CAUTIONARY TALE OF MARIO MONTEZ

So shame was not merely repressive then—something to be gotten rid of, in Spanish *un lastre*, in English dead weight, so much "baggage" to unload, as we'd say in our contemporary psychospeak. It could also be productive, generative, a source of transformation and renewal for those whom Eve Kosofsky Sedgwick had called in her groundbreaking 1993 essay on queer performativity the "shame-prone." "If queer is a politically potent term, which it is," she would claim, "that's because, far from being capable of being detached from the childhood scene of shame, it cleaves to that scene as a near-inexhaustible source of transformational energy" (Sedgwick 1995 210).

And yet the politically transformative potential of shame for the "shame-prone" could also be disabled and blunted if, instead of focusing on the traumatized or marked subject's creative straining for reconnection, we fixed our gaze on his/her scene of violation and trauma, freezing it. If we gazed on that scene and searched there for the marked subject's ontological difference or "truth," if we asked it to speak, that is, the way Foucault described modern sexual science as asking "sex" to speak the subject's truth (60–62), we would end up, not engaging with an interlocutor, but creating a subjected subject instead—a subject-for-us, that is, for us to know, to conquer, to possess. We would be evening out and erasing the subject's uncomfortable, inscrutable otherness by fitting it into our own pre-established epistemological schemes, as Doris Sommer in her reading of Emmanuel Levinas, the Jewish philosopher of ethics and alterity, had warned (Levinas 43–44; Sommer 1999 27–28). And we would be adding to the marked subject's burdensome sense of hypervisibility the weight of our own scrutinizing gaze, congealing him or her, locking him or her into place.

So fixed, so locked into place, the marked subject could then be rendered "serviceable," in Toni Morrison's apt term (1993 8). It could even be perversely used to form others' (more powerful others') individual and communal sense of identity, as indeed happens in one of the most recent and influential elaborations on Sedgwick's call to pay heed to the productivity of queer shame, Douglas Crimp's "Mario Montez, for Shame."

Countering what some queer theorists and activists had called the current mainstreaming, homogenization, and de-sexualization of gay community life and culture under the banner of Gay Pride, a group of queer scholars and activists committed to a politics of difference had gathered at the University of Michigan in Ann Arbor, in March 2003, for a conference that would promote its exact opposite: *Gay Shame.* Crimp's essay on Andy Warhol's film, *Screen Test #2* (1965), "Mario Montez, for Shame," an ostensibly ethical, Levinasian approach that proposed shame—not pride—as a way to reclaim the "differences and singularities" of queer community life (58), was to serve as a primary text for discussion, as a rallying text of sorts. But, as queer cultural critics Lawrence LaFountain-Stokes, Judith Halberstam, and Hiram Pérez would note in their incisive review of the conference, Crimp's proposal for the formation of a queer community respectful of differences would in the end rest ironically on the exposed, shamed, and fixed body of the 1960s underground queer actor of color of Warhol's film, Mario Montez. And not uncoincidentally, almost all of the conference speakers and participants would also be—ironically again—white lesbians and gay men.

How could a gay community respectful of differences be based on shame?, asked Puerto Rican cultural critic LaFountain-Stokes in his sharp, unsympathetic review. And who was this Mario Montez anyway, prior to and beyond his incarnation in Crimp's essay as a founding figure of sorts, *malgré lui*, of gay shame?

Mario Montez, né René Rivera, was a Puerto Rican postal worker who lived in the then densely populated New York Puerto Rican community of the 1960s Lower East Side, before this section was rebaptized by a first generation of New York Puerto Rican or *Nuyorican* poets in the early 1970s with the Spanglish name *Loisaida* (see chapter five). The Lower East Side was home then to a lively avant-garde, underground film and theater arts movement whose undisputed master was the queer filmmaker and performance artist *avant la lettre*, Jack Smith, and Montez, who would go on to star in his notoriously censored films, *Flaming Creatures* (1961) and *Normal Love* (1963), would became Smith's preferred underground actor.

Both Smith and Montez shared a penchant for what the New York film critic J. Hoberman has called "the tropical and excessive" (Smith 15); both drew inspiration from the tropicalizing and orientalizing gestures of 1940s Dominican-born Hollywood B-movie diva, Maria Montez; and both met in that unstable, irreverently sacred ground of discarded grandeur we might call *avant la lettre* "Loisaida kitsch."

Consonant with postmodern definitions of kitsch (Olalquiaga 46–55), Smith and Montez pursued an aesthetics that consisted in recycling, in Smith's term, the "moldy" or devalued images of Latin/Spanish/Oriental femininity in old Hollywood films (the "cobra woman," the "white savage," the Scheherazade, and the vamp figures of Montez's early 1940s films) in order not so much to camp them up, or parody them, as to foreground instead the artfulness, imagination, passion, and sheer sublime willfulness and belief with which exoticized subjects, such as Maria Montez, negotiated their emergence onto public visibility, their ephemeral, Warholian "15 minutes of fame," an art the Latino cultural critic José Esteban Muñoz has aptly called a "survivalist" aesthetics.

"She believed and thereby made the people who went to her movies believe," declared Smith in his flamboyant 1960s film manifesto, "The Perfect Appositeness of Maria Montez":

> Maria Montez Moldy Movie Queen, Shoulder pad, gold platform wedgie Siren, Determined, dreambound, Spanish, Irish, Negro?, Indian girl who went to Hollywood from the Dominican Rep. Wretch actress . . . why limit her? Don't slander her beautiful womanliness that took joy in her own beauty and all beauty—or whatever in her that turned plaster cornball sets to beauty. Her eyes saw not just beauty but incredible, delirious, drug-like hallucinatory beauty. (25)

And Mario Montez's performances in Smith's films, *Flaming Creatures* and *Normal Love*, in Warhol's *Harlot* (1964), *Mario Banana* (1964), *Screen Test #2* (1965), and *Chelsea Girls* (1966), and in the Puerto Rican underground filmmaker José Rodríguez-Soltero's *hommage* to "Mexican spitfire" of the 1920s and 1930s, Lupe Vélez, *Lupe* (1966), all attest to a similar kind of acting whose goal was, in Smith's own words, not to change the actor but the world through the expression of an extravagant, excessive form of belief (20).

Drawing inspiration from Maria Montez, who had herself drawn inspiration from the notorious nineteenth-century Irish-born dancer Eliza Rosanna Gilbert, who under the pseudonym of Lola Montez (of "Whatever Lola wants, Lola gets" fame) would make a career as a seriously flawed, if popular, Spanish dancer and courtesan to the rich, Mario would appropriate, like them, the whole range of tropicalist/orientalist gestures and images in order to transform them by infusing them with his own hyperbolic form of belief.

"She," claims a semi-fictional character in the experimental playwright Charles Ludlam's vignettes about the New York underground scene, was "the first Puerto Rican artist who knew she was Puerto Rican and used it" (150). And indeed in the Lower East Side of the 1960s where Puerto Rican expressions of spirituality and hybrid, syncretic, neo-Baroque cultural forms must have appeared as kitsch proper, or as what Celeste Olalquiaga has called "first-degree kitsch" (that supposedly unmediated, "genuine" relationship of belief members of more traditional cultures have vis-à-vis their sacred objects, as seen from the perspective of more "modern," alienated subjects; Olalquiaga 42–44), Mario Montez's cross-dressed emergence onto the Lower East Side underground scene must have seemed as the act of a Puerto Rican who was self-consciously performing Puerto-Ricanness, or as kitsch that knew it was kitsch.

In Crimp's rallying essay, however, Mario Montez or simply "Mario," as he calls him, is a diminished figure, unaware of his own humiliation in Warhol's *Screen Test #2*—in short, pathetic. Interrogated off-camera by the playwright/screen writer Ronald Tavel in Warhol's film, Mario is ostensibly auditioning for the role of Esmeralda in a future Warhol remake of *The Hunchback of Notre Dame*. Shown throughout in close-up and wearing a seductively disheveled wig, dangling oversize earrings, a silk scarf, and long white evening gloves, Mario is asked by the off-camera Tavel as part of his supposed audition to perform a series of acts, by turns ridiculous and degrading: to repeat the word "diarrhea," purportedly the name of a movie producer, "exactly as if it tasted of nectar," to mime biting the head off a live chicken as if he were a "female geek," to show how he'd seduce three different characters from *The Hunchback of Notre Dame*, to lift up his skirt, unzip his fly, and take out his penis, and, finally, to repeat after Tavel in a supplicating pose, "Oh, Lord, I commend this spirit into Thy hands."

"Taking it out and putting it in—that sums up the movie business," Tavel explains, as he urges Montez to submit to his orders to literally expose himself. Montez, however, resists: he looks at the camera, not as the prying, invasive instrument Warhol's camera was known to be ("I can see you were trying to bring out the worst in me," Montez had complained to Warhol after a viewing of *Hedy* (1966), his portrayal of 1950s tragic diva Hedy Lamarr; Warhol 91), but as if it were a mirror, his own private mirror, in his own private closet, dressing room, or boudoir. Appearing to feign inattention or indifference to Tavel's requests, Montez adjusts his unruly hair with the aid of a silk scarf, as though he were immersed in the most private of moments, causing Tavel to repeat over and over his demands: "Will you forget about your hair for a moment?! Miss Montez, you're not concentrating!"

No, he's not. He can't help it: his hair keeps getting in the way. But only to reveal unexpectedly, after much vacillation, a perfectly constructed pose: Montez's almond-shaped, Egyptian-like, operatic eyes peering out of his tangle of hair and into the camera in a vampy, devouring gaze.

"Poor Mario Montez," Crimp exclaims, quoting from another moment reported by Warhol in his book, *POPism*; he always "got his feelings hurt" (Crimp 58; Warhol 181). "Poor Mario," Crimp repeats throughout his essay, registering thus a sympathy that simultaneously cuts a structuring swath in its wake: on one side, "Mario's" side, is self-absorption and delusion; on the other, Tavel's, Warhol's, and ours as spectators and readers of Warhol and Crimp, the side of those off-camera, those who can look without being seen, is distant, self-reflexive, magnanimous awareness.

"Hoodwinked" by Tavel, lulled by his words of encouragement ("That was delightful, Miss Montez . . . I think we're going to sign you up immediately . . ."; 61), Montez does not realize, according to Crimp, that he's being set up for a fall, that the aim of Tavel/Warhol's supposed audition or screen test is not only to expose his "gender illusionism" but, more importantly and ruthlessly, the very shame that lies at the heart of his gender "illusions" (59). And indeed toward the end of Tavel's grueling, seventy-minute interrogation, Montez, who, as Crimp explains, quoting Warhol, was "Puerto Rican and a very religious Roman Catholic," looks finally, according to Crimp, "bewildered and terrified" (62), visibly shaken and ashamed, as Tavel asks him to repeat in a supplicating pose, "Oh, Lord, I commend this spirit into Thy hands." An abject lesson of sorts, Mario Montez's final shaming is the climax of Crimp's essay—the concrete, visible representation toward which his essay builds and from which its title/conclusion derives its moral, programmatic force: "Mario Montez, For Shame!" Playing on the double meaning of "for," "because of" and "in favor of," Crimp's title/conclusion paradoxically suggests both the classically defining operation of shame, its projection onto others, in this case Montez (Shame on you, Mario! *For Shame!*), and a call to rally around shame, or more specifically shaming, in order to constitute ethically inclusive communities respectful of difference (*For Shame*, in the name of shame, in favor of, or for the cause of shame!).

But how can shaming, or the (often phobic) projection of shame, be constitutive of ethically inclusive communities one might ask, following on LaFountain-Stokes's initial reserve? How can (phobic) projection and inclusion derive both from the same scene? Following on Sedgwick, Crimp argues, somewhat tautologically, that "in those already shamed, the shame-prone, the shame is not so easily shed, so simply projected: it manages to persist as one's own" (66).

In those already shamed, that is, ostensibly Warhol, Tavel, and Crimp but also "us," their "ideal" queer spectators and readers, projection is never fully accomplished; it leaves inevitably a residue—a certain discomfiture or unease, which is the trace of our "own" shame. Watching the shaming of Montez, or reading about it, this ideal, shame-prone spectator or reader, who participates in the shaming, however vicariously, will experience not so much Montez's shame but *his* or *her* "own" shame. Crimp explains:

> I'm thus not "like" Mario, but the distinctiveness that is revealed in Mario invades me—"floods me," to use Sedgwick's word—and my own distinctiveness is revealed simultaneously. I, too, feel exposed. (67)

And it is this residue of one's own shame that Crimp offers, quoting theorist Michael Warner (66), as a common ground for the constitution of new queer communities-in-difference.

"In taking on the shame, I do not share in the other's identity. I simply adopt the other's vulnerability to being shamed. In this operation . . . the other's difference is preserved . . . ," Crimp affirms (65). True enough, the other's difference is preserved, but it is preserved *and* contained, for the difference *within* the homogenizing category of the "shame-prone," which had initially been deferred for argument's sake, now returns, and is preserved, in the strictly hierarchical division of labor between Montez and "us." Whereas Mario Montez is pressed into performing his shame in public for us, we, who experience our shame vicariously and in private, off-camera and off-site, are ironically free to flex our theoretical muscles and strain toward the abstraction of a utopian queer community-in-difference, as Pérez in his critical reading of the *Gay Shame* conference has incisively noted (Pérez 179).

Our mobility, our capacity, that is, not only to experience shame but to transform it into public theorizing and agency is predicated, one might say, on Montez's immobility, on his being locked into place; our irreducible singularity and self-possession on our total "knowingness" about him. After all, Mario Montez's supposed shame about his cross-dressing we "know" derives from his being identified as a "Puerto Rican and a very religious Roman Catholic" (62)—an identification that elicits no further explanation in Crimp's essay, which stands as self-evident, as the necessary tautology on which others' differences might be recognized, built, promoted.

Of course, there are other readings of Montez's performances, less pathetic, less pathologizing ones. First and foremost, there's Warhol's, for whom Mario's apparent lack of awareness was strategic, a way to elicit his audiences expectations, to capture them, as it were, in order to subvert them:

> Mario had that classic comedy combination of seeming dumb but being able to say the right things with perfect timing; just when you thought you were laughing at him, he'd turn it all around. (A lot of the superstars had that special quality.) (181)

And then there's Wayne Koestenbaum's appraisal of Montez's "imperturbable surface" in *Screen Test #2* in his learnedly dishy biography of Warhol:

> In one of Mario's greatest roles for Andy, *Screen Test #2* (1965), scripted by Ronald Tavel, she auditions for the part of Esmeralda, love object of the Hunchback of Nôtre Dame, while the offscreen Tavel shouts promptings that might seem sadistic were it not for Mario's imperturbable surface, more concerned with maquillage than with thespian success . . . (2001 102)

And film critic Gary Morris's observation that *Screen Test #2* recalls Warhol's other portraits, his silkscreens and serial paintings, for instance, "in its doomed attempt to penetrate the human face."

ART AND ENGAGEMENT

I myself would rather dwell on Mario Montez's own insistently minimal gestures: the brushing of his unruly hair, his distracted listening to Tavel, his staring at the camera as if it were his own private mirror in his own private boudoir, his sudden, unexpected turn to the camera, through his tangle of hair, in a vampy, devouring gaze. I myself would rather listen to the language spoken by these gestures—resistant, ambiguous, dense, as all language must be that must traverse the silencing barrier of shame.

"Poor Mario!," Crimp exclaims; he doesn't even know that he is being set up. Poor Crimp! Poor Tavel! They don't even know that Mario's gestures are calling their bluff, disarming them, and in so doing inviting them *not to identify or find their image through him* but to engage.

The point of acknowledging difference, Doris Sommer has argued in her reading of Levinas from the perspective of American minority texts (Sommer 1999 27–31), is not to know it, or to expose it till it yields its secret, its artifice, its art, so that it becomes, in Warhol's words, "so for real" (181)—so for real for us, that is. The point of acknowledging difference is not even to venerate the mystery of the other's inscrutable, ever-receding, sacred face, as Levinas recommends. It is more simply—and more difficultly—to engage with that difference.

For ten years I had stopped. For ten years I had been paralyzed with shame—overcome by the possibility that a word, a word of mine might damage, betray. But the art in Juan's voice—its hesitations, elisions, detours—kept prodding me, urging me on to strain, to reconnect. And then one day, I just got up—as Juan would say, deferring interpretation—and fortified by the thought that such minimal deviations were not only a command but a hope, I decided to pick up the phone and answer his call.

CHAPTER 5

What's in a Name

THE PLACES

Baths/Bathhouses

Built originally at the turn of the century to serve the personal hygiene needs of urban populations in major U.S. cities such as New York, Los Angeles, and San Francisco at a time when most households lacked a private bath (only one in forty families in the densely populated tenement district of New York's Lower East Side lived in an apartment with a bathroom then; Chauncey 1994 208), bathhouses would become, according to historian George Chauncey, "[t]he safest, most enduring, and one of the most affirmative of the settings in which gay men gathered in the first half of the twentieth century" (207). Although there was vigilance of homosexual activity in these bathhouses, many either tolerated discrete homosexual behavior or protected it from harassment and persecution by the police. By the 1930s and 1940s "baths that did not cater to gay men had begun to decline in number and popularity as indoor plumbing and private bathing facilities became more widely available," Chauncey explains (217). And after World War II, baths would cater almost exclusively to homosexually inclined men. In these bathhouses, gay men would build environments that were safe and affirmative of homosexual practices and cultural expressions. As noted by many writers, including Keith Haring in the late 1970s (Gruen 1991 43), the baths would foster an environment where people would be judged by their physical attributes rather than by the displays of status, education, or wealth that were then prevalent in the gay bars and other areas of gay social life. True, most bathhouses in New York City were segregated by race and class until the 1970s, but so were most bars, gay and straight, and most neighborhoods. Yet within these structural limits, which would be increasingly questioned by gays of color after the 1970s, the baths would encourage a certain communal egalitarianism, a certain feeling of sameness among its patrons, a feeling of engaging in sex with peers that was foreign to the hierarchical relations that had prevailed in New York between "fairies" and the "normal" men, or "trade," they "serviced" in the early part of the century (Chauncey 65–97). Thus as the Stonewall Rebellion of 1969 ushered in an era of gay liberation, which would openly celebrate sex among peers who shared a common gay identity, lavish new bathhouses would be launched by gay entrepreneurs, now featuring disco dance floors, cabaret lounges, massage parlors, sauna rooms, TV rooms, cafes, Olympic swimming pools, sun decks, and "fantasy environments," which recreated, as in a sort of sexual amusement park, illegal and dangerous erotic situations, such as cruising in the park or in public bathrooms, within the safe confines of the baths. As the 1970s rolled on a sexual subculture would evolve whose mass appeal may be gauged in the establishment of the first nationwide chain of gay baths, the Club Baths. By 1973, the Club Baths would have almost 500,000 card-carrying members (Hogan and Hudson 73). And a bathhouse such as New York City's Continental Baths, where performers Bette Middler, Barry Manilow, Peter Allen, and Cab Calloway entertained towel-clad audiences, would become an important venue to launch a show-business career. With the advent of the AIDS pandemic in the 1980s the lesbian and gay community would be split by the debate on whether to close down the bathhouses as a means to fight the spread of AIDS or to use them to educate its patrons about "safe sex." It was during this time that Juan and C . . . would go to the baths, as Juan says (see chapter two, "One of These Days!"), to have sex with each other and no one else, and perhaps to bask in that atmosphere of sexual freedom and camaraderie that the baths had created, and which would soon come to an end. In April 1984, the San Francisco Department of Public Health would close down the city's baths claiming that they contributed to the spread of AIDS. And in November 1985, New York City officials would follow suit using a "nuisance abatement" statute.

Coney Island

A desolate and remote sandbar at the foot of Brooklyn, which served during the nineteenth century as a beachside resort and a haven for illicit activities, including gambling and prostitution, Coney Island would become by the first decades of the twentieth century the most extravagant and modern playground the world had ever known. Incorporating the latest in technological advances, Coney Island's "staggering concentration of resources and mechanical devices" would be unprecedently "deployed," as Michael Immerso has noted, "purely for the purpose of pleasure" (3). Known as "Sodom by the Sea" and the unofficial capital of America's new mass culture, Coney Island represented then, as John Kasson and Woody Register have argued and as the exile Cuban writer José Martí had already suggested in his classic urban chronicle of 1881, a break with a nineteenth-century Victorian ethos of moral restraint. By promoting a lax environment in which the sexes mixed freely and anonymously and encouraging consumption for the fun of it, Coney Island would take Americans from the Victorian age into the modern world. Its three amusement parks, Steeplechase, Luna Park, and Dreamland (burned down in 1911), offered, as described by Ric Burns's documentary *Coney Island* (2002), "a riot of rides, restaurants, recreated disasters, freak shows, and historical displays. There was a simulated trip to the moon, the largest herd of show elephants in the world, and huge moving panoramas showing the Creation, the End of the World, and Hell. There were re-enactments of the Boer War and the Fall of Pompeii, and an Infant Incubator where premature babies were placed on display. Strangest of all was Lilliputia, a perfect miniature town inhabited by 300 little persons year-round." At its height in the 1920s Coney Island's amusement parks and beach area would receive a million visitors a day during the summer months. But by the 1950s, as the white working-class immigrant population that had sustained its economy during the first half of the century began to move out of the city and into the suburbs, Coney Island's amusement area would experience a long, protracted decline, which would peak in 1964 when Steeplechase, the first of the original turn-of-the-century amusement parks, closed down. During the next two decades Coney Island would become an economically depressed urban area of ruined mechanical rides such as the Parachute Jump (declared a historic landmark in 1988) and surviving 1920s rides such as The Wonder Wheel and The Cyclone roller coaster, and dilapidated, architecturally fanciful old hotels and bathhouses, surrounded by X-rated movie theaters, strip joints, and cheap side shows—an area associated in the popular imagination and the media with prostitution, gang warfare, and the drug trade (see, for instance, the 1979 film *The Warriors*). True enough, by the mid-1950s Coney Island had seen better days. But what would effectively turn Coney Island into a blighted area, into a slum, by the 1970s was, according to Charles Denson's evocative and richly detailed memoir, *Coney Island: Lost and Found*, the "urban renewal" policies of New York City's Park Commissioner Robert Moses.

Starting in the 1950s, Moses would launch a "scorched-earth" policy that would designate entire areas of Coney Island, the residential Gut and West Side areas for instance, for demolition. And while the city prepared to raze these areas, he would have the city's poor, by and large Puerto Rican and black, relocated to these zones. Concentrated thus in areas with deteriorating housing (housing landlords would refuse to repair because it had already been slated for destruction), the black and Puerto Rican poor would become increasingly vocal, and racial strife in Coney Island would significantly rise (in 1968, about 3,000 people of color rioted down Mermaid Ave.; Denson 143). The city would eventually build rows of mid- and low-income public housing projects in Coney Island's razed zones, but by then, the mid-1970s, its severe fiscal crisis would forced it to discontinue building. By the time the 1970s would come to a close, the city had almost gone into bankruptcy and urban renewal had left Coney Island, in Denson's words, a "devastated" area, rife with abandoned or burned-out buildings, vacant lots, and rows of new housing projects with little or no financial support. It had also left the poor stranded in the midst of this ruined phantasmagoric, modern amusement park. For them, the ruined amusement park area and the unfulfilled promise of modernity, of "urban renewal," seemed to mirror each other. And yet in the midst of these ruins, the 1920s Cyclone and Wonder Wheel were saved and kept operating, and some popular, old-time Coney Island side shows would manage to survive, and a corporation formed by concerned citizens, the Astella Development Corporation, would begin to build affordable low-rise, single-family homes on the grounds the city had razed, and a burgeoning black and Puerto Rican youth, hip-hop culture would emerge. It was then, in the early 1980s, that a group of enterprising young artists, interested in American popular culture and contemporary performance art, and drawn by Coney Island's peculiar mix of ruins and vitality, decadence and promise, would begin to revive and reinvent old–Coney Island popular art forms and to mix them with downtown avant-garde theater and performance, slam poetry, breakdancing, and other hip-hop art forms (228–31). It was surely then that Juan Rivera and Keith Haring would visit Coney Island, as is told in Juan's interview (see chapter two, "Paradise"). And Haring, like those other postmodern artists, must have also been taken with Coney Island's contradictory ambience, an ambience that, for Haring, was perhaps no better exemplified than by the sight of black and Puerto Rican hip-hop boys riding that old survivor from modernity's utopian age, The Cyclone.

East Rock, New Haven

A trap rock hill that rises 400 feet above the city of New Haven on its Northeast side, East Rock features on its summit a column-like, phallic monument that dominates the city's landscape and is visible from the surrounding towns. The monument, which was built in 1887 to commemorate Connecticut's soldiers fallen in the Wars of Independence and of 1812, the Mexican-American and Civil Wars, has become a symbol of New Haven. Accessed through a winding road, East Rock's summit, which offers spectacular views of New Haven and the Long Island Sound and opens onto many hiking trails, has been traditionally both an area of recreation and a lovers' lane, as it indeed appears in Juan's tale (see chapter two, "Fly, Robin, Fly").

El Barrio/East Harlem

In Spanish, the neighborhood, the community, the down home country district or turf, El Barrio refers to a geographically shifting section of Manhattan's East Harlem, also known as Spanish Harlem, which stretches from 96th to 142nd streets, between the East River and Fifth Ave., approximately. So named by its Latin American immigrants toward the first decades of the twentieth century, El Barrio, then a multiethnic, multilingual, working-class European immigrant enclave, bordering black Harlem on its North and West and the affluent WASPish Upper East Side on its South, would become increasingly Latino and specifically Puerto Rican after 1917, when with the imminent entry of the United States into World War I, the U.S. Congress would grant its territorial subjects of Puerto Rico American citizenship, making them thus eligible for the draft (for more information on the Jones Act of 1917, see Cabranes). As Puerto Ricans, now U.S. citizens, migrated in increasing numbers to El Barrio, the number of European immigrants would decrease as the Congress, echoing a generalized feeling of xenophobia fueled by the War, passed laws restricting the influx of Europeans. European immigrants' anxiety about being displaced by Puerto Ricans in El Barrio would erupt into what the press would call the "Harlem Riots" of 1926, in which European men wielding sticks would rampage through the streets of East Harlem vandalizing Puerto Rican and Latino businesses. Reports from the times show that much of this anxiety must have derived from what the European immigrants and the press viewed as the Puerto Ricans' peculiar mix of ethnicity and race, which defied American standards of racial categorization. As reported by *The New York Times*, "the bad feeling [among white immigrant residents of East Harlem] is said to have been caused by the rapid influx of Latin and West Indian negroes who describe themselves as Porto Ricans" (qtd. in Sánchez Korrol 151).

Negroes who describe themselves as Porto Ricans is the telling circumlocution with which *The Times* captures what must have seem to European immigrants then, and to the general readership of *The Times*, the Puerto Ricans' evasion of clear and distinct American standards of racial classification, which declared them simply "Negro." The Puerto Ricans' insistence on defining themselves as other than, or more than, "Negro," must have been a great source of anxiety for a population of recent immigrants who aspired to leave behind their ethnic roots, which symbolically racialized them, and assimilate into American society by becoming simply "white." In the following decades Puerto Ricans would continue to resist assimilating into American racial categories, and El Barrio would become what it is to this day—a multiracial, multilingual, multiethnic, transnational urban space. A center for Latin American, Puerto Rican, and Afro-Cuban music, composed and performed both by Puerto Ricans and Cubans, El Barrio would develop since the 1920s into a major circuit for the exchange of Latin American, Caribbean, and African American popular cultures. Much of what is now considered the canon of Puerto Rican popular music and song, for instance, was composed, as the historian Ruth Glasser has shown, outside Puerto Rico—in El Barrio—and transmitted there and to Latin America from New York. Using the Afro-Cuban rhythms (*bolero, son, guaracha*) that were popular then both in Puerto Rico and New York, Puerto Rican immigrant artists, such as Rafael Hernández and Pedro Flores, would compose and record in El Barrio between the two world wars the songs that would end up identifying Puerto Rico in the Island and for the rest of the world (Glasser 1995). Decades later, in the 1960s and 1970s, another generation of New York Puerto Rican artists, the children of the "Great Migration" that followed World War II, would build on this transnational tradition by combining Afro-Cuban rhythms with indigenous Puerto Rican, Latin American, and African-American beats to create the sounds that, popularized as *salsa*, would travel to Latin America and the world, spawning a transnational urban movement (For a history of salsa, see Flores; Flores and Valentín-Escobar; Quintero Rivera; and Rondón). If between the wars Puerto Ricans were the largest Latino group in multiracial, multiethnic East Harlem, after World War II, with the mass migration of working-class Puerto Ricans to New York, El Barrio would become majority Puerto Rican. Displaced by the Island's process of modernization promoted by the populist *Partido Popular Democrático* and its leader Luis Muñoz Marín, which resulted in high rates of unemployment in the Island's leading economic sector, agricultural production, and encouraged migration as a "safety valve," Puerto Ricans would arrive in El Barrio ironically as it was undergoing its own process of modern development, known as "urban renewal." Designated as far back as 1937 by federal legislation for slum tenement clearance, El Barrio would inaugurate in 1941 the high-rise public housing residence, or "project," which served as a model for subsequent public housing development in New York City in the 1950s and 1960s (Dávila 32). Old tenements were to be cleared and tenants placed in modern, hygienic residential public structures. But before tenants were placed they would have to be screened for their suitability as part of an aspiring "submerged middle-class" (31), and Puerto Ricans, considered a "transient" population by social workers and anthropologists, whose "hedonistic," "short-range" values, as anthropologist Oscar Lewis had described them, were resistant to middle-class stability (1965 li–ii; see chapter four, "Listening Speaks (II)"), would have to organize politically in order to gain admittance into these new housing projects, avoiding thus further dislocation. Although there are no statistics available for the number of Puerto Ricans displaced by urban renewal in El Barrio, anthropologist Arlene Dávila wryly notes, "their numbers were likely to be great, as indicated by estimates from 1959–61, when Puerto Ricans accounted for up to 76 percent of the people displaced from various urban renewal sites in the city" (31). Faced once again with displacement driven by state development policies, Puerto Ricans in El Barrio would not only organize to fight for inclusion in the new housing projects, they would also center their cultural and political struggles throughout the 1960s and 1970s on the overarching demand for "community control" of institutions and development policy. And this call for community control of space, institutions, resources, and development policies would fuel most of the literature, arts, and politics of El Barrio of the times, from Piri Thomas's foundational text of Nuyorican literature, *Down These Mean Streets* (1967), which ends in an impassioned reclaiming of El Barrio's "mutilated" streets (Thomas 298), to the performative work of visual artist Rafael Montañez Ortiz, who would found there in El Barrio, in 1969, the first Latino museum in the United States, El Museo del Barrio, and the political activism of the Young Lords Organization, later the Young Lords Party (YLP). Emblematic of this movement for community control, the YLP, an anticolonial, pro-Puerto Rican independence, Third-World, socialist, community-action group, made up mostly of first–generation New York Puerto Rican college-age youth from working-class homes, would also be founded there in El Barrio in 1969 (for a history of the Young Lords, see YLP and Abramson, Melendez, Guzmán, and Morales; see also Morales's documentary film, *¡Palante, Siempre Palante! The Young Lords*). Inspired by a Chicago Puerto Rican gang of the same name, which had operated there since the 1950s, becoming politicized in the struggles against the uprooting of Latinos from their neighborhoods by the city's urban renewal projects (Morales 212), the YLP would advocate a concept of development or progress (*pa'lante!*, in Spanish "forward," would be its rallying call) based on the community's control of the institutions that serviced it (YLP and Abramson 150). A highly photogenic, image-conscious group, these New York Puerto Rican young men and women, wearing black leather and army-surplus jackets and donning purple berets (hardly the image of rural immigrants from the Third World), would savvyly manage to garner the attention of the city's press in a series of "operations" that would take over, or occupy, some of El Barrio's most prominent institutions in order to pressure them into meeting the community's urgent needs. By 1976 however the YLP had all but disbanded, as a result of internal dissension over the growing hard line of its Maoist central committee leadership, which would increasingly alienate the group from its community base, and of external FBI persecution (Melendez 189–98). And although the YLP's struggle for community control would leave a legacy of activism that would result in, among other things, the creation of the first bilingual school district in the city (see Pedraza), in its wake an indigenous, Barrio-raised Puerto Rican political leadership would gain ascendancy by managing the funds for the Great Society/War on Poverty programs created by the Johnson administration to channel (and to quell) inner-city unrest. By the end of the 1970s this local leadership had attained almost complete control of El Barrio's politics and development policy (Dávila 34). But ironically by then the city would go bankrupt, and the federal government, under the leadership of Ronald Reagan, would dismantle the remaining Great Society programs of the so-called "welfare state." Not unlike the indigenous leadership of some Third World postcolonial nation, El Barrio's local leadership would gain political control, but they would also inherit a massive and decaying public infrastructure with dwindling or no public funds. By the mid-1980s, as the city moved to dispose of hundreds of tenements it had reluctantly acquired from tax-delinquent landlords, who had abandoned them as urban renewal projects devalued them, El Barrio would have one of the largest concentrations of public and publicly managed housing in the city (36). Throughout the 1980s and into the 1990s El Barrio would become a prime example of urban blight: deteriorated housing, littered vacant lots, diminished social services, lack of jobs (as the manufacturing industries that employed many of its residents moved out of New York), and a flourishing drug economy based on crack cocaine (see Bourgois). It was then that a cultural movement to reconstruct the sense of *barrio* or neighborhood the twin forces of urban renewal and federal/city disinvestment had almost destroyed would emerge: residents would begin to convert drug-infected lots into gardens with brightly colored, Puerto Rican country homes or *casitas* at their center (Aponte-Parés 1995, Flores 2000 63–78), and private and nonprofit developers would renovate abandoned buildings for special-needs housing, such as housing for people living with AIDS, and artists, including Keith Haring (whose *Crack Is Wack!* mural still stands on Second Ave. and 127th St.), would paint graffiti and murals celebrating El Barrio's Latino heritage and memorializing the victims of violence and the drug trade, and a new Mexican migration would reenergize restaurants, festivals, and streets. It is this *barrio*, a neighborhood caught between urban blight and communal initiative, that Juan Rivera would return to in the late 1980s (see chapter two, "'I'm Juanito Xtravaganza': An Epilogue"). By the time he tells his tale in the mid-1990s however, the neighborhood would be on the brink of another struggle—the struggle over "gentrification," or the selling of El Barrio to private developers by packaging its complicated, highly politicized history for consumption as "heritage tourism" and as middle/high-income housing (see Dávila).

Loisaida, East Village

Hispanicized or Spanglish version of the "Lower East Side" given to this old New York neighborhood by its Puerto Rican residents to designate the area that runs from Houston to 14th streets and from Avenue A to the East River, also known as "Alphabet City," or the eastern part of the East Village, or simply, the Lower East Side. First coined by poets and cultural activists Bimbo Rivas and Chino García, members of the New York Puerto Rican or Nuyorican literary movement of the mid-1970s, this Spanglish renaming of the Lower East Side, they hoped, would help to stem the tide of its predominantly poor, working-class Puerto Rican residents leaving the area (during the 1970s nearly half of all Loisaida residents would be forced to relocate; Mele 182) by affirming the neighborhood's Puerto Rican/Latino cultural identity and forestalling thus real estate companies' plans to resettle the district with middle- and upper-middle-class residents, that is, to "gentrify" the neighborhood (see Ševčenko). At a time when Loisaida was littered with boarded-up tenements and abandoned schools, rubble-strewn lots, drug dens, and deteriorated public and private housing, as a result both of extensive private real estate disinvestment and municipal neglect (the City of New York was undergoing then its worst fiscal crisis since the Depression), cultural activists such as Bimbo Rivas, Chino García, and Miguel Algarín, cofounder, with playwright Miguel Piñero, of one of the neighborhood's longest-lasting and most influential social institutions, The Nuyorican Poets Cafe, would propose to set in motion the process of materially reconstructing the neighborhood by reconstructing it culturally, that is, by reconstructing people's sense of communal belonging and commitment to place. As has been argued by Ševčenko, this Loisaida cultural politics of place derived from the movement for "community control" of the late 1960s and early 1970s, a movement led by radical first-generation New York Puerto Rican groups such as the Real Great Society of the Lower East Side (see Aponte-Parés 1999) and the Young Lords of El Barrio (see El Barrio), which had sought to gain control over space, institutions, resources, and development policies in Puerto Rican/Latino neighborhoods. (Interestingly enough, though El Barrio-based, the Young Lords Organization had made its political debut on Loisaida's Tompkins Square Park on July 26, 1969, at a demonstration celebrating the tenth anniversary of the Cuban Revolution; Melendez 87). And in his "Introduction" to *Nuyorican Poetry: An Anthology of Puerto Rican Words and Feelings*, a poetic manifesto of sorts for the Loisaida cultural movement, Algarín would acknowledge as much: he would argue for taking over space and establishing an "alternative street government" (10) through the compellingly representative story of a gang that, not unlike the Real Great Society or the Young Lords, had turned from "outlaw" street practices to legally acquiring an abandoned lot and transforming it: "To stay free is not theoretical," he would declare. "It is to take over your immediate environment" (12). And yet it is not so much this alternative street government, which would be the realization of the community's control of space, that would intrigue Algarín as those "outlaw" street cultural practices, or "tactics" as the French theoretician of space Michel de Certeau has called them (88), through which Nuyoricans "hussled" or "juggled" the legal restrictions, or norms, of dominant social spaces in order to survive and express themselves (10). And of all of these practices none more emblematic than the unsanctioned, and often derided, linguistic practice of Spanish-English code-switching or Spanglish. How to "legalize your 'risks'" (13), how to turn "outlaw" street cultural practices into an alternative government or a "geographical identity" (14) without "damaging" their "disruptive," subversive edge, their "creative intuition" (19) would be the central questions that Algarín would address as he proposed a new cultural politics of place for Nuyorican communities, especially his, Loisaida. And his response would be a vanguard Spanglish artistic practice, which could both "juggle" present normative structures, as street cultural practices do, and envision new forms of community. Loisaida then was a capacious term; it designated more than a geographic, ethnic, or racial identity. Like the Spanglish practice that had produced it, it was also a call for community (trans)formation through participation in an open multicultural practice of reusing or recycling space. It indexed the multiple specific cultural practices, such as home-steading, graffiti writing, mural painting, and gardening, through which Puerto Ricans and other Loisaida residents would seek to revitalize and give value in the 1970s and 1980s to this economically depressed and physically devastated area. Puerto Ricans had arrived in the Lower East Side at the turn of the twentieth century to work as skilled cigar makers, forming small enclaves (Sánchez-Korrol 136). But it was not until the late 1940s and early 1950s, with the industrialization of Puerto Rico and the clearing of city slums, under the urban renewal policies of Robert Moses, that Puerto Ricans would be massively displaced and end up in considerable numbers in the Lower East Side. Puerto Ricans arrived as earlier white, ethnic immigrants moved out of the ghetto and into the suburbs. Initially, as Mele asserts, Puerto Rican labor would "salvage small firms with slim profit margins," such as those in the garment and apparel industries (126–27). But as the city began to deindustrialize toward the end of the 1950s and on through the 1970s, becoming principally a global finance and communications center, manufacturing jobs would relocate out of New York (Between 1960 and 1975, fifty-five percent of all of the city's manufacturing jobs would be displaced; Turner 307, 312), locking working-class Puerto Ricans out of what had been traditionally the immigrant's path to upward mobility and consigning them to long-term poverty. Perhaps like earlier immigrants Puerto Ricans would be identified in the media and public policy discourse as the cause of slum conditions, rather than as its victims. (In this logic, a logic that survives to this day in a muted form, as evinced in the still prevalent practice of boarding up buildings on Fifth Ave. along the path of the Puerto Rican Day Parade to protect from the onslaught of the Puerto Rican poor descending from their neighborhoods, to eradicate poverty meant to remove Puerto Ricans and thus urban renewal plans were significantly nicknamed "Puerto Rican Removal Plans"; Bowles; Mele 131). But unlike earlier white ethnic immigrants, and like African Americans, Puerto Ricans, unable to move to the suburbs, would have to develop practices of recycling urban detritus and devastation in order to give themselves and their communities value. Drawing from a long-standing Creole tradition of combining heterogeneous materials, remnants of devalued and discarded cultural forms, Puerto Ricans would make, as one says in Spanish, *de tripas corazón*, out of the guts a heart, out of their devastated urbanscape a community, a *barrio*, a neighborhood. But certainly Puerto Ricans were not the only ones to lay claim to the Lower East Side, investing it with value. As early as the 1960s disaffected suburban youth from middle-class homes would follow the opposite paths of their parents and return to the Lower East Side, where they would project onto the image of a deteriorated slum neighborhood their own visions of alternative community. At a time when suburbanization and urban renewal were creating living spaces segregated by class, ethnicity, and race, and when success meant approximating the ideal of becoming white, monolingual, monocultural, heterosexual, and middle class, this, what John Gruen called "the Combine Generation" of the 1960s, would project onto what appeared to them a more plural, more authentic, less consumer-oriented neighborhood the dream of alternative community. And in deploying this image of the Lower East Side as an alternative to the oppressively homogeneous suburb, and even to the gentrified old bohemian neighborhood, the Greenwich Village, in using, that is, its lived space, cultures, and peoples as a vantage point from which to launch their communal visions, they would reinvent the Lower East Side north of Houston, which included the Puerto Rican/Latino sector, what would later be renamed Loisaida, for middle-class, rebellious youth as a place of desire and identification, recasting it as east of the Village, or as the "East Village." It was a new Bohemia, not gentrified like the Village, further to the left, East. True enough, the Lower East Side was a multiracial, multicultural, multilingual, even multiclass neighborhood, but it was by no means a harmonious mosaic. Successive projects of urban renewal had turned the area, as Mele recounts, into a patchwork of "fractured communities," with diverse, disparate histories, whose "interaction was often conflictive" (137). But in projecting their alternative visions onto the Lower East Side to counter a homogeneous suburb and a gentrified bohemia, these middle-class rebels would smooth out the tensions among those communities and homogenize their uneven, disparate histories. Middle-class youth would cast their difference as migrants from suburbia as analogous to their neighbors' marginal condition as poor immigrants or displaced inner-city, working-class residents, their neighbors' exchangeable marginality often standing in for their own voluntary exile from suburbia. As a writer from the major community newspaper of the time, the *East Village Other*, would state, "People are here in the East Village because they could no longer make it in Harlem or Poland or Russia or Suburbia or Puerto Rico or what have you" (Mele 170). Suburbia or Puerto Rico or what have you, it was all the same. The same in difference, or the same indifference. Of course, quite a few members of the "underground," the East Village's artistic movement of the time, could themselves claim a marginal status, for the underground was peopled with women, Jews, and especially queer artists (Allen Ginsberg, Andy Warhol, Jack Smith, and Charles Ludlam, for instance). And their identification with, and desire for, the (ethnic or racial) otherness that the Lower East Side represented to them could also be seen as an identification with, and desire for, the (sexual and gendered) otherness that they themselves were. Perhaps in speaking for the marginality of the Lower East Side, they were also attempting to speak for and give value to their own devalued lives as queer artists. This was certainly the case for queer artists such as Charles Ludlam and Jack Smith, and even for Warhol, whose intense interest in marginal lives (drag queens, hustlers, "low lifes," "trash," as they are significantly called in Warhol and Morrissey's film of the same title) has been seen by critics as a way to process his own shame as a gay man, whose most notorious symptom was his paradoxically exhibited "shyness" (Sedgwick 1996 139–40). Practicing what has been called a gay camp "trash aesthetics" (Bottoms 216), these queer East Village artists sought to critique middle-class heterosexual norms by representing and giving value to the socially devalued, the "moldy," as Smith would call it, the extravagant, even the grotesque. "Our slant," Ludlam would explain referring to his "ridiculous theater," "was . . . especially [to] focus[. . .] on those things held in low esteem by society and [to] revalu[e] them, giving them new meaning, new worth, by changing their context" (Ludlam 31). And thus Maria Montez, the 1940s Dominican B-movie actress, who, according to Smith could turn "plaster cornball sets to beauty" (Smith 26), and Mario Montez, a Puerto Rican Lower East Side drag performer, himself, according to Ludlam, a great recycler of Lower East Side junk (Roemer 68), would become both for Ludlam and Smith the perfect vehicles for their artistic vision. A "superstar," the term coined by Smith and appropriated by Warhol to refer to the untrained street artists whom he would feature in his films, Mario Montez would appear in Warhol's first movie, *Harlot* (1964), and subsequently in *Mario Banana* (1964), *Screen Test #2* (1965), and *Chelsea Girls* (1966); in Smith's films, *Flaming Creatures* and *Normal Love*; in the Puerto Rican underground filmmaker José Rodríguez-Soltero's *hommage* to "Mexican spitfire" of the 1930s and 1940s, Lupe Vélez, *Lupe*, and in many of Ludlam's plays. And yet, despite its admiration for the powers of Maria and Mario Montez as recyclers and for Lower East Side Puerto Rican culture, or what Ludlam would call the "Puerto Rican Mystique" (150), in speaking its (sexual) difference through these artists, in ventriloquizing them, in using them as leverage to critique and subvert middle-class heterosexual norms, the queer underground, one could also argue, as Frances Negrón-Muntaner has done (114), would perhaps end up turning these artists and their production into mere metaphors, or tropes, for its own artistic project, effacing thus their agency and reducing the difference of their cultural forms. Decades later as the history of the underground was told, Negrón-Muntaner would charge, the impact of Puerto Rican cultural forms on the creation, and creativity, of the underground would be absent from most accounts (106). But the relationship of Loisaida to the East Village as generative of culture and art would continue, resurfacing on the world stage in the 1980s, as the East Village would transform from a marginal neighborhood into an international arts movement and lifestyle. As recounted by Mele, by the late 1970s the East Village would spawn a new underground arts movement centered in experimental music, art, and performance spaces such as CBGB, Club 57, and the Mudd Club (which, though located in TriBeCa, would become one of the first venues for the East Village's new underground). Informed by a punk sensibility, this new underground would embrace, assume, and deploy many of the signs of the Lower East Side's, especially Loisaida's, urban decay, against a rapidly privatizing cityscape, turning them into an internationally recognizable, contentiously ironic, resistant, in-your-face style. "Thus, the symbols and images of abandoned buildings, empty lots, . . . and a thriving drug economy [would] serve [. . .] as a foundation of an urban aesthetic inclusive of music, art, fashion, and literature," as Mele contends (221), but so would those "outlaw street" practices, identified by Algarín, through which predominantly African American and Puerto Rican/Latino inner-city youth would render themselves visible by remapping and reclaiming public space, and of these none more impacting than graffiti. Perhaps there is no more emblematic image of this moment of convergence between a punk-inspired underground and an inner-city, outlaw, youth culture than the scene in Charlie Ahearn's film about graffiti and the emergence of hip-hop, *Wild Style* (1981), when the underground film actress and art dealer, Patti Astor, who plays a well-connected downtown journalist and socialite, enters a hip-hop club and joins a circle of breakdancers, showing off some of her own idiosyncratic moves. "Even today," art critic Dan Cameron reflects, "th[is] image has lost almost none of its capacity to evoke a moment in popular culture when the divides of race and class in American life could be so awkwardly, and charmingly, summed up and dispensed with" (Cameron 49). An utopian moment if there is one, this documentary-styled film, which follows real-life graffiti writer George-Lee Quiñones as he struggles with the symbolic (and not-so-symbolic) seductions of turning his outlaw art into painting-on-canvas-for-sale, ends, despite its obvious reservations about mainstreaming, with an "outlaw party" or jam in an abandoned Loisaida band shell that is renovated by the artists for the event and at which everyone is welcome to participate, including the downtown journalist and socialite played by Astor. Featuring all the hip-hop arts and most of its artists at the time, the film would seem to suggest, through effective crosscutting, that hip-hop arts recycle and renovate devastated urban space such as Loisaida's. Coming on the heels of the press's recent "discovery" of hip-hop culture, *Wild Style* would also seem to argue, not unlike Algarín, against mainstreaming and for the harnessing of hip-hop's "outlaw street" practices, such as graffiti, for the reconstruction of plural, multiclass, multiracial, and multicultural communities. And it is the desire to participate in practices such as these, which are "outlaw" yet open to cross-class, cross-race collaboration, which would draw artists to the East Village in the early 1980s, giving rise to the myth of the East Village and to its short-lived art boom. In 1981, the School of Visual Arts–trained Keith Haring would join street artists Fab 5 Freddy and Futura 2000 in organizing an exhibit of "graffiti-based, -rooted, -inspired works," as the handbill announced (Cameron 44), at the Mudd Club, which would become typical of the East Village gallery scene. Titled *Beyond Words*, this show, which "displayed photographs of graffiti-ridden subway trains and spray-painted pieces of scrap metal" (Mele 228), would include both street and school-trained artists, such as Kenny Scharf, Rammellzee, Lady Pink, George-Lee Quiñones, SAMO (Jean-Michel Basquiat), and of course the show's organizers, Frederick Brathwaite (aka Fab 5 Freddy), Futura 2000, and Keith Haring, who would go on to form the core of one of the East Village's most representative galleries, Fun Gallery. In a role not unlike the one that she had played in Ahearn's film, Patti Astor and her partner, Bill Stelling, would open Fun Gallery in 1981. Located on East 11th St. in a tiny storefront, Fun Gallery's openings would bring together, as reported by the press, "[t]een-age graffiti writers, . . . radio-blaring youths from the nearby housing projects, . . . Park Avenue matrons and art world celebrities" (Deitch 13) in an ambient environment that recreated the outlaw party represented in *Wild Style*, with rap music, breakdancing, and graffiti (now on canvas) on the wall. As is also described by Juan Rivera in relation to Keith Haring's exhibits and "events" (see chapter two, "Paradise"), in these openings, the traditional hierarchies that sustained the art market then (street versus gallery, high art versus popular culture, art versus life) would be suspended, as the boundaries of class and race blurred under the banner of Fun. And fun it was, and profitable. Soon local and international mainstream art collectors and dealers would also want to get in on the Fun. And when Basquiat's show opened there in 1982 the trail of limousines could be seen winding down all the way from Third Ave. to Loisaida. By 1984, at the peak of the East Village's art boom, over 70 commercial galleries could be seen operating there, among these the trend-setting Gracie Mansion's Loo Division on East 10th St. and Avenue B, right in the heart of Loisaida. But the boom would soon go bust, and as early as 1985 many of the neighborhood's most prominent galleries would be looking to relocate to the traditional art areas of SoHo and 57th St., and many of its major artists, such as Haring and Basquiat, would "graduate" from the East Village galleries to the world's premier art venues in SoHo, Europe, Japan, and Brazil. By the end of the decade almost all of the galleries had migrated out of the East Village. In retrospect, it would seem to some that the much-vaunted alternative independence of the East Village had, after all, been, as Cameron has put it, its own "myth" (63). Successful artists and gallerists, whether they had planned it or not, had all to varying degrees deployed the myth of the East Village as leverage to enter the mainstream. And predictably, once they had done so, some of these artists would disavow the impact of their East Village experience on their artistic career and work. One could argue then that the 1980s East Village art movement did not change much in its brief lifespan—but something had changed, perhaps irrevocably. If nothing else, the 1980s East Village art movement had made the neighborhood as a political/ cultural statement and a lifestyle an intense object of desire for a large middle-class audience, making real estate prices there soar and increasing gentrification, as Mele has contended (233). If nothing else, it had made the racial, cultural, and class difference of disinvested Loisaida stylishly marketable. An indeed while the multicultural East Village art movement of the 1980s raged on, between twenty-five and fifty percent of the Puerto Rican/Latino residents of the southern and eastern blocks of the East Village, that is, Loisaida, were displaced (Mele 250). And Loisaida, the capacious term for an "outlaw" practice of recycling and a cultural politics of space would become "merely" an avenue instead, as Ševčenko has lamented (under pressure from local groups, the city would rename Avenue C in 1987, from Houston to 14th St., Loisaida Ave., in "recognition of the community's [cultural] diversity"; Ševčenko 310). Yet the cultural politics of space that had been initiated in the dark days of the 1970s as a way to recycle urban detritus into community agency would continue in the work of local activists and artists, such as the New York Puerto Rican writers Tato Laviera and Edgardo Vega-Yunqué, the Cuban American queer per-formance artist, Alina Troyano (a. k. a Carmelita Tropicana), and the multiethnic poets of Nuyorican Poets Cafe.

Paradise Garage

See chapter three, "A Love Interlude: The Paradise Garage."

Shibuya, Tokyo

See chapter three, "Pop and the Limits of Universalism: Shibuya, Tokyo."

Times Square and the Sex Trade (42nd and 53rd Streets, and Third Ave.)

From the late nineteenth century the 42nd St./Times Square area, then known as Longacre Square, has been identified with sex—the selling, consuming, marketing, managing, and policing of sex. And though much of the writing on the area, as well as almost all the development initiatives proposed for it, including the 42nd Street Development Project, which culminated in its present-day renovation, have been fueled by the goal of recapturing an earlier pristine, golden era, devoid of sexual commerce, historians of the Square have argued (Chauncey 1991; Gilfoyle; and Senelick, for instance), there is no period in the area's history that has not been identified with sex and its commerce. Not really a square but the place where two of the city's major avenues, Broadway and Seventh, converge to form a triangle, the famed zipper-signed Times Tower where the "ball drops" every year on New Year's Eve, as they approach 42nd St., the Square is literally and symbolically a crossroads, a crossroads most often referred to nowadays as the "Crossroads of the World" in recognition both of the Square's prominence as a center for corporate global entertainment and media (MTV, ABC, NBC, Disney, Condé Nast, AMC and Loews theaters, Virgin, Madame Tussaud) as well as a magnet for the diverse populations that make up and visit New York. A place of convergence for a racially and ethnically diverse population of passersby on their way to one of the city's major subway stations, the Port Authority Bus Terminal, the movies and theater, the fast food chain restaurants and cafes, and a multitude of global retail and tourist shops, where show business people, street artists, movie and theatergoers, tourists, and workers on their way home, the middle-class, the affluent, and the poor, the young and the aged mix, the Square provides what looks like a gigantic stage for the chance encounter of people across racial, ethnic, gender, class, and age lines. If the erotically charged experience of mixing across hierarchically set boundaries, looking at people, being looked at, and looking at being looked at, is, according to urban historian Marshall Berman (1982 148–64; 1997), the quintessentially modern experience, then Times Square is, to a degree greater than any other location in the city, and perhaps the United States, emblematic of the pleasures and risks of modernity. No wonder that from its early days as a center of male saloon culture to its later incarnations as a gay cruising ground, a haven for the 1950s Beat generation and for 1960s lesbian, gay, and transgender runaway kids, the Square has figured so prominently in literature, memoir, and film as a space of liberation from the constraints of sexual normativity and convention. (Even one of its most enduring images, the famous 1945 Eisenstaedt photo of an exuberant sailor kissing a surprised nurse in the midst of the Square's World War II victory celebration, representative as it might be of the nation coming together at the end of the war under the sign of heterosexual union, derives its erotic charge from its association with the Square's transgressively spontaneous encounters.) But the Square has also been the target of successive campaigns to police and eradicate sex as a sign of social decay, as well as of literary and cinematic critiques of the ways it has turned sex into a business, commodifying its liberating potential, as in John Rechy's 1963 novel about hustling, *City of Night*, and James Leo Herlihy's 1965 *Midnight Cowboy*. In the interstices, between the Square's modern impulse toward chance encounters across conventionally set lines, the state and social forces that have policed and curtailed these encounters, and the market interests that have profited from them, individuals have forged alternative sexual communities and cultures with their own "dynamics, semiotic systems, and territories," as George Chauncey has proposed (1991 322). Known as Longacre Square before it became Times Square at the petition of *The New York Times*, which relocated there in 1904, the Square would emerge at the northern edge of what was then the Tenderloin District, a male entertainment area, running from 24th to 40th streets on Sixth Ave., and composed of concert saloons offering a mixed fare of cheap performance with liberal access to prostitution and gambling (Buckley 286). As an extension of the Tenderloin, Longacre Square, aptly nicknamed then "Thieves Lair" for its honky-tonk ambiance, would become by the early twentieth century the "sex capital of New York" (Gilfoyle 299). Already in 1901, an antiprostitution citizens association, the Committee of Fifteen, investigating the area would identify "132 sites where prostitutes pl[y] their trade in the area bounded by Sixth and Eighth Avenues and 37th and 47th Streets" (Gilfoyle 299; Traub 30). And on 43rd St., between Broadway and Eighth avenues, where *The New York Times* would relocate, most brownstones on the southern side of the block, then known by the suggestive theatrical moniker, Soubrette Row, served as brothels (Traub 30). It was in this atmosphere where the line between entertainment and prostitution, stage and street often blurred that the "legitimate" Broadway theater would develop, as well as successive campaigns to eradicate sexually suggestive entertainment and prostitution. Beginning in 1900, "progressive," anti-vice citizens associations, such as the Committee of Fifteen (1900–02) and the highly successful Committee of Fourteen (1905–32) (Makagon 54), would target prostitution and public displays of sexuality in the Square as a way to undermine the immigrant "sporting" male culture of the concert saloon, which they believed to be at the root of society's ills, chief among them the increasing commodification (and degeneration) of people's private or family life. Targeting the venues where prostitution was either encouraged or tolerated and sexually suggestive material presented— hotels and restaurants but also theaters—the societies would manage to drive the sex trade underground by the 1920s, if not eradicate it (Gilfoyle 311). But ironically, with the passage of the Volstead Act of 1919, which enacted a national Prohibition against drinking, "in part to control public sociability . . . and . . . to destroy the immigrant, working-class male culture of the saloon," as Chauncey has claimed, the sexual underworld of the Square would be expanded and the ability of the police and anti-vice societies to control it undermined (Chauncey 1991 319). Overnight hotels and restaurants that depended on liquor revenues would be forced out of business, and those that survived would have to resort to allowing prostitutes and speakeasies to operate out of their premises (319). As the venues for illegal activity proliferated, encouraged by popular resistance to Prohibition and protected by the Mob, so would the tolerance for unconventional, non-normative sexual behavior and lifestyles. It is in this atmosphere of expanded clandestine activity, which would become more pronounced with the onset of the Depression, that effeminately flamboyant working-class gay young men, forced out of their more insulated city neighborhoods by homophobic hostility from neighbors and family, would seek refuge in the Square (315–16). Like later Latino runaway kids Sylvia Rivera and Holly Woodlawn in the early 1960s, these self-identified "painted queens" would survive in the Square by serving other self-identified gay and "normal," often working-class immigrant men from neighboring Hell's Kitchen, as prostitutes, forging, in the process, a highly visible gay community and subculture (321–22). But as the Depression deepened, a new type of straight-identified prostitute, aggressively masculine in presentation, often young men from economically devastated areas, sometimes sailors and servicemen, would come to the Square to sell sexual favors in order to support themselves (322). Known as "hustlers," or in gay parlance, "rough trade," this latest influx of young men into the Square would come to dominate the sex trade in The Deuce, or 42nd St. between Seventh and Eighth, forcing the "fairy" prostitutes, or "queens," onto Bryant Park on 42nd and Sixth Ave. while a well-dressed, more "mannered," gay-identified hustler from an earlier era would continue to ply his trade to the East, along Fifth Ave. (321), or on Third, along the stretch of antique stores that extended then from 42nd to Bloomingdale's (on 59th and Third; Friedman 114). Successive migrations of young men into the Square would consolidate this geographical pattern, whereby The Deuce would be associated with straight-identified, working-class "rough trade," Bryant Park with effeminate, transvestite, and transgender sex workers, and the East with gay-identified prostitutes for a more middle-class gay-identified clientele. (This pattern would hold all the way into the 1990s, when The Deuce would become a ghost town of boarded-up storefronts and porno theaters, Bryant Park would be renovated and cleansed, and Third Ave., which had been known during the first decades of the twentieth century and into the 1950s as New York's "Gay Street," would continue to develop into a neighborhood of high-rise office towers and luxury apartments.) In fact, the opening of the Port Authority Bus Terminal in 1950 would, if anything, turn The

Deuce into rougher terrain. With white, middle-class flight to the suburbs after World War II, the Square would become, like so many other downtown areas of industrial cities across the United States, a magnet for those left behind by a suburbanizing America, for those whom the writers Jack Kerouac, Allen Ginsberg, and William Burroughs would call, including themselves, "the Beat Generation," a name appropriately coined for them by Herbert Huncke, an old-time Times Square hustler, drug-addict, and spellbinding narrator who would be their guide to the Square's underworld (Bianco 127–31; Huncke 72). And whereas the literary Beat would find in the marginal state of the Square during this period a sort of poetic resistance to a suburbanizing America, others such as Thomas Painter, a sexual researcher on male prostitution and one of sexologist Alfred Kinsey's most thorough homosexual collaborators and informants, long a denizen of the Square, were highly distressed. Streets and bars were now packed with "juvenile delinquents of the most obviously criminal or depraved nature, who hustle[d]," complained Painter (qtd. in Friedman 112). He longed for the good-old Depression days of "polite trade," as Friedman has called them, when straight-identified sailors and servicemen knew how to serve their older paying gay customers, or johns. And he would find in the "active," straight-identified masculinity of the recently immigrated Puerto Rican men who hustled on East 14th St. and the Lower East Side "a throwback to the honest young sailors he [had] met during the Depression and war years" (114). This is not to say that, in his sexual relations with Puerto Rican men, Painter would assume a "feminine" or "receptive" role. On the contrary, "what was particularly satisfying" to Painter, the sexual historian Henry L. Minton has observed, was to be "able to assume the active masculine role . . . with his virile [Puerto Rican] partners" (Minton 200). As proof of his own troubled sense of masculinity, Painter would place "his partners in the position where they had to 'submit' to and accept his initiatives" (200). "I want to control, tame, hold, this strong, violent aggressive male—to 'have' him," Painter would confess in the multivolume journal or "life record" he would produce at Kinsey's request (qtd. in Minton 200). Against this increasingly marginal character of the Square in the 1950s, relished by the Beats, Painter's Puerto Rican sexual partners would offer him, or so he thought, the possibility of a return to a more primitively homo-erotic world of intense male bonding where sexual relations among men were not only available but ordinary, neither especially nor spatially segregated but diffused throughout the entire culture (Minton 196–97), where straight-identified men could still have sex with other men and remain straight (and conveniently so, one might add, so that he, Painter, could fulfill his racial/sexual fantasy of controlling, or "taming," them). (In Painter's view, one could argue then, the spatial marginalization of the Square was not so much a resistance to an imposed postwar, suburban, heterosexual normalization of American society as the precursor to another sort of normality—the normality of the marginal that a later gay identity politics would realize, an evolution perhaps most evident in the work of the Beat poet Allen Ginsberg.) Painter's sexual nostalgia, and preservationist spirit, would eventually send him traveling to San Juan, encouraged by Kinsey, who would counsel him that in Latin America "homosexual relations are for free and for fun among children and older males who engaged with their peers," although, alas, recently, "American contacts have [also] introduced the subject of pay," as Painter would soon find out (qtd. in Friedman 114). His attempt to recover an earlier, more innocently homoerotic world of male–male sexual relations through his relations with Puerto Rican men would perhaps initiate a long-standing association of Puerto Ricans in New York City (and especially the Square) with "trade" and with intense, homoerotic male bonding, more generally. Chauncey, for one, has argued that during the late 1950s and early 1960s New York City would "experienc[e] a massive influx of queer *boricuas*, who [would] 'electrif[y]' the local gay sex scene the way working-class Italians had done during the 1920s" (Negrón-Muntaner 107). And Negrón-Muntaner has followed his cue by proposing that the Puerto Rican immigrant male characters presented on *West Side Story* could have been read by a gay audience then, including the librettist, choreographer, lyricist, and composer of the play, all of whom were Jewish and gay, as much desired ethnic "trade" (Negrón-Muntaner 71). Indeed, *West Side Story* seems to have had the retroactive effect of influencing hustler fashion in the Square; at the time, as noted by Friedman, young men coming into the Square would signal their availability and desirability as hustlers by imitating the gang style that they had seen on the screen in *West Side Story*, the film, and which had been made famous just a few blocks up, on the Broadway stage (Friedman 120). During the ensuing decades of the 1960s and 1970s, the Square would become, if anything, even more marginal, and the aura of liberation it had once had would begin to tarnish. The rebellious atmosphere fostered by the sexual liberation movement and a bourgeoning "gay" consciousness would draw teenagers from all over the country to the Square in search of escape from the physical and mental abuse of their homophobic neighborhoods and homes, as well as in the hope of finding a sense of community or belonging. As remembered by Sylvia Rivera, the New York Latina transgender activist who had been a child prostitute there and would go on to become a participant in the Stonewall Rebellion of 1969, when she arrived in the Square in the early 1960s as an eleven-year-old scrawny male runaway she was "euphoric . . . at discovering that so many queens hung out and hustled there" and would soon become a member of their community by literally being rechristened into it and changing her name, from Ray to Sylvia (Duberman 66–67). And Puerto Rican drag performer Holly Woodlawn, who had run away from her Miami home at age sixteen during the same time, would recall in her memoir, *A Low Life in High Heels*, the many empathetic queens and hustlers who would take her under their wing, as she tried, rather unsuccessfully, to survive by hustling in Bryant Park (Woodlawn 54–55). But already around that time, in 1962, the Texas Chicano author John Rechy's first autobiographical novel *City of Night* would sound a different, more disillusioned note, whose echo would resonate throughout the 1970s. In Rechy's novel, Times Square was no longer a place of resistance to an imposed suburban, "mainstream" normality that had taken over America but rather its ultimate, most representative space: "Later I would think of America as one vast City of Night stretching gaudily from Times Square to Hollywood Boulevard— jukebox-winking, rock-n-roll-moaning: America at night fusing its darkcities into the unmistakable shape of loneliness" (Rechy 9). With this retrospective realization on the part of its protagonist that all the utopian urban spaces where he had sought to escape the traumatic loneliness of his childhood and find community were no more than the most emblematic sites where that loneliness was being replayed, Rechy's novel would begin. At bottom, what would trouble Rechy's protagonist most was money, or the way money in the Square seemed to mediate between people in order to protect and to distance them from the kind of vulnerability that might produce real communication: In his novel, the fee exacted by the hustler from the john was simply his way of protecting himself from having to face the possibility of loving another man, of surrendering himself, from having to acquire a more expansive notion of masculinity, one that would allow for recip- rocal relations (54, 341). And it was also simultaneously the john's way of defending himself from the unbearably painful admission that he yearned to love and be loved by another man—his way of sullying and degrading that illusion, so as not to have to face it—and its utterly painful improbability (54). Hustling would become then in Rechy's novel a metonymy for the increasing commercialization that mediated personal relations in America, both marginal and mainstream, and the loneliness that such commodification had produced. Money, true enough, had always mediated the relationship between hustlers and johns, in the Square as elsewhere. It determined the extent of intimacy, the length and frequency of contact, who (and of what race, ethnicity, gender, age, and class) would assume what sexual role, and though these factors were predictable, given a broader knowledge of American society, they were never fixed, were always historically contingent or bound. But as the 1960s rolled into the 1970s the reach of money, it seemed, had deepened, and the pace of its exchanges accelerated. By then a large number of kids had landed on the Square, forced out of their impoverished inner-city neighborhoods by a de-industrializing economic downturn that had swept major American cities, such as New York. And the Square had decidedly become black and Latino, except for a population of passersby on their way to the Port Authority Bus Terminal and middle-class white men who went there to "slum it." The Square had also fallen on hard times—facing competition from the newly created home video technology, the row of 42nd St. "grind" movie theaters that had subsisted there since the Depression days, had had to avail themselves of the recently passed 1966 U.S. Supreme Court decision that extended First-Amendment protections to explicitly sexual material and turn porno in order to survive. As a matter of fact, the entire street had become a huge porno emporium of dilapidated theaters turned venues for porno flicks and live-sex acts (such as the notorious *Show World Center* where, according to urban chronicler Josh Alan Friedman, a porno star named Tara Alexander had once brought eighty-three men, including her husband, to orgasm in a one-night record-breaking "spermathon"; Friedman 1986 89 and ff.), storefronts turned "massage parlors" where sex was regularly sold, camera shops and gadget stores turned bookstores for sexually explicit material, with booths, or "peepshows," where for a mere twenty-five cents a man could pay to watch the private parts of a woman for the specifically timed period of forty seconds, or engage in sex with another man, generally a hustler, for the same amount of time—and all of this oiled and fueled by the ubiquitous presence of drugs. For more than sex it was drugs that was the glue that held Times Square together during this period, speeding up its transactions, making everyone crave more, turning everything into cash. Perhaps there is no better image of the increasingly intimate and frantic pace of sexually oriented transactions in the Square than the peepshow. Introduced into the Square's porno bookstores in 1966 by Martin Hodas, a small-time jukebox vendor who would turn into the Square's most prominent porn filmmaker, the peepshows were coin-operated movie machines, common in arcades, where for a quarter one could watch a brief film clip of a woman stripping, but Hodas would outfit his with his own far more salacious nude loops, producing a boom in bookstore patronage. By 1970, the number of adult bookstores in the Square would more than double, becoming so profitable that Hodas would be forced to share control of the peeps with the Mob (Bianco 165–69). It was at the height of this boom that Hodas's collaborator, Garrett Williams, would revolutionize the sex industry by innovating the live peepshow. Now instead of a machine, there was a private booth with a window whose metal curtain would open at the drop of a quarter. On the other side of the window a naked woman would materialize twisting and turning in sexually suggestive poses on a revolving drum, disappearing forty seconds later, and forcing the titillated viewer to drop another quarter to complete orgasm, as in a kind of Vegas-style sexual slot machine (Friedman 1986 65). Like crack cocaine, which would become the drug of choice in the Square among female prostitutes and hustlers, the live peepshows would offer a cheaply attainable high while dangling the promise of yet another more satisfactory one at the drop of the next coin. By the end of the 1970s, the use of crack would be so widespread among hustlers that it would upend all trade protocol, making receptive "bottoms" out of active, insertive "tops," cheapening their rates, and generally installing in the area an atmosphere of such desperation that a vial of crack would become the price of almost any act, the most common (yet ephemeral) currency of exchange. It is this world overrun by a far-reaching and intensive sexual emporium, fed by a surplus of impoverished, runaway (and thrownaway) inner-city kids, and fueled by drugs that Juan Rivera would arrive in during the late 1970s, as he relates in his interview (see chapter two, "Just Telling Stories"). Perhaps no one has captured this moment so eloquently, and so problematically, in the lives of Latino, mostly Puerto Rican, young men hustling in the Square than the controversial photographer Larry Clark in his book *Teenage Lust* (1983). In a series of beautifully shot black and white photos, Clark has captured what no one else had: the very gaze of Latino (Puerto Rican) kids hustling in the Square, as they sold themselves. There is a sense of despair in their eyes, but also of menace, which is sexually charged, as if they understood that it is their very despair and menace, their abject condition, that they are selling their customer, the john. As explained by Clark in the book's concluding essay, "Because the main thing about 42nd St. . . . about all those pictures . . . is . . . the kids' eyes, the way a kid looks at a man, and . . . when he's looking at the camera, he's actually looking at a man . . . The picture is of what the kid is offering . . . [And what he] is offering [is] himself . . . It's a way of seeing things, but it's all polished up. It's point of sale." Clark would claim that, in capturing these boys' ambiguous point-of-sale look, he had captured them, but one could suggest as well that they also seem to have captured him—in his absence, in his camera's probing gaze, for these kids seem to understand the sexualized gaze that elicits theirs as the look of a john. And indeed, Clark's Times Square photographs, which are steeped in nostalgia, would seem to invite the viewer to participate in a largely bygone homoerotically charged world of male bonding through gazing at the eroticized bodies of these Latino/Puerto Rican young men. "[S]ince i became a photographer," he would confess in the preface to his book, "i always wanted to turn back the years. always wished i had a camera when i was a boy fucking in the back seat. gangbangs with the pretty girl all the other girls in the neighborhood hated . . . in 1972 and 73 the kid brothers in the neighborhood took me with them in their teen lust scene. it took me back." Not unlike Painter, who was also a photographer of (principally) hustler nudes, Clark might be said to attempt to recover then, through these pictures, an earlier, more innocently primitive childhood world of homoerotic male bonding, which Puerto Rican young men who hustled in the Square, among others, would signify for him. But unlike Painter's romanticized view of Puerto Rican men and culture, Clark's photos seem to exude a menacing aura of violence, as if the john's dream of communion with (and "taming" of) the hypermasculine ethnic male had somehow by the end of the 1970s gone awry. By then the frenetically violent, drug-induced pace of the sex trade in the Square would force runaway kids who landed there and ended up hustling, like Juan Rivera (see chapter 2, "One of These Days!"), to displace themselves toward the East Side where an alternate, more middle-class, gay-identified hustling scene had survived throughout most of the century in bars such as The Rounds, The Cowboys, The Haymarket, and The Ice Palace (see Delaney 42–43; Whitaker 2). For those who stayed in the Square however, generally the most destitute, straight-identified, or transgender inner-city black and Latino kids, without access to the media or the Internet (Friedman 2003 225), the Square would become a harsher, more dangerous space, as the twin forces of urban development and AIDS would ravage the place. Beginning in the 1980s the city would unveil a plan to redevelop 42nd St., the 42nd Street Development Project, by rezoning its sex shops, condemning its porno theaters (the New Amsterdam, the Lyric, the Victory, the Apollo), and turning them over to corporate owners who would restore them while building office towers to offset their cost (Traub 140). And as the city began to condemn sex trade venues on the grounds of rezoning and prevention of AIDS, theater owners and others critical of the city's plan would sue to halt its implementation (forty-seven suits in all), freezing all development there as well as all upkeep, and thrusting the neighborhood into a slow, protracted death (Traub 149–50). By the early 1990s, when the last suit was settled, the Square would look like a ghost town or war zone of boarded-up theaters and storefronts covered with graffiti and marked with white, stenciled "Post No Bill" signs. It was then that sociologist Robert P. McNamara, surveying the neighborhood for an ethnographic study of the impact of AIDS on the sex trade, would characterize street hustling there as a market "organized along ethnic lines to the extent that most hustlers are Hispanic while most clients are Caucasian" (McNamara 3): "Ninety percent of all hustlers out here are Puerto Rican . . . [A]t one time, a lotta blacks were goin' with the tricks, but it ain't that way no more. Now it's like, maybe, 10% black and the rest is Puerto Ricans that they go with," one of McNamara's informants, an older, twenty-one-year-old Puerto Rican youth nicknamed Apache, who had been hustling there for the past seven years, would explain (37). And he would add, "Clients want a young, skinny-looking Puerto Rican, not a white boy" (37), referring perhaps to his clients' penchant for the kind of "rough trade" nostalgically identified in the Square with the "good-old" pre-AIDS, pre-Stonewall days. It is true that during the 1980s the city and federal government would begin to recognize the problem of runaway youth involved in prostitution, as a response to extensive (and often sensationalist) media coverage (Friedman 2003 212–20), and shelters such as Covenant House, initially located in the Square and founded by the Franciscan priest, Fr. Bruce Ritter, would garner much attention and funding (Baker). But portrayed in the media (in films such as *Taxi Driver*, 1976) and by private charities such as Ritter's Covenant House as a problem of mostly middle-class youth who had run away from their middle-American homes to fall into prostitution (Ritter 1987; 1988), the solutions to this problem would not address the needs of the kids who hustled in the Square, who were mostly black and Latino from inner-city neighborhoods devastated by de-industrialization, federal disinvestment, and drugs (Baker). On the contrary, private programs such as Covenant House's, which offered by and large "critical care" (shelter, limited counseling, and food) for a short-term period, would serve the Reagan administration as a justification for defunding federal services to poor and minority families and generally dismantling the "welfare state" (Baker), further aggravating the conditions that had originally sent most of the kids in the Square into the streets. Throughout the 1990s, as development began in earnest in the Square, Bryant Park and the Port Authority Bus Terminal would be renovated and cleansed of sexual activity. The sex trade would move to the periphery of the Square, Eighth Ave. above 42nd St., and the New Times Square, dominated by Disney, MTV, ABC, NBC, AMC, and Virgin, would be purged of the sex trade, though not of sex. Sex, now corporate, would continue to sell products on billboards and electronic signs, video screens, Internet, and the air waves. But perhaps no sign would be more indicative of this new Times Square than the renovated AMC Empire 25 multiscreen movie theater on 42nd St. Originally built in 1912 and named after the Square's top female impersonator, Julian Eltinge, this new twenty-five-screen movie theater would recycle the façade of the old Eltinge 42nd Street Theater and install a vertical old-fashioned, blinking-lights marquee from which would dangle an alluringly revolving 25, reminiscent of the twenty-five-cent peeps.

THE PEOPLE

Anthony, Florence

Celebrity columnist and author of the best-selling novel *Keeping Secrets, Telling Lies*, Anthony was the first African American to work on the *New York Post*'s notoriously powerful celebrity gossip column *Page Six*. It was during her tenure there that she would contribute to an article about Juan Rivera's economic condition and his relationship with the Keith Haring Foundation after his lover and partner's death. Characteristically titled "AIDS Fund Stiffs Founder's Pal," the article would appear on Friday, October 30, 1992.

Arman, Yves and Deborah

Son and daughter-in-law of the French American artist Arman, well known for his "accumulation art" or assemblages of everyday consumer objects, such as his "Long Term Parking" (1982), a towering sculpture made of sixty cars embedded in 1,764 tons of concrete and exhibited at Jouy-en-Josas, France. A close friend of Haring, Yves, who was a car enthusiast and a reckless driver, as told by Juan in his interview (see chapter two, "Paradise"), would die tragically in February of 1989 while driving to meet Haring at the international ARCO art fair in Madrid. For Arman's funeral, Haring would be asked to paint the coffin. As he would write in his *Journals*: "Painting the coffin was an incredible (to say the least) experience. It was effortless, also, pouring out of my heart and hands. I painted with silver enamel on the shiny black Spanish coffin. Originally I intended to do just the angel, which he had adopted as his 'sign,' but found it necessary to complete the whole thing. At the bottom were a mother and child. And then I wanted to write FOREVER + EVER, but because the R didn't fit, it turned into this FOR EVE R AND EVER" (Haring 1997 243). Identifying with Arman, Haring would speak thus at his funeral: "I want people to be able to say about me what I said about Yves [at his funeral]— that every day he lived to the fullest and his life (our life) was and always will be complete" (243).

Basquiat, Jean-Michel

Major American visual artist of the latter half of the twentieth century. Born in 1960 in Brooklyn to a Haitian father and a first-generation New York Puerto Rican mother, Basquiat is considered both by his admirers and detractors alike perhaps the most emblematic American painter of the 1980s. As such, Basquiat has been the subject of a major Whitney Museum retrospective (1993), a Hollywood film, written and directed by his fellow 1980s Neo-Expressionist painter, Julian Schnabel, and multiple biographies, catalogues, and art journal essays since his untimely death in 1988 at the age of twenty-eight from a drug overdose. Basquiat, who would first become known to the media and the art world through his participation in the late 1970s graffiti art movement, would begin his career by scrawling ironic aphorisms and slogans with his partner, subway writer Al Diaz (also known as Bomb-1) on the buildings and streets of SoHo and TriBeCa in New York City under the identificatory tag SAMO, an abbreviation, as Basquiat would later explain, for "the same old shit" (Hoban 25). Like other New York City graffiti artists of the late 1970s and early 1980s, Basquiat and Diaz would appropriate public space (in their case, significantly, the space of the downtown art scene) in order to question established meanings and hierarchies. Rather than offering a political alternative, SAMO's aphorisms and slogans were a very post-modern intervention that sought to expose the commodification of contemporary culture and mock the pretensions of ideologies that claimed to be real alternatives to commodified culture: god, religion, new-age spirituality, and the downtown avant-garde art world: "SAMO as an alternative to god. SAMO as an end to playing art. SAMO as an end 2 Vynil Punkery. SAMO as an expression of spiritual

love. SAMO for the so-called avant garde. SAMO as an alternative
2 playing art with the 'radical chic' sect on Daddy's$funds. SAMO as
an alternative to the 'meat rack' arteest on display" (Hoban 28). In a
final sarcastic turn, SAMO's aphorisms, which exposed the contemporary commercialization of culture through irony, would also appear
trademarked (SAMO©). In the span of a few years, Basquiat would go
from scrawling on the walls of SoHo and TriBeCa to exhibiting his
works on canvas in some of SoHo's most prestigious galleries, for
instance, the Annina Nosei and Mary Boone-Michael Warner galleries
in which Basquiat would have one-artist shows in 1982, 1983, and
1984, which were major media events. René Ricard, the well-known
poet and critic, would consecrate Basquiat in a long, glowing article,
titled "The Radiant Child," for *Artforum*: "If Cy Twombly and Jean
Dubuffet had a baby and gave it up for adoption, it would be Jean-
Michel. The elegance of Twombly . . . and . . . the brut of the young
Dubuffet" (Ricard 35–43). But almost immediately critics would also
question the mass-media marketing of Basquiat by an art world driven
by rampant speculation and the commodification of the latest cultural
margin or edge. Still Basquiat would exhibit throughout the 1980s in
some of the world's major galleries: the Bruno Bischofberger, Larry
Gagosian, and Tony Shafrazi galleries in Zurich, Los Angeles, and
New York. His meteoric rise to art-world superstardom, however,
would continue to be haunted by the "taint" of his beginnings as a
graffitist. And for some Basquiat would always remain more of a
"primitive" than a "primitivist," as has been analyzed recently by
Frances Negrón-Muntaner (130). Unlike his mentor Andy Warhol,
the most famous living Pop artist of his time, and unlike other contemporary figures of the 1980s art and music scenes, notably Keith
Haring and Madonna, Basquiat would appear in countless anecdotes
as unable to use popular mass culture or the street, urban, subaltern
styles of Latino and black inner-city youth as a subject matter for high
art while effecting the "cool," distant, and abstract gaze that Warhol,
for one, was famous for ("Make it simple and plastic and white," was
Warhol's motto when dealing with popular or subaltern subjects;
Warhol and Hackett 91). In Juan's tale, for instance, this inability is
manifested in Basquiat's incredible discomfort at art-show openings,
where he would often withdraw into the bathroom to do drugs (see
chapter two, "Paradise"). For Basquiat's art, unlike Warhol's, was not
solely about appropriating the popular, or celebrating and continuing
it in high-art forms, like Haring's. His art, as has been noted by critics,
was a commentary on the ethical and political problems inherent in
such appropriations, especially for an artist who was often perceived

by many in the art world to be as much of a "primitive" as his subjects. Basquiat's inability to assume a cool, distant stance vis-à-vis the subject matter of his work—the appropriation and commodification of popular, subaltern cultures and racialized bodies—would often register in the commentaries of many of his critics and friends as either an artistic or emotional flaw. For Mary Boone, SoHo's premier art dealer throughout the 1980s, it was a sign of Basquiat being "too conscious of his place in the world." "He was too externalized," she would add; "he didn't have a strong enough internal life," which was, according to her, the mark of a great artist (Hoban 236). For others, such as Madonna, it confirmed Basquiat's emotional fragility: "He was one of the few people I was truly envious of. But he didn't know how good he was and he was plagued with insecurities . . . When I heard that Jean-Michel had died I was not surprised. He was too fragile for this world" (Hoban 166–67). Yet a careful examination of Basquiat's paintings would show that this inability was also the result of a conscious aesthetic choice. As the art critic Dick Hebdige has shown, Basquiat's art project was, if anything, too self-scrutinizing, too hard on him: "Basquiat always looked back at himself—as well as us—from the place of the Other. This is what, for all its exuberance and generosity, is ultimately so austere about his project. He never let up. He never gave himself a break" (62). Instead of assuming a cool, distant gaze, Basquiat's work's relentless self-examination would seem to undermine any position of comfort from which a viewer could gaze at the "primitive" or subaltern other. In the end, he would offer himself and others no rest, and this is what is so disturbing about viewing his work. But it is also Basquiat's particular artistic achievement: at a time when the art world was driven by speculating on the commodification of subaltern cultures and lives, Basquiat would force us to watch the impact of this commodification without the comfort of an outside, distant gaze, implicating us in the process. His work artistically exposes as such what Ricard's comment had so presciently identified at the launching of his career: "We are no longer collecting art, we are buying individuals. This is no piece by SAMO. This is a piece of SAMO."

Caroline of Monaco, Princess (a. k. a HRH the Princess of Hanover)

Eldest child of Monaco's Prince Rainier and former Hollywood movie actress Grace Kelly, Princess Grace. After the tragic death of her mother in 1982 from a stroke while driving on the narrow, twisting roads above Monte Carlo, Caroline would assume her mother's charitable work, becoming the ceremonial, if unofficial, first lady of Monaco. In 1983 she would become chair of the Board of Trustees of the Princess Grace Foundation, a philanthropic organization dedicated to the promotion of education and training in the arts. It was in this capacity that she would be introduced to Keith Haring by Yves Arman, and would dine at Arman's home where Juan would be charged with making dinner, as is told in his interview (see chapter two, "Paradise"). After Arman's death in 1989 Caroline would commission Haring to paint a mural in his memory for the Princess Grace Maternity Hospital. That year Haring would also be awarded the title *Chevalier de l'Ordre du Mérite Culturel* by the Principality of Monaco for the execution and donation of this mural.

Dubose, Juan

A New York African American DJ, Dubose would become Keith Haring's partner and live-in lover at the start of Haring's artistic career in 1981 and separate from Haring at its peak in 1986. Even after separating, Haring would continue to paint while listening to music mixes prepared by Dubose, and at Haring's parties for the "downtown cultural elite" (Madonna, Grace Jones, Warhol) and at his installations, Dubose would regularly deejay. At Haring's 1984 show at the Tony Shafrazi Gallery, for instance, Dubose would deejay for a group of breakdancers who would take part in Haring's black light disco installation with fluorescently painted walls (Gruen 1991 111). Dubose would also keep home for Haring while he worked: "When Juan and I began living together, my life seemed to be more or less settled. I now had a home and Juan was taking care of it— cooking and so forth, and I could really just concentrate on work" (80). Haring had met Dubose at the Saint Mark's Baths, a place he frequented because he preferred its atmosphere to the cruising scene at the gay bars: ". . . everyone at the baths was sort of on an equal level . . . all class distinctions were gone. You were a common, united, connected group of people" (43). And initially it was their commonality, rather than their racial and class differences, that would attract Haring to Dubose: "I decide this is the right person for me—he's black, he's thin, he's the same height as me, and he's almost the same age" (77). But, with time, as Haring's career would soar, Dubose would grow more silent and introverted, Haring's friends would report (80). Of his early period of blissful home life with Dubose, Haring would say: "I'm terrifically comfortable with Juan. But then,

I'm always comfortable with people of color—much more than with white people . . . I feel that . . . my spirit and soul is much closer to the spirit and soul of people of color. And, yes, I have an erotic attraction for people of color, because there is no better way to be wholly a part of the experience than to be sexually involved. I firmly believe that a sexual relationship—a deep sexual relationship is a way of truly experiencing another person—and really becoming that other person" (88). By 1986, however, Haring would outgrow Dubose, and Dubose partly in response, Haring admits, would turn to drugs (138). Haring and Dubose would separate that year, and in 1989 Dubose would die of AIDS, almost one year before Haring himself would pass away from complications related to AIDS.

Gruen, John

Cultural journalist and critic, author of the most frequently cited biography of Haring, *Keith Haring: The Authorized Biography* (1991). Gruen's biography, which is organized as a series of first-person observations and anecdotes about Haring as told by his family, associates, and friends, and by Haring himself, traces Haring's life and artistic career from his childhood in the small Pennsylvania Dutch farm community of Kutztown to his final memorial service there following his death in 1990 at age thirty-one. Between Haring's childhood and memorial service at Kutztown, Gruen would paint a picture of Haring's rise from struggling New York City art student to international 1980s art-world Pop star. Yet the framing of his narrative by Haring's hometown would seem to suggest the singular importance of Kutztown in shaping his life and art, as has been argued in chapter three. Significantly, Haring's distinctive use of a strong cartoon-like line seems to be traced here to his childhood experience of bonding with his father through art. As told by Haring's mother, Joan: "Before Keith was even a year old, he used to sit on his dad's lap after supper just drawing some gobbly-goo with crayons he'd been given. Then, later, Allen, who was very good at drawing cartoon things, would show Keith how to draw circles. Then, he'd make a circle into a balloon or an ice-cream cone or make a face out of it, and put ears on it or make all kinds of animals. Or Allen would put down a line and then ask Keith to put down a line, and then Allen would put down another line—and they'd make something out of it" (4). And in closing his biography, Gruen would quote Haring's sister, Kay, at a memorial service held for him at the Cathedral of St. John the Divine: "I remember that Keith was always drawing . . . it was his hobby, his pastime, his vehicle of expression, his very being. So, you see, it has always seemed to me that the brother I grew up with is the same brother that all of you know. Only the neighborhood get-togethers became the Manhattan club scene; the art projects with kids grew to include thousands and thousands of youths; his generous nature reached to touch virtually millions; and the canvas on which he drew became the whole world" (220). In contrast, Haring's *Journals* would associate his style and approach as an artist with his decision to migrate from his childhood home of Kutztown (see chapter three). In January 2003, a musical version of Haring's life, titled *Radiant Baby*, would open at New York's Public Theater. Written by Stuart Ross and directed by George C. Wolfe, its book would be based on Gruen's biography.

Gruen, Julia

Personal assistant to Keith Haring from 1984 to his death in 1990, Gruen would become the executive director of the Keith Haring Foundation upon his death. In her father's biography, *Keith Haring: The Authorized Biography*, Gruen would recall the effect that meeting Haring in 1984 had on her: ". . . a lot of people would concur that, once having met Keith—male or female, young or old—there always comes a point where you do almost fall in love with him. It's crazy. I myself have fallen in love with plenty of gay men, and have suffered for it. But it wasn't like that with Keith—it wasn't about that. I mean, I wasn't attracted to him. It's just that there was this inexplicable something in him—an essence of goodness or trust or the essence in believing in someone, and an innocence and generosity that just absolutely made you fall in love with him"(Gruen 1991 126). From then on Gruen would become Haring's personal assistant and studio manager, helping him to organize his calendar, keep his books, negotiate his contracts, and formalize his business and public relations, even track down a prop when needed for an event (118, 126). She would often be asked by Haring to travel with him around the world to attend openings, parties, dinners, and public events: "In a way, I think [Keith] was glad there was someone along who wasn't as tongue-tied as some of his other traveling companions might have been," she would explain (199). And she would add, referring to Haring's penchant for surrounding himself with black and Latino youth while he worked: "As always, [Keith] surrounded himself with young Hispanics and black kids. I mean, the flow of these young people into the studio was constant—constant! I didn't analyze it, but often wondered, 'How can he work?' But he did. And with terrific concentration. These kids would either sit and watch him work or they'd hang out in a corner of his studio, smoking pot and listening to music. Obviously they inspired Keith in some way. I once asked him about it. He said they helped him to keep up a certain rhythm, a certain beat, a certain closeness to the street life that he wanted to be a part of" (199–200). In 1989 as Haring realized that his life would be cut short by AIDS, he would create the Keith Haring Foundation to insure his artistic legacy and name Gruen as its executive director. On his death in February 16, 1990 Gruen would help Haring's family to organize a memorial for him in Kutztown, his hometown, to which she would carry his ashes, strewing them on a field where he used to go meditate, as is narrated in Gruen's biography (218–19) and Juan's interview (see chapter two, "Paradise"). In her current capacity as executive director of the Foundation, Gruen has for the past 18 years been responsible for overseeing museum and gallery exhibits of Haring's work, such as his retrospective at the Whitney in 1996 (see Sussman), the publication of material on his life and work, such as the *Keith Haring Journals*, and the production of a musical play on Haring's life, titled *Radiant Baby* and based on her father's biography. She has also organized on-line exhibits, and written essays on his works (see, for instance, "Haring All-Over" and "No Boundaries" in the Foundation's website: www.haring.com/essays), and worked with AIDS and children's organizations to continue to promote the causes that Haring dedicated himself to during his lifetime, as the Foundation website explains.

Hampton, David

A handsome and talented African American gay youth from a middle-class family in Buffalo, New York, Hampton would become notorious in the early 1980s for gaining entrance into the homes of Manhattan's white, Upper-East-Side cultural elite by posing as the Ivy-League son of famed African American actor Sidney Poitier. At a time when New York and the rest of the nation were caught in the grip of conspicuous consumption and the cult of celebrity and fame, Hampton would leave what he considered his parochial, mediocre native Buffalo in search of stardom and "fabulousness." One night in 1983, as he and a friend tried to get into the legendary New York disco Studio 54, whose admission policy was well known for selecting every night from among a throng of young hopefuls to mix with their glamorous guests, he decided to pose as Sidney Poitier's son and his friend as Gregory Peck's. They would soon be ushered into the club, gaining admittance into the inner sanctum of New York celebrities' early 1980s' playground. From then on he would repeat this performance at the homes of many New York personalities, among them, actress Melanie Griffith, actor Gary Sinise, designer Calvin Klein, and the dean of the Columbia University's Graduate School of Journalism, Osborn Elliot. Claiming to be a friend of their children who had just been mugged while waiting to catch a plane to meet his father, Sidney Poitier, and had been robbed of his belongings, including a Harvard term paper titled "Injustices in the Criminal Justice System," Hampton would charm his hosts into either giving him money or putting him up, or both. At other times, he would perform this impersonation at expensive restaurants, where he would allege to be waiting for his famous father who would never show up. Feeling sorry for Hampton, who had already eaten a lavish meal, the manager would invariably cancel the check or pick up the tab. Hampton's conceit, however, would soon catch up with him, and for impersonating the rich and famous and gaining access to their homes he would be formally charged with attempted burglary and sentenced to twenty-one months in jail. Meanwhile stories of Hampton's impersonations would continue to circulate among the wealthy of New York, and two of his victims, Osborn and Inger Elliot, who had been shocked to find the alleged son of Sidney Poitier in bed with a man the morning after they had taken him in, would relate their anecdote to playwright John Guare who would turn it into a play. Titled *Six Degrees of Separation*, Guare's play would open in May of 1990 at the Vivian Beaumont Theater of Lincoln Center, becoming a long-running show and spawning a film starring Stockard Channing, Donald Sutherland, and Will Smith in the role based on Hampton's life. The play, generally considered Guare's finest, certainly his greatest success, explores the notion of "who we let into our lives," according to Guare, in a world obsessed with the creation and selling of celebrity and fame. Using as literary conceit Stanley Milgram's 1967 sociological theory that everyone in the United States is connected to everyone else by a chain of six people, Guare's *Six Degrees of Separation* comments on the interconnectedness of people's lives in our contemporary world and on the opportunities such interconnections present. As Stockard Channing in the role of Ouisa Kittredge, the upper-class Upper-East-Side society lady who trades on other people's art works, a role for which she would win an Academy-award nomination, reflects, "I read somewhere that everyone on this planet is separated by only six other people—six degrees of separation between us and everyone else on this planet, the president of the United States or a gondolier in

Venice . . . It's a profound thought . . . How every person is a new door, opening up into other worlds." In the film, whereas Ouisa's husband, Flan, refuses to embrace the Hampton character's irruption in their lives as an "opening [onto] other worlds," turning it instead into an anecdote, which he will later recount with relish at society functions, Ouisa will take advantage of that irruption to reflect on her own life, dominated as it has been by trading in the right people, the right contacts, the right circles, and confront its lack of meaning or what she calls its "structure." As she will exclaim at the end of the film: ". . . we turned him [Hampton's character, Paul] into an anecdote, but it was an experience. I will not turn him into an anecdote. How do we keep what happens to us? How do we fit it into life without turning it into an anecdote? . . . Oh, that reminds me of the time that impostor came into our lives! Oh, tell the one about that boy! And we become these human juke boxes spilling out anecdotes—but it was an experience. How do we keep the experience?" Ironically, soon after the play would open, Guare himself would be caught up, like his characters, in his own "six degrees of separation." Infuriated at having his life used without his consent, Hampton would return to New York from a Hawaiian vacation to crash the play's producer's party, threaten Guare into giving him what he thought was his fair share of the play's profits, and grant scathing interviews to the press. But unlike Ouisa Kittredge, his liberal character, Guare would refuse to acknowledge the real Hampton's rights to his play's story, or embrace Hampton's challenge as an opportunity for self-reflection. Insisting until Hampton's death that he was an "amoral sociopath" and "a waste of a life," Guare would seek instead a restraining order against him in April of 1991 (see www.dailynews.com, July 22, 2003). Unable to obtain compensation, Hampton would sue in turn for $100 million in civil damages, claiming Guare had stolen the copyright to his person. One year later, in April of 1992, the N.Y. State Supreme Court would rule against Hampton, but by then his case had acquired such notoriety that famed liberal lawyer William Kunstler would offer to take up his defense in a subsequent appeal. In July of 1993, Hampton's lawsuit would finally be settled as the N.Y. State Appellate Division upheld the 1992 State Supreme Court ruling. It was during this time, while he appealed his case, that Hampton would meet Juan Rivera, encouraging him to pursue his own case against the Keith Haring Foundation (see chapter two, "Paradise"). He would also arrange for the publication of Juan's story on *Page Six*. For the next ten years, until his death in June of 2003 at age thirty-nine, Hampton would continue to ply his impersonations. And every time he did, he would mesmerize his victim with the proposition that he or she could also live, through him, through his stories and connections, the lives of the rich and famous. "It was performance art on the world's smallest possible stage, usually involving an audience of only one or two," his friend attorney Ronald Kuby would note at the time of his passing (see www.nytimes.com, July 19, 2003). Even after the embarrassment and rage of realizing that one had been duped, one last victim, who had been in the throes of a post-9/11 depression the day he had met Hampton, would confess, "Honestly? It was one of the best dates that I ever went on" (www.nytimes.com, July 19, 2003). At the time of his death at Beth Israel Hospital from AIDS complications, Hampton had been living in a small room at a home for AIDS patients where he had been trying to turn his life into book.

Jones, Grace

Perhaps the most emblematic of the gay disco divas of the late 1970s, Jones was an immensely successful high-fashion runway model before becoming a mesmerizingly haunting singer, a brilliant performance artist, and a riveting presence on stage and film. And no one would seem more shocking, more outrageous, more sexually uninhibited, or more fun than Jones. Born Grace Mendoza in Spanish Town, Jamaica, Jones would move to Syracuse, New York, as a teenager to live with her father, a preacher at a local church, and encounter there the theater instead. She would study drama at Syracuse University, but would soon leave college for New York City where she would land a contract with Paris designers Yves Saint Laurent, Claude Montana, and Kenzo Takada to model on their runways. In Paris, her unusually angular features, high cheek bones, full-bodied lips, and statuesque, muscular body would cut a strikingly handsome figure, which would enthrall the French. While in Paris she would discover disco, which was then all the rage. And she would return to New York, the epicenter of the phenomenon, to launch her career as a major singing star and an already legendary disco diva of sorts, as the titles of her albums, *Portfolio* (1977), *Fame* (1978), and *Muse* (1979), and her remake of classics such as Edith Piaf's *La Vie en Rose* suggest. And she would appear at many of the city's top gay discos, The Gallery, Paradise Garage, and Studio 54, singing what would then become the gay male anthem of the late 1970s, *I Need a Man*, a song in which Jones would waste no time pining for the proverbial man that got away, but would declare instead—unapologetically and with gusto—her immediate, carnal need for *a* man, "a man to make my dreams come true."

"Perhaps that man is you," she would add, invitingly. Remixed by Tom Moulton, the most prolific and influential gay disco mixer and producer of the times, this song would rise to #1 in the U.S. Hot Dance Club Play Chart, catapulting Jones to "Queen of the Gay Discos" status. But the unabashed, brazenly assertive sexuality of Jones's songs would not be her only appeal—so would be her sexually charged performances. In a much-reproduced image of the times, an invitation to a 1978 Roseland show, Jones would pose naked, on all fours, and wearing a tiger's tale inside a cage tagged "Don't Feed the Animal" (Goude 1981 105). Conceived in collaboration with her artistic director, the French photographer Jean-Paul Goude, who would subsequently direct her videos, especially her 1983 Grammy-nominated *A One Man Show*, and later marry her, this image seemed to hark back to, or at least to signal, old colonial stereotypes about the threateningly alluring sexuality of Africans projected onto the black female body, as the art critic Miriam Kershaw has proposed. And indeed the show, which recreated the decaying industrial scape of Manhattan's lower West Side, with corrugated metal curtains, scaffolding, and hunky Puerto Rican conga drummers providing the atmosphere for an urban jungle theme, as Goude would recall in his tellingly titled book of photos, *Jungle Fever*, seemed to reinforce this view. (Subsequent commentary by Goude on his recent autobiography, *So Far So Goude*, would also confirm what one might generously call his ambivalently colonial gaze: "Initially, [Grace] was flattered by all my attention," he would explain in an interview. "[And] she let herself be taken over, but then she suspected that I had only fallen in love with her image. Of course it was [true]! [But t]hat's the story of my life," he would wistfully conclude [Hodgkinson].) And yet as the show progressed, it would become fully evident that Jones was no threateningly alluring caged kitty posing for the scopic enjoyment of the white colonial male gaze (as film critic Laura Mulvey in another context has proposed), that one would do well to heed the warning on the cage not to feed the "animal" with one's objectifying gaze. At the peak of her show a live tiger in a cage would be rolled out onto the stage. And as 6,000 fans shrieked and screamed, Jones, covered in a tiger's coat, would sing, snarl, and hiss at her opponent, the caged beast. And then as the beast became fully angered and aroused, Jones would open the door of the cage and the lights would suddenly go off. For a full ten seconds the theater would go pitch dark and the music would stop as everyone's heart sank and the threat of the angered beast hung in the air, permeating the space. And as the audience was about to come out of its stupor and rush the door, the roar of two fighting tigers would be heard, paralyzing them in their place. And then all of a sudden the roar would stop and the lights and music would come on, and Jones would be standing there all alone on stage, singing and chewing on a big fat piece of steak. Delirious applause would erupt and screaming and hollering ensue as one realized, as she would later sing in one of her most famous remakes, Smoky Robinson's soul classic *The Hunter Is Captured by the Game*, for her 1979 reggae-influenced New Wave album, *Warm Leatherette*, that here, as in so many of her subsequent performances, the "hunter" had indeed been "captured by the game." Jones's ability to incorporate, to literally eat up the damaging racial and gender stereotypes that would disable her, turning them, through a shocking and witty inversion, into an occasion for empowerment would henceforth become her signature artistic move. And her mouth, her sensuous, full-bodied mouth, opening wide to show her large, perfectly aligned white teeth in a sort of growl or self-satisfied laughter or smirk would become her most frequently used metonymy for this ability, as is shown in her 1984 video *Slave to the Rhythm* where her mouth cut by a stiletto knife and outstretched seems to incorporate all—even herself. Jones's ability to incorporate damaging stereotypes in order to empower herself would be most brilliantly put to use in her 1983 Grammy-nominated video *A One Man Show*, directed by Jean-Paul Goude. As the video begins Jones is introduced through a series of photographs that tease and tantalize the audience's scopic desire by showing Jones in front of the camera naked and exposed: as a little girl lifting her skirt to show her private parts, as a female tiger in a cage, and as a runway model hounded by interviewers and photographers. But as her live performance commences, she will be seen displacing the objectification implicit in these photos by standing atop a twenty-foot long stairway like a female King Kong, breaking out of her gorilla outfit, and proceeding to impersonate or perform a series of stereotypes of dangerously threatening black masculinity—from the phallic jazz sax player to the James-Brown-type soul-funk stage performer and the contemporary breakdancing and moon-walking b-boy—dressed in a man's suit and sporting a cropped, manly "fade" haircut with a difference: high heels and her signature blood-red lip gloss. This small-though-highly-significant gap between Jones's male impersonation and her high heels and aggressively protruding red lips would once again under-score her ability to empower herself by incorporating and manipulating the stereotype, by eating it up, as it were, yet keeping it at a distance, always eluding it, always refusing to be fixed by it. Jones and Haring would first meet in 1984 at the pinnacle of their internationalizing careers, as they both gained broad mass-cultural success. Jones was starring then as the Amazon Zula in *Conan the Destroyer* and would soon play the smolderingly fatal May Day in the James Bond movie *A View to a Kill* (1985). And Haring was exhibiting all over Europe and Japan where he was being greeted with the media fanfare of a rock star and would soon begin planning the opening of his new commercial venture, a retail store, the Pop Shop, first on Lafayette Street in New York City and later in Tokyo (see chapter three, "Pop and the Limits of Universalism: Shibuya, Japan"). They would be introduced by Warhol, who wanted Haring to paint Jones's body the way he had done earlier with dancer-choreographer Bill T. Jones for a photograph by the then notoriously famous Robert Mapplethorpe for the cover of his pseudo-tabloid magazine, *Interview*. Both Haring and Mapplethorpe were well known by then for their strongly desiring gaze at black and Latino bodies, to the point of fetishization, some claimed (see Mercer). And Warhol himself, who had been nicknamed "Drella," a conflation of Cinderella and Dracula, had become notorious for his voraciously voyeuristic desire for media celebrities as well as the eccentrically subaltern subjects he would make through his studio, the "Factory," into "superstars" (Warhol and Hackett 153). But if anyone could match these artists' invasively desiring gaze with her own elusively disruptive and creative artistic moves it was Jones, as we have seen. She had after all thrilled her audiences and made a name for herself both by eliciting and eluding, inviting and inverting that kind of look. And yet in her collaborations with Haring during these years for Mapplethorpe's photograph and Warhol's cover, for her performances at the Paradise Garage (1985), and the video *I'm not Perfect (But I'm Perfect for You)* (1986), Jones would appear uncharacteristically static, weighed down by the Haring-inspired jewelry of designer David Spada and almost absorbed by the immense graffiti-covered canvas skirt Haring had created for her, a homage to Josephine Baker's famed banana skirt at the Folies Bergères and one under which Juan Rivera, his partner and assistant, would invisibly labor, as he would recount in his interview (see chapter two, "Paradise"), in an attempt to prop her up. For Haring Jones was, it would seem, as he would later tell his biographer John Gruen, the ultimate "embodiment of everything that [was] both primitive and pop," the "ultimate body to paint" (Gruen 1991 116), and as such she would look to him more like a totem or icon, adored yet fixed, than the outrageously elusive debunker of old colonial or African tribal myths she had up to then been. Haring and Jones would remain friends throughout his brief lifetime, often crossing each other's paths at airports around the world or meeting in Monte Carlo to spend time with their goddaughter, Madison, the daughter of their friends Yves and Debby Arman. Toward the early 1990s, after the death of Haring and of many of Jones's friends from AIDS, she would take a much-needed hiatus (it was a very hard time for her, she would later explain; www.andwedanced.com/artists/grace), from which she would finally emerge in 2004 to sing at a tribute concert for music producer Trevor Horn one of her old signature songs, which he had produced, "Slave to the Rhythm": "Work to the rhythm. Live to the rhythm. Love to the rhythm . . . Never stop the action. Keep it up, keep it up!," she would once again command.

L.A. II

A New York Puerto Rican graffiti writer whose tags, LA II and LA ROCK Keith Haring had long admired, as he wandered through his Lower East Side or Loisaida neighborhood, for their beauty and perfection (Gruen 1991 80). Angel Ortiz or Little Angel II, LA II, would become one of Haring's major collaborators and an important influence. As discussed in chapter three, they would meet during one of Haring's strolls through the neighborhood in the summer of 1981 as he spotted a group of boys spray-painting graffiti or "piecing" the courtyard of a local junior high school, P.S. 22. Haring was then twenty-three, LA fourteen. And during the next five years, as they collaborated in hundreds of works, they would become especially noted for their sculptures and vases, faux archaeological artifacts and classical statues painted in bright, Day-Glo colors on which Haring would draw his iconic subway figures, LA II filling in the negative, empty space with his swerving, interlocking, multidirectional, calligraphic tags. Initially Haring would ask LA II to tag a junked taxicab hood he had found, adding later his homeboy, barking dog, and crawling radiant baby figures to LA II's scrawls. But after he had finished combining both their marks, LA II would insist that they fill in all of the remaining negative, empty space. "I like it when everything's covered," he would later explain to Katherine Dieckmann in an interview for a special memorial issue of the *The Village Voice* devoted to Haring's art on the occasion of his death (Dieckmann 115). And it would be this dense, all-over pattern, with its tension between Haring's simple, outlined figures and LA II's aggressively swerving calligraphic tags, that would end up dynamizing Haring's art and propelling it to wider recognition and appeal, as has been noted by cultural critics and journalists Katharine Dieckmann, Colin

Moynihan, and most recently Ricardo Montez. (Even Julia Gruen, executive director of the Keith Haring Foundation, who has at times failed to credit LA II on her Foundation's website, would point to one of their collaborative pieces in her on-line exhibit "Haring All-Over," a 1982 painting, as a key moment in the evolution of Haring's art toward what she would call a "more complex," "all-over," "surface pattern" [www.haring.com/cgi-bin/essays; Gruen 1999], as has been observed by Montez 347). Indeed following their encounter, Haring and LA II would produce some of the pieces that would in time become most associated with Haring's art, collaborative pieces such as a 1982 Day-Glo statue of a siren sitting on a pedestal, a 1982 Day-Glo statue of *Venus on the Half Shell*, as Haring would call it (Gruen 1991 85), a 1982 Day-Glo *Statue of Liberty*, a 1983 Day-Glo bust of Michelangelo's *David*, and their very familiar graffiti-covered, faux-classical terracotta vases and columns, which have often been shown or reproduced without properly crediting LA II (see, for instance, the 1997 catalogue for the Whitney exhibit, *Keith Haring*; Sussman 148–51; and the Keith Haring Foundation's Internet art archive for the years 1982, 1984, and 1985: www.haring.com/art_haring/index.html). During the next five years LA II and Haring would travel around the world, creating onsite works in some of the world's major galleries: Tony Shafrazi's in 1982 and 1983; the Galerie Watari in Tokyo in 1983; Robert Fraser's in London in 1983; Salvatore Ala's in Milan in 1984. But as graffiti would begin to lose its appeal for the art-world market, Haring would, as he says, increasingly "*dis*associate" himself from it (Gruen 1991 89), and LA II, with few resources and no formal art education, would struggle, like other graffiti writers, to support himself as an artist. The years that followed his collaboration with Haring would be particularly hard for LA II. He would work in a pizzeria and as a bicycle messenger, sleeping on friends' couches on the Lower East Side, in order to support himself, as Colin Moynihan in his article for *The Village Voice* twelve years after Haring's death would report. And yet ironically as LA II struggled to support himself, Haring's artwork, which included some of his collaborative pieces with LA II, would be regularly sold for six-figure prices, according to Moynihan. But LA II would not be able to share in this art-market boom because the Keith Haring Foundation, which possessed ten to fifteen of the collaborative pieces, would neither recognize LA II's claim to part ownership of them nor put them up for sale, depriving him thus, according to him, both of potential income and art-world acclaim (Moynihan). Finally in 2002 the Clayton Patterson Gallery and Outlaw Museum on the Lower East Side would host a month-long exhibit of LA II or Angel Ortiz's latest work. Significantly titled *Setting the Record Straight*, the show would be advertised as a way to rectify the lack of acknowledgment and compensation LA II had suffered. Yet by making his acknowledgment contingent, not on the inherent beauty or skill of his art, which was what had initially attracted Haring, but on rectifying his contribution to Haring's work, the show would end up stressing LA II's dependence on Haring. And it would do so by recycling the old images or tropes of sexual seduction and racial and class dominance that had hovered over their relationship from the very beginning, images in which LA II was supposed to play the presumably "straight," Puerto Rican, barrio homeboy to Haring's voraciously desiring, white, upper-middle-class, gay sugar daddy or john, as has been astutely observed by Montez (436). Unfortunately the exhibit at the Lower East Side's Patterson Gallery would not solve LA II's money problems, and on June 2003, one year after his come-back show, he would be arrested for allegedly selling heroin to an undercover cop in the old Loisaida neighborhood where he had first met Haring, which was now gentrified, Avenue D, and he would be sentenced to two to four years in jail (September 3–9, 2003, *The Villager*: www.thevillager.com).

Levan, Larry

See in chapter three, "A Love Interlude: the Paradise Garage."

Madonna

Madonna.

Scharf, Kenny

Along with Keith Haring and Jean-Michel Basquiat, one of the major figures to emerge out of the East Village arts movement of the 1980s. Like them, Kenny Scharf would be influenced by popular culture, especially by the animated cartoon characters of the early 1960s prime-time TV shows, *The Flintstones* and *The Jetsons*. And he would famously rework these characters into cosmic, mythic tableaux, as in his 1982 *Elroy Mandala II* or *Tantric Judy* (see www.kennyscharf.com). But unlike Haring and Basquiat, Scharf would not incorporate popular culture forms as a way of establishing a common vocabulary with which to dialogue with urban "street" art. Instead what programs such as *The Flintstones* and *The Jetsons* would provide Scharf with was a view of a total, self-enclosed world in which the stereotypes of American middle-class life could be transposed into popular art and rendered, in Kirk Varnedoe and Adam Gopnik's words, as "timeless verities" (Varnedoe and Gopnik 383). Closer to the *faux-naïf* urban cartoon art of the Hairy Who, the Chicago school of painting, than to the work of Haring and Basquiat or to graffiti art, as Varnedoe and Gopnik have observed (383), Scharf's work would appropriate the suburban, middle-class vocabulary of the 1960s animated TV shows in order to create his own internal, total world of imagination and wit whose constantly metamorphosizing cartoon figures and shapes would culminate in his elaborately stylized, Pop-Surrealist landscapes of the 1990s and 2000s (see www.kennyscharf.com). Like the emblematic 1983 piece that opens his website, *The Funs Inside*, Scharf would integrate spray-painted graffiti but only as a backdrop of incomprehensibly tangled shapes that would serve as a contrast to his own transparently clear, futuristic, internal landscapes of endless transmutations and "fun." His work, like the gaping mouth of the cartoon creature that seems to invite the viewer to the "fun inside" in *The Funs Inside*, would invite the viewer to enter other, more person-ally utopian worlds, where standard vocabularies and logics might be altered and displaced but where communication was always possible, productive, accessible, and immediate. If Haring and Basquiat had adopted the East Village as a vantage point from which to launch their critique of American mainstream culture, Scharf, one could say, had discovered there instead the necessary distance from which to recover the ideal of total, unmediated communication and access promised in the 1950s and early 1960s by American middle-class, suburban modernity. And out of the erotic charge of this promised "brave new world" Scharf would create his zany, "groovy" aesthetics. Like Haring, Scharf had arrived in New York to study at the School of Visual Arts in 1978. They had soon become friends, and with John Sex, another SVA student, Drew Straub, an art student from Haring's hometown, Kutztown, and Tseng Kwong Chi, who would become Haring's collaborating photographer, they would create a sort of posse, often hanging out and performing at the East Village underground venue, Club 57 (see chapter three). Scharf and Haring would be very sup-portive of each other's projects and ambition during these early years. They would both participate in the groundbreaking exhibitions of underground art of the times, *The Times Square Show*, in 1980, and its larger survey the following year, *New York/New Wave*, at P.S. 122, and Scharf would collaborate with Haring in his 1980 *Club 57 Invitational* and his 1981 exhibit of "graffiti-based, -rooted, [and] -inspired works" at the Mudd Club, *Beyond Words*, co-organized with Fab 5 Freddy and Futura 2000 (Cameron 44). But as Haring began to be noticed by collectors, gallery owners, and critics for his subway drawings and his street-inflected art, Scharf would become jealous at being bypassed, and their relationship would suffer. They shared then a loft near 42nd St., and every time collectors would come to visit, Scharf would recall, "It was exciting because I thought they'd look at my work too. But it turned into this horrible experience. Everybody went right to Keith's work. It was really hard on me. I felt just terrible" (Gruen 1991 75). And when Haring became world famous and was catapulted to the status of international media celebrity, like no other artist of his generation, their relationship would become more than strained; it would become estranged. Scharf would feel then that Haring had shut him out and that his life was irremediably absorbed with the "pursuit of famous people[,] fabulous celebrities[,]" and "these gay Puerto Rican hustlers," by whom he meant people such as Juan Rivera, whom he felt were "dragging Keith down" (139–40), as Juan in his interview would confirm (see chapter two, "Paradise"). Still Haring would continue to visit Scharf and his family in their country home in Brazil. And though Haring's AIDS diagnosis would put a further strain in their relationship, as Scharf would admit, they would once again regain their "original, true closeness" shortly before his death (188). At the moment of Haring's death in 1990 Scharf would be one of the first persons called. Despite their divergent artistic paths, Haring would always insist that, along with Francesco Clemente, Jean-Michel Basquiat, and George Condo, Scharf was one of his favorite artists (195).

Vazquez, Gilbert

See chapter three, "Pop and the Limits of Universalism: Shibuya, Tokyo."

THE TERMS

ARC

AIDS-related complex, a condition in which some of the symptoms of HIV infection, such as fever, persistent lymphodenopathy, or lymph node disease, and weight loss, are already present, but none of the opportunistic diseases associated with full-blown AIDS. A term used at the beginning of the AIDS pandemic to designate the condition of individuals whose immune system had already been compromised and whose T-cell count had already decreased, ARC would often be seen as a precursor to AIDS. This diagnosis, which would be given to Juan when he found out that he was HIV-positive (see chapter two, "Paradise"), is no longer recognized by the CDC (the U.S. Centers for Disease Control; see Hubert and Gillaspy; Watstein and Stratton).

Cristal

Originally developed in 1876 by Louis Roederer for Tsar Alexander II of Russia, *Cristal*, France's premier champagne, which is known to wine connoisseurs for its straightforward and smooth "attack" and its long, sustained finish and sells for $400 to $600 a bottle, would become the preferred drink of Keith Haring and his coterie of 1980s art-world friends. Since the 1990s it has become the drink of choice of successful hip-hop producers and artists, such as Puff Daddy, Sean John Combs or P. Diddy, Jay-Z, Snoop Dogg, and Mary J. Blige. References to it appear regularly in rap music and video, and in 2003, it was the drink most often cited in American popular music, according to the website Americanbrandstand.com, which tracks product mentions in American music. More recently, however, Jay-Z has launched a boycott of *Cristal* in all of his clubs alleging racism on the part of its company's managing director Frédéric Rouzaud who told *The Economist* that his company viewed the affection rappers had for its product with a mix of "curiosity and serenity" (June 15, 2006; www.msnbc.msn.com).

Dominant/Passive; Macho/Pato (Maricón); Hustler/Pargo; Top/Bottom

The various terms used by Juan throughout his interview to denote sexual positions and the social identities and practices associated with them in sex between and among men, dominant/passive, macho/ pato (*maricón*), hustler/*pargo*, top/bottom are not fixed, stable, or equivalent binary pairs that designate equally fixed, stable, or analogous sexual identities and practices. Rather, they seem to designate in Juan's interview, as Roger Lancaster has proposed in his observations on sexual categories in Latin America, "Sexual Positions: Caveats and Second Thoughts on Categories," possible sexual scripts whose power relations and meanings are determined at any given point by the limits imposed by specific social contexts and the individuals' ability to negotiate them (Lancaster 1997 12–14). Like Michel Foucault's notion of power, power in these male–male sexual categories and scripts in Juan's tale is not something that someone (the "active" or "dominant" partner, for instance) possesses to the detriment of the other (the "passive" or dispossessed; Foucault 94). Instead, power appears to be here a dynamic relationship, susceptible to being redefined, reconfigured, and resignified in daily interaction and practice, as has been shown by Richard Parker's, Mathew C. Gutmann's, and most recently Héctor Carrillo's research on contemporary male sexuality in Mexico and Brazil. Whereas some critics had long proposed a single, unified, specifically Latin American system of sexual categorization, whose basis was the traditional, patriarchal, gender-inflected distinction between (male) inserting partners and (female or male) receptive ones or, as is known, the *activo/pasivo* sexual regime, contemporary Latin American sexual cultures, Parker has convincingly been arguing for some time now, are the result of competing local and foreign or international adopted models of understanding and practicing sexuality, such as the current Euro-American model of sexual classification that privileges the distinction homosexual/heterosexual as the dominant marker of sexual practice and identity. And it is this incongruence between models of sexual categorization, or lack of fit, that gives Latin American sexual cultures their dynamism and allows local subjects to reinterpret and rearticulate classifications from those interstices or gaps for the purpose of achieving pleasure and a measure of leverage or agency in controlling their sexual lives (Parker). U.S. sexual cultures are no less the result of competing sexual systems than Latin American ones. Along with indigenous and vernacular models of sexual categorization and practice, U.S. sexual cultures are continuously being impacted by new immigrant ways of conceiving and practicing sex. Some studies of American sexuality have focused on the imprint or legacy of the Latin American patriarchal *activo/pasivo* sexual regime on the lives of U.S. Latinos (see, for instance, Almaguer); more recent research however has concentrated instead on the incongruence between this model and other dominant U.S. sexual models and on how U.S. Latinos have creatively negotiated it (see, for instance, Muñoz-Laboy). In his interview Juan's varied deployment of sexual categories may be said to represent creative (though by no means ideal) negotiations of this sort. His interview, which spans Juan's awakening as a sexual subject in the Puerto Rican, immigrant, working-class neighborhood of The Hill in New Haven, Connecticut, during the years this neighborhood was undergoing severe deterioration, as a result of de-industrialization and disinvestment, in the 1970s (Glasser 1997 133–43), his participation in the sex trade in Times

WHAT'S IN A NAME ✤ 169

Square at the height of its transformation into the city's premier sexual and drug emporium, in the late 1970s (see chapter five, "Times Square and the Sex Trade"), and his involvement in an abusive ("S&M," he would call it) relationship with a second-generation West-Indian American named C . . . , who had recently "come out" as "gay," and with the East Village, avant-garde, 1980s Pop artist Keith Haring, allows us to appreciate how binary sexual categories are redeployed and resignified in varied economic, racial, social, and cultural contexts, acquiring thus diverse meanings and nuances, referring to different, modified sexual power dynamics and scripts. While growing up in The Hill neighborhood in New Haven, Juan's greatest fear (and most intense attraction) was the possibility of "falling" into (or being "seduced" into accepting) the receptive position of *pato* (literally a "duck") or *maricón* [faggot] to the anally insertive position of a macho, as prescribed by the local version of the Puerto Rican/ Latin American *activo/pasivo* sexual regime then in force. As has been analyzed by cultural critics and anthropologists as diverse as Octavio Paz, Rafael Ramírez, Richard Parker, Tomás Almaguer, and especially Roger Lancaster (1992), the insertive males in this first, New Haven section of Juan's interview do not consider themselves, or are considered by others, anything other than simply macho or male, whereas the penetrated male or *pato* is considered feminized, degraded (or even "demonic"), and less than male. In addition, as discussed by Lancaster (1992), it is the *pato* here who bears the brunt of the individual and family disgrace and shame that results from such socially stigmatized behavior, making it possible thus for the macho to engage in same-sex activity without having to socially pay, as it were, with the burden of stigma or shame. And it is he who can make intense homosocial desire among men materialize and transform into actual same-sex sex by absorbing all (homosexual) desire, by taking it upon himself, as it were, and absolving thus the macho from all personal responsibility for disgrace and shame, as is shown in the East Rock scene of this first Hill section of Juan's interview (17–18). And yet, though this local, Puerto Rican version of the *activo/pasivo* regime is dominant in this Hill section of Juan's interview, there are also other competing models that interpellate Juan as well: For one, there is, in addition to the *pato* and the macho, the model represented by the *locas*, or rather, as Juan qualifies them, the "loud *locas*" (18). Literally crazy women, as in the French *folles*, the *locas* are not just effeminate men, or *queens*, but *patos* who have decided to assume the feminization imposed on them and wield it with a vengeance, as a weapon. Closer to the bitch, these *locas* would seem to refuse to accept the binary system whereby the *patos* are symbolically relegated to the feminine, domestic sphere, discreetly (and abashedly) serving or "taking care" of the "men." Instead, like fallen women, these loud *locas* in Juan's tale would rather prowl the streets in flamboyant, self-advertising outfits, displaying their desire in public, making their claim both to the visibility of their desire and to public space. And if a macho rejects their advances, they do not simply yield their claim to expressing themselves in public, or take responsibility for all (homosexual) desire onto themselves—quite the opposite, they project it: It is you who are the *pato*, they shout back. You who desire me! Needless to say, these *locas* present a challenge to the patriarchal, gender-inflected *activo/pasivo* regime in the Puerto Rican Hill neighborhood, but they do so at peril to themselves: "Until then [that is, until he went to his first gay disco] my image of gay people were these loud *locas* like M . . . , F . . . , and J . . . ," Juan would explain. "They'd walk down the street swishing and shaking their bangles, and if they spooked a boy, and the boy got loud with them, they'd read him and threaten to punch him out. Eventually, they all died—were killed. M . . . was found in his apartment cas . . . trated. And F . . . was killed in a bar in *Six Corners* (remember *Six Corners?*) . . . —they stuck a pipe up his butt. And J . . . died . . . —of an overdose" (18). Additionally, there is, in this Hill section of Juan's interview, an emerging "gay" model of same-sex sexual practice and identity that appears to center on the experience of mutuality and sameness fostered by the disco, represented here most vividly by the multiple, specular reflections on its mirror ball (see chapter two, "Fly, Robin, Fly," and chapter three, "Clones Go Home!"): "And then I found *The Neuter Rooster*, my first gay night-club. It had this huge statue of *un pájaro* [literally a bird, and thus allusive to the category *pato*] about to take off, and as you walked in you could hear the club's theme, '*Fly, robin, fly* . . . ,' and you'd see your face reflected in all of these mirrors and all these pretty boys' faces, and I felt . . . like flying, reborn, and I flew, and flew . . . far away" (18). The sexual categories deployed by Juan would once again mutate when he arrived in Times Square, New York in the late 1970s and ended up participating, like so many other gay runaway youths, in its then booming sex trade (see chapter two, "Just Telling Stories"). Instead of *activo/pasivo*, the prevailing model of sexual practice in this section will become dominant/*pargo*. A version of *activo/pasivo*, dominant/*pargo* appears to describe here not so much the practice of being a macho or *pato* through the assumption of a specific sexually symbolic position as the act of performing "dominance" for a paying client or *pargo* who is looking to experience what is for him an earlier mode of sexual practice, which has by then in the age of gay liberation and identity been superseded and which Latinos, especially Puerto Ricans, have come to signify in the Square's sex trade since at least the 1950s (see chapter five, "Times Square and the Sex Trade"). A nostalgic trade then, the hustler's art would seem to consist in selling the *pargo* (in Spanish literally the porgy or fish and figuratively and pejoratively, as in English, the gullible, the dupe, the chump) the fantasy of participating in an older, more "primitively" alluring, archaic sexual regime from which he the hustler is often ironically (or even tragically), as in the case of Juan, trying to escape. That this act of "dominance" is obviously a performance, rather than merely the assumption of a sexually symbolic position, is underscored by the fact that Juan, like so many other gay runaway kids (see chapter five, "Times Square and the Sex Trade"), is being paid here to perform not the category he had always had to assume in his New Haven Puerto Rican neighborhood, that of *pato*, but its very opposite: that of macho. And it is further underscored by the fact that the goal of this paid performance is not so much to "dominate" the *pargo* as to provide him with the occasion, or script, to assume the *pasivo* role strategically, that is, so that he can then invert the power relations of the *activo/pasivo* sexual regime and end up on "top," which is ultimately, as Juan suggests, the *pargo*'s fantasy: "Practically every *pargo* I ever dealt with wanted me to dominate him so he could end up on top . . . That was the fantasy they were paying for," he would explain (24). In his subsequent relationships with the second-generation West-Indian American who had just "come out" as gay, C . . . , and with the small-mid-American-town-young-man-turned-media-celebrity, 1980s Pop artist Keith Haring, Juan would attempt to build loving "gay" relationships based on mutuality, or at least complementarity. But these relationships would continue to be haunted by the power dynamics of the *activo/pasivo*, dominant/*pargo* sexual regimes, which would once again mutate. Whereas *activo/pasivo* would transform into the gay categories top/bottom, that express, rather than opposite gender/ sexual identities, mere positions in the enjoyment and fulfillment of gay sex, dominance, now detached from these positions assumed during sex, would remain a determining category in Juan's relationships, signaling, according to his interview, a difference in his control over his circumstances due to class, education, culture, psychology, or race. Thus, although Juan would be "top" in both these relationships, he would continue to struggle under the psychological, educational, racial, cultural or class dominance of C . . . and Haring, respectively, a dominance he would attempt to negotiate.

Ecstasy, E

A synthetic, psychoactive "designer" drug, first synthesized in 1912 by the German pharmaceutical company Merk in search for a good styptic to reduce bleeding, MDMA (3, 4 methylenedioxy-methamphetamine) or Ecstasy would be rediscovered in the late 1970s by the controversial California chemical researcher of psychedelic drugs, Alexander Shulgin, who would introduced it to his friends, many of whom were professional therapists. Shulgin and his therapist friends would note among the drug's mind-altering effects a lowering of defensive barriers and an openness to the world and others that was particularly valuable in therapeutic practice. MDMA, they observed, promoted a feeling of empathy for the world and others while simultaneously enhancing, not diminishing, the subject's sense of self-worth, self-forgiveness, and self-acceptance (Eisener). By the early 1980s, MDMA, then known as "Adam," for its association with a feeling of return to a natural, prelapsarian state of innocence, before guilt and shame, was being used by over a thousand therapists in private practice. But soon the artisanal production of MDMA for therapeutic purposes would expand into full mass production as MDMA, now marketed as "Ecstasy," made its entrance into dance culture through the gay discos. Fostering both empathy and self-worth, Ecstasy would become the perfect compliment at major gay discos, such as New York's The Saint, where a crowd of mostly white young men, who had just "come out of the closet" and were living the experience of being "gay" after the Stonewall Rebellion and the emergence of the gay liberation movement, shed all inhibition and social stigma as they celebrated their common oneness under what was then the largest planetarium dome over a dance floor (Collin; Silcott and Mireille). From New York Ecstasy would spread to other American cities, such as Dallas-Fort Worth, which was caught then in the grip of a conspicuous consumption modeled on its namesake, the extravagant night-time TV drama, *Dallas*. Perhaps as a reaction to this individualistic ethos of the Reagan era, Ecstasy, which was distributed openly in bars and nightclubs, purchased with credit cards from toll-free numbers, and bought at convenience stores under the tongue-in-cheek label "Sassyfras," would end up replacing cocaine as the drug of choice among Dallas-Fort Worth's upwardly mobile young urban professionals. Profiled in major newspapers and magazines as the hottest new trend in the search for happiness through chemistry, MDMA's fame would spread. Spurred by sensationalist media reports of abuse and alleging scientific evidence that showed that MDMA caused damaging effects on serotonergic axons in animals, the U.S. Drug Enforcement Administration (DEA) would move in 1985 to place the drug in Schedule 1 status, the most restrictive of all its drug categories. But by then MDMA's fame had crossed the Atlantic. First introduced in Europe by the disciples of the Indian guru Bhagwan Shree Rajneesh, the *sannyasins*, or perfect renunciants, after the Sanskrit word *sannyasa*, Ecstasy would make its way to the dance floors of the Spanish island resort of Ibiza where it would mix with American house music, giving birth to what the British would call acid house. By the summer of 1986, Ibiza was popularly known among Brits as "XTC Island," and returning young tourists and DJs would take this musical experience back with them, organizing the country's first "raves," clandestine parties in abandoned warehouses or open fields outside of London's M25 Orbital motorway where young people would gather to take Ecstasy, dance acid house, and socialize while connecting with each other in a spirit of what was called then PLUR (peace, love, unity, and respect). It was probably during this time that Keith Haring and Juan were introduced to Ecstasy, as they toured Europe. In its heyday, during what would come to be known as the "Summer of Love" of 1988, tens of thousands of British youths would attend these semi-spontaneous, clandestine parties (see Reynolds). But soon moral panic would set in as the British press would begin to represent the rave scene as a threat to the nation's youth. Finally, after much media controversy, the conservative government of Margaret Thatcher would pass in 1994 a Criminal Justice and Public Order Act, criminalizing spontaneous gatherings of one hundred or more in which music with "sounds wholly or predominantly characterised by the emission of a succession of repetitive beats" (that is, house music) was played (see Collin). By then, however, Ecstasy, the American export, had spread globally and come back to California transformed as part of rave culture. And in cities such as San Francisco, Los Angeles, and New York raves would be promoted and held legally in major dance clubs, where they would become part of the intense 1990s commercial competition among club owners for patrons and the lucrative drug trade. This dark underside of utopian rave culture would be finally exposed by the media in 1996 when Michael Alig, famed club-kid promoter for the church-turned-disco, the Limelight, would be arrested for the gruesome murder and dismemberment of the in-house drug dealer, Angel Meléndez (see Owen). An aggressive national campaign to close down rave venues and the drug trade associated with them would ensue resulting in multiple anti-rave city ordinances and the federal Ecstasy Anti-Proliferation Act of 2000, which would exponentially increase sentences for distribution and possession of Ecstasy (Rosenbaum). Today, despite this campaign, Ecstasy remains not only popular among youth, but its use seems to have become more mainstream. According to the National Institute on Drug Abuse (NIDA), Ecstasy is nowadays widely available among high school and college students, both in rural and suburban as well as urban areas (www.drugabuse.gov).

Graffiti

See Basquiat, Loisaida in chapter five; and chapter three.

Keith Haring Foundation

Founded in 1989 by the artist, shortly before his death in 1990, the Keith Haring Foundation would be established, according to its official website, "to sustain and expand public awareness of Keith Haring and his artwork" and to continue Haring's work with AIDS-related and children's charities, as Juan contends (see chapter two, "Paradise"). "One organization that was specifically named in Keith's will," the website notes, "was Children's Village, a residential treatment center and community service organization meeting the needs of homeless and runaway children, disadvantaged children, youth and families" (www.haring.com).

Page Six

Notorious, no-holds-barred, daily gossip column in the *New York Post*, this powerful column about the private lives of the nation's "movers and shakers" has been known, as *Arena* magazine observes, to "launch a bestseller, break a contract, fill a restaurant—even end a marriage" (Phillips). Begun by British newspaper mogul Rupert Murdoch after acquiring the *Post* in 1976, *Page Six* was originally conceived by its former editors, James Brady and Neal Travis, and has been edited since 1985 by Richard Johnson. As Juan Rivera relates (see chapter two, "Paradise"), an article on his request to the Keith Haring Foundation for money to visit a homeopathic doctor and buy vitamins and food would appear on October 30, 1992, characteristically titled "AIDS Fund Stiffs Founder's Pal," penned by Frank DiGiacomo and Joanna Molloy, with Florence Anthony. Contacted by the press, Julia Gruen, executive director of the Foundation, would explain, "Juan didn't say specifically that he wanted money to go to the doctor. He said he needed food. I said we'll arrange to have that done. He said he had other problems. I said we'd arrange for counseling. Then he said he needed cash. This we don't do" (6). And she would add, "The will [of Keith Haring] says we must give money to organizations, not individuals. He's somebody we've all known for years. But we have discussed the situation here and we have made a determination about what he would do with the money. We just do not hand money out to people. Even Keith's lovers" (6).

Outlaw Parties

See Loisaida, East Village in chapter five.

Spooking

From the verb to spook, meaning to frighten, startle, or unnerve someone the way a spook, a specter, or ghost would, spooking, as used by Juan throughout his interview, would appear to be the act of frightening, startling, unnerving, outwitting, or simply looking intensely at someone in order to uncover or reveal his or her dissimulated, hidden, closeted desire or identity. "I spook the guys and the girls in my neighborhood, and I have this method when I walk toward a pretty boy," he would explain. "I always pretend I'm looking straight, but meanwhile I'm trying to check whether he is gonna spook me first. 'Cause if you spook him first, he'll say 'oh you faggot!' But if you let'em spook you first ('cause I don't know what it is they see when they pass me but they always end up spooking me), then you can catch'em later spooking you. *Y ellos te viran la cara* [and they turn their face away], like saying you caught me" (21). An act of unveiling or revealing someone's dissimulated, ghostly, or spectral desire or identity, someone's desire or identity, that is, as a spook, as someone haunted or possessed by another, socially unacceptable or stigmatized desire or identity (consider here that "spook" in U.S. slang refers also to an undercover agent or spy and, pejoratively, to African Americans), spooking would seem to require that the person who does the spooking also expose himself or herself. Because it risks vulnerability and self-exposure in the act of uncovering or "catching" someone else, spooking is also a game of power and wit in which performance plays a large role and whose stakes are only raised by the ever-present possibility of violence.

Tímido (Jíbaro)

Spanish for timid or shy, *tímido* would appear to signal in Juan's interview an affect that he associates both with Puerto-Ricanness, as his linguistic code-switching from English to Spanish suggests (see chapter six), and gayness. It would seem further associated in his interview with the gender-coded domestic sphere to which the feminine and the effeminate male or *pato* are restricted (see chapter five, "Dominant/ Passive; Macho/*Pato* (*Maricón*); Hustler/*Pargo*; Top/Bottom"), as his childhood recollections confirm (". . . I sat at home like . . . *la nena de la casa* [the little girl of the house], . . . and as they grabbed me, I felt *tímida como una nena* [timid like a girl]" [16]). And it would appear in all of these cases to be an affect that must be overcome in order to express oneself as a person or an individual who is a member of a stigmatized group. "I really wanted to get up and kick this guy's ass! But I was too timid . . . I was a little faggot," Juan will explain as he tells the story of the family friend who sexually assaulted his sister and him, blaming his victimization or inability to strike back on his being "timid" or "a little faggot" (15). And later, as he recounts his growing assertiveness in his relationship with his abusive partner C . . . , he will state, "I was such a little *tímido* kid from New Haven when I first met C . . . that, whether I'd kick him back or not, he pulled something out of me that made me feel stronger . . . And I stopped being that little Puerto Rican *tímido* kid from Connecticut and started kicking back" (19–20). Yet timidity is not only an affect to be overcome in Juan's interview, it is also a very visible condition on the basis of which he will recognize (and even desire) others with whom he feels he shares, as he does with the interviewer, a stigmatized identity. "When I knew you back then I always thought 'cause of your voice and 'cause you were timid that you were gay," he will tell Cruz-Malavé, to his surprise ("Because I was timid?") (11). And he will further amplify this connection between timidity and gayness by identifying Cruz-Malavé's timidity with his Puerto-Ricanness: "And 'cause of the way you spoke—very soft, Puerto Rican . . . ," adding slyly, "And I've always been attracted to guys that are shy" (12). Timidity in Juan's interview would seem to function then, as Eve Kosofsky Sedgwick in her analysis of the work of queer artists Andy Warhol and Henry James has proposed, as a symptom or indicator of a sort of queer shame that is not only paralyzing (and as such something to be transcended or overcome) but also productive, generative, a source of personal and communal formation and renewal, as she states (Sedgwick 1993, 1995, 1996; see also chapter four). If at least superficially the connection between shyness and queerness would seem to be so culturally coded and sanctioned that it appears natural or commonplace ("Remember the 50s?," Lily Tomlin once joked. "Nobody was gay in the 50s; they were just shy" [qtd. in Sedgwick 1996 137]), the association between Puerto-Ricanness and timidity will however seem counterintuitive to most North Americans, especially given most media representations of Puerto Ricans in the United States as brazen or simply loud. Yet there is a long-standing association of Puerto-Ricanness with timidity in Puerto Rican culture through the mediating term *jíbaro*, the Puerto Rican Spanish word used to refer to the Island's inland peasants and their culture. And it is this connection that undergirds Juan's code-switched usage of *tímido*, as is confirmed in his description of Haring's New York Puerto Rican collaborator (see chapter five, "LA II"), LA II, as "*tímido*, you know, *un jibarito*" [timid, you know, a little *jíbaro*]: "He was a pretty young boy but kinda *tímido*, you know, *un jibarito*, when Keith first met him" (44). First used during the eighteenth century to designate the Island's mixed-race, inland, "squatter" peasant population, as the anthropologist Sydney Mintz has called it (148–49), *jíbaro* was a pejorative, racially charged term deployed by the urban elites who lived in the Spanish colonial port city and military garrison of San Juan to refer to those who lived outside its walls a "seminomadic," itinerant existence and who were thus considered barbaric, wild, beyond the pale of the city's civilized order, unrepresentable (Scarano 1414–15). And yet, as studied by Francisco A. Scarano in his groundbreaking essay, "The *Jíbaro* Masquerade and the Subaltern Politics of Creole Identity Formation in Puerto Rico 1745–1823," the rapidly changing economic conditions of Puerto Rico at the turn of the nineteenth century, precipitated by the independence of Haiti and the demise of its plantation economy, would encourage the local Creole elite to adopt the "mask" of the *jíbaro* and its culture in order to claim local authority vis-à-vis the Spanish Crown and recently immigrated landowners who were intent on promoting an export-oriented plantation economy (1428–31). It would not be the last time that the unpresentable *jíbaro* would be used to represent local or national interests. The figure of the *jíbaro* as a trope for the Puerto Rican people would be famously put to use by the Puerto Rican *Partido Popular Democrático* (Popular Democratic Party) of Luis Muñoz Marín in the 1940s and 1950s, whose policies of industrialization and modernization would ironically lead to the mass migration of Puerto Ricans, especially from *jíbaro* backgrounds, to the United States (see chapter five, "El Barrio/East Harlem"). And it would be successively rehabilitated by pro-independence activists throughout the 1960s and 1970s as part of their call for Puerto Ricans to take control of their land and resources both on the Island and the United States. Still the mark of unrepresentability, of wiliness and wildness originally associated with the figure of the *jíbaro*, what Puerto Ricans tellingly call the *jíbaro*'s *mancha de plátano*, or the plantain's (indelible) stain, would never disappear completely from Puerto Rican culture, and "timidity," both as a symptom of stigma and shame and as a strategic resistance to appear, to be represented in and by official discourse as well, would continue to play an important role in Puerto Rican popular culture production, as it certainly does in Juan's interview.

Wasting

Associated with the progression of disease in patients living with AIDS and the imminence of death, AIDS-related "wasting syndrome," as is it has been called, is defined as the involuntary loss of more than ten percent of body weight accompanied by persistent, chronic diarrhea, weakness, and fever for a period of more than thirty days (see *The Body: The Complete HIV/AIDS Resource*, www.thebody.com). Recognized as an AIDS-defining condition by the U.S. Center for Disease Control and Prevention (CDC) since 1987, wasting, which is characterized by a loss not only of fat but, more importantly, muscle mass, and gives patients suffering from this condition a gaunt look that is described in Juan's interview (see chapter two, "Paradise"), continues to be a problem for people living with HIV/AIDS. Along with Kaposi's sarcoma lesions, wasting, which for a period in the 1980s became the very public face of AIDS, is perhaps the most visibly shocking indicator of AIDS. Its causes are low food intake as a result of diminished appetite, lack of energy and/or funds to prepare food, poor nutrient absorption by the body, and an increased metabolic rate (see *HIV in Site*: hivinsite.ucsf.edu). As poignantly expressed by Juan at the end of his interview, both poverty and severe anxiety about one's condition as HIV-positive and poor can physiologically contribute to or trigger the onset of wasting syndrome.

Xtravaganza, House of

One of the original or "legendary" drag ball houses of New York City, the House of Xtravaganza would be founded in the early 1980s by a young Puerto Rican gay runaway, Hector, who would adopt the performance name Xtravaganza as his new family name. By then drag balls had had a long history in New York City, a history that dated back to the great masquerade balls of the 1920s and 1930s when queer men and women cross-dressed and danced, oftentimes in lavishly bejeweled and feathered costumes in the Lower East Side, the Village, and Harlem. As the number of cross-dressed dancers grew at these balls some time in the 1920s, so did the spectators who would go there simply to watch or gawk at what the poet Langston Hughes called their fabulous "spectacles in color" (Garber). By the 1930s the annual masquerade ball at Harlem's Hamilton Lodge, sponsored by the Grand Union Order of Odd Fellows and informally known in the neighborhood as "the Faggot's Ball," had become the city's most popular and largest of such gatherings, with attendance hovering at around 7,000 between spectators and dancers (Chauncey 1994 258). It was then a magnificent and highly anticipated event covered by the local media and attended by local black working-class lesbians and gay men as well as white lesbians and gay men from other parts of the city, the white avant-garde, and the artistic, professional, and financial cream of Harlem society. And it was a tellingly rich indication of what the historian Eric Garber has described as the complex, multiclass, multiracial lesbian and gay social world of African American Harlem in the Jazz Age. The contemporary African American and Latino queer ballroom scene, such as it has been presented in the documentary films *Paris Is Burning* (1991) by Jenny Livingston, and *How Do I Look* (2004) by Wolfgang Busch, and the faux-documentary or docudrama *One Moment in Time* (1992) by Félix Rodríguez, is heir to these Jazz Age Harlem masquerade balls, which continued to be held, albeit in a lower key and sponsored now by the participating drag queens themselves, in places like the Harlem's Elks Lodge on 139th St. throughout the 1950s and 1960s (Cunningham). However the contemporary organization of the ballroom scene, structured as it is around "houses," associations, or "gangs," as their members have described them, that compete at balls for increasingly proliferating categories, seems to have emerged, as the ballroom historian Marcel Christian has proposed in the recent documentary, *How Do I Look*, out of the intense competition between Puerto Rican/Latino and black drag queens at these balls in the late 1960s. Their intense gang-like "battles," he suggests, would translate into what would come to be known in the 1970s, following the model of the then popularly available designer culture, as "houses." This development, one could say, might be seen as part of a long and creative cultural interaction (and competition) between Puerto Ricans/ Latinos and blacks in mixed and contiguous neighborhoods such as Harlem, El Barrio, and the South Bronx, and in hang-outs such as the

Christopher Street piers, which had manifested itself in El Barrio, for instance, in the black and Latino lesbian and gay dance parties held in abandoned lofts along Second and Third avenues, between 116th and 125th streets, throughout the 1960s (Lawrence 45–46). By the early 1970s the first ball houses had begun to form around the leading figures of some of the balls' most famous "walkers," veteran winners of many drag competitions, such as Dorian Corey, Pepper LaBeija, Avis Pendavis, and Paris Dupree, who could trace their beginnings in ballroom culture to the late 1950s and early 1960s and who would rule as "mothers" of the Houses of Corey, LaBeija, Pendavis, and Dupree, respectively. But as the number of gay runaway and thrown-away kids began to flood the streets by the late 1970s and early 1980s, the houses would become more than fashion houses; they would turn into alternative kinship structures with a "father," a "mother," and a band of oftentimes unruly "children," places where a whole generation of abandoned kids would find protection, status, and love. And the ballroom scene, which had been informed till then by images from Hollywood and Broadway and Vegas shows, as Dorian Corey in *Paris Is Burning* has so eloquently recalled, would concomitantly evolve to absorb these kids' culture, with its popular media referents, its allusions to the world of media celebrities, TV stars, designers, and supermodels, and its street-inflected arts. This new generation of kids would introduce into the balls' competitive runway walk new survival arts that had been worked out and honed in correctional facilities, parks, dance clubs, and streets against those who would have had them diminished or erased: the shady art of insult or "reading," the stylishly martial art of "voguing," and the apparently-simple-yet-dangerously-daring art of walking down the street cross-dressed without being detected or "spooked," without being bloodied. If the older generation had shown how to create fabulously fanciful selves out of the unimaginative and trite gender binary male–female, this new generation of "children," as they called themselves, would find the extraordinary and exceptional in the chameleon-like art of dissimulation, in the grandness of the small gesture of surviving in the streets one more day through one's elusive, Ninja-like wit. And in thus dissimulating the other, in thus imitating it in the most faithful or "real" way, they would find not only survival but a sort of compensation or pay back: they would end up not only absorbing the "original" but making it look in comparison poor and stale, as Jenny Livingston's parallel montage in *Paris Is Burning* has so astutely captured. True, this art of dissimulation or "realness," as it would be called, was in the end more "ambivalent" toward hegemonic or dominant gender and racial norms than "subversive" of them, as the queer theorist Judith Butler in her response to African American cultural critic bell hooks would argue (Butler 1993 125). But it was a tactical art, an art on the run, as befitted the always provisional, precarious life of its subjects, which demanded recognition and respect: "We [black people] have had everything taken away from us," one of the ball children in *Paris Is Burning* would combatively affirm, "and yet we have all learned how to survive." Perhaps no house would be more emblematic of this generational shift in ballroom culture from the showy parade of fabulous bodies to the in-your-face runway walk of the street arts of survival and realness than the House of Xtravaganza. Founded by the young Puerto Rican runaway, Hector Xtravaganza, and headed by a sixteen-year-old "mother," Anji Xtravaganza, a New York Puerto Rican native of the South Bronx who had been on the streets since age fourteen (Cunningham), the House of Xtravaganza would achieve international fame through voguing and realness. And Anji Xtravaganza, its first mother, would be especially exemplary of this shift. Not a classically feminine, or femme queen, beauty, she would achieve in record time a legendary status only accorded to veteran mothers such as Dorian Corey, Pepper LaBeija, Avis Pendavis, and Paris Dupree, becoming with them one of the so-called "Terrible Five" (Cunningham), by molding her figure and attire with such unassailable taste that she would go on to win at balls repeatedly for most convincingly impersonating a model, especially her walk (Cunningham). She would also rise to stardom in the ballroom community for being a stern yet caring and protective mother to her "children," for keeping them, as one of her awards read, "intact" (*Paris Is Burning*). By 1993 when she died she had achieved a brief international fame of sorts through her notable appearance in *Paris Is Burning*. And her house, the House of Xtravaganza that she had helped found, had also come to be known around the world through the incredible corporal dexterity and wit of two of its voguing children, Jose and Louis Xtravaganza, whose performance in Madonna's video, *Vogue* (1990), and documentary film, *Truth or Dare* (1991), would help propel a voguing craze, as well as through the tragic death of one of its most extraordinarily "real" femme queens, *Venus Xtravaganza*, whose shimmering presence in *Paris Is Burning* would keep scholars of gender, sexuality, and race writing for years to come (Butler 1993; hooks; Yarbro-Bejarano). Although Juan Rivera had hung out with the original posse that had formed the House of Xtravaganza in the early 1980s, he had grown distant from them during the years he was partner of Keith Haring, who had formed his own house. But on returning to El Barrio in the

1990s he would once again renew his bond with them. And at the "grand march," when hosting houses introduce their members at the balls, he would hear himself being formally acknowledged as one of their own (see chapter two, " 'I'm Juanito Xtravaganza': An Epilogue").

Today the House of Xtravaganza continues to host balls and perform, with voguer extraordinaire, Jose Xtravaganza, as its father, and femme queen "face" par excellence, the model Giselle Xtravaganza, as mother, at the helm. (To view their stunning performances, see Wolfgang Busch's film *How Do I Look.*)

CHAPTER 6

Spanglish Glosses

The following would aspire to be not a glossary of Spanish-English definitions but a list of glosses, returning thus that overly precise and reassuring term with which so many ethnographic books end, "Glossary," to its properly humble meaning: a commentary, an approximation. For Spanglish is not a language, and there are no monolingual native speakers of Spanglish, to my knowledge (and as a New York Puerto Rican, or a Nuyorican, I suppose, I should know, for both Puerto Ricans and Chicanos share the burden, and the advantage as well, of being identified as the primary practitioners, if not the inventors, of this often derided linguistic form). Instead, Spanglish is, as the linguist Ana Celia Zentella has proposed, a practice of switching from one language code or system to another at grammatically permissible boundaries in a sentence and within a single speaking turn in order to underscore or highlight specific rhetorical effects, such as a change in a speaker's role—from speaker to quoter of someone else's speech, or from narrator to evaluator of his/her own speech—or to control his/her interlocutor's behavior by stressing a demand, requesting a clarification, or appealing to a shared value or goal (80–114).

Usually considered simply filler or a "crutch" for a speaker who is at a loss for words in one language, and who is therefore thought to have a deficient knowledge of that language, Spanglish code alternation is in fact most often a redundant and excessive practice, rather than the result of language lack or loss. As Zentella has proven in her extensive analysis of code-switching among New York Puerto Rican children in El Barrio/East Harlem in her sensitive and meticulously researched study, *Growing Up Bilingual: Puerto Rican Children in New York*, up to ninety percent of what the children code-switched they knew how to express in either language and still they chose to code-switch (109), a fact that has led some linguists and cultural critics to judge their practice as unnecessary and chaotic, as a meaningless "mongrelizing" flourish, in short a vice.

But even when code-switching is triggered by a sense of loss, that loss is not often the loss of simple denotative meaning, or reference. It is instead the recognition of the inadequacy of any one language to translate the wealth of associations that determine the specifically contextual meaning of a word or expression in another language, what linguists since Ferdinand de Saussure first established their discipline have called "value" (114–19), and what much of U.S. Latino literature persistently signals by calling attention to what the Cuban American writer Gustavo Pérez-Firmat has termed its mournful (and yet joyful) "bilingual blues."

Whether Spanglish code-switching is the result of the recognition of loss or a willfully redundant practice, both its excess and lack with respect to referential monolingual meaning induce its interlocutor, most often another bilingual who is also adept at switching codes, to reach for a meaning or meanings that are beyond simple denotation, to interpret redundancy as a performative or rhetorical act, to establish sets of association or genealogies that are extraneous to the first or target language—associations that are sometimes contradictory, sometimes comical.

Like all literary language, Spanglish calls for interpretations, glosses, approximations. It forces us to contemplate the incongruity between linguistic sign and its referent, as Doris Sommer has most recently stressed (2004 xviii–xix). But it does not make us linger there in self-absorbed melancholy (in fact, Puerto Rican children's smooth, quick-as-lightning alternation between codes has often been remarked as well as held against them as a sign of the meaninglessness of their craft; Zentella 92), as befits a fundamentally nontragic, comic, or pragmatic view of the world. Instead, it invites us to reinterpret loss, as well as excess, as a productive occasion to play what Sommer, following the multilingual Austrian philosopher Ludwig Wittgenstein, has called "language games" (157 and ff.), that is, to create new value by importing associations from one language to another, by contaminating one system with the other. As the Puerto Rican writer Luis Rafael Sánchez has remarked (1994 22), Spanglish and the language arts it represents are a way of trafficking or smuggling between linguistic and cultural ports, often with hilarious (as well as political) consequences. In what follows I have thus no ethnic secrets to reveal, no absolute or fixed cultural terms to report, just a possible and tentative trajectory of smuggling between codes to gloss.

Fly, Robin, Fly

12 "He was *hot*. I mean, I never thought I'd get into *un chino* but . . . Yeah, I remember . . . This guy *was* cute": Switch to the Spanish vocative *chino* (a Chinese man and, by extension, an Asian or "Oriental"), perhaps to indicate a racial and cultural difference and distance, even a stereotypical foreignness, as well as to stress a break in expectations, as the passage suggests, which is reinforced by the adversarial conjunction "but."

13 "JR: My first sexual turn on was in my grandma's house. I remember sleeping and when I woke up my cousin was feeling me up. AC-M: *¿Tu primo?* JR: *Prima*. A real pretty girl": Switch to the Spanish gendered noun forms for cousin, *primo* (male cousin) and *prima* (female cousin), to request and receive clarification.

14 "'Cause if you spook him first, he'll say, 'oh you faggot!' But if you let'em spook you first ('cause I don't know what it is they see when they pass me but they always end up spooking me), then you can catch'em later spooking you. *Y ellos te viran la cara*, like saying you caught me": Switch to the Spanish independent clause *Y ellos te viran la cara* (And they turn their face away) perhaps to capture and linguistically perform what the very topic of the passage describes: the intense game of power and wit of dissimulation and unveiling, avoidance and exposure, "catching" and "turning away," which is the act of "spooking," or disclosing (or "blowing") someone's (heterosexual) cover in the middle of the street. For a more detailed description of spooking, see chapter five, "Spooking."

15 "He was married to this fat woman, a *santera*, and he was a born-again Christian, an *aleluya* kind of guy. I really wanted to get up and kick this guy's ass!": Change to the Spanish apposition *santera* (a *Santería* priestess) to further specify this subject and to sketch her character. Shift to the Spanish noun *aleluya* (Hallelujah!), used here as a descriptive adjective to refer metonymically and dismissively to a member of the Pentecostal faith. The metonymy *aleluya*, the praise of god often associated with this faith, ironically contrasts here with this second subject's less-than-holy deeds, as Juan describes them.

15 "Yeah, I knew I was gonna be gay, but I couldn't figure it out. And every time *que pasaba un pato por casa tú veías a todos estos hombres pitándole y gritando*, '*Mira a ése le gusta coger por el culo*,' and I'd go, 'Oh, noooo!!, that's not gonna be me. Please, God! . . .' Ha! Ha! Ha!": Switch to an almost full Spanish sentence (a *pato* [faggot, literally a "duck"] passed by the house you could see all of these men whistling and yelling, "Look at that one, he likes to get it up the ass"), perhaps to distinguish between the recollection of an event and its evaluation ("Yeah, I knew I was gonna be gay, but I couldn't figure it out . . . and I'd go, 'Oh, nooo!!, that's not going to be me . . . '"), following a pattern identified by Zentella in her analysis of Spanglish code switching as a "narrative frame break" (Zentella 94) and by Lourdes Torres as an "evaluation device" (Torres 83–8).

15   "And I guess he *knew* I was gonna be *un mariconcito*, 'cause I was in the fifth grade and he was in sixth, and I don't know exactly what we said, but by the time we finished our conversation, we were going to the bathroom and I knew I was gonna get fucked": Shift to the Spanish noun *un mariconcito* (a little faggot), perhaps both to mark the pejorative sense of the term *maricón* (faggot) and to mitigate it through the endearing diminutive suffix *ito*. For a more detailed commentary on categories and terms related to *maricón*, see chapter five, "Dominant/Passive; Macho/*Pato* (*Maricón*); Hustler/*Pargo*; Top/Bottom."

16   "My father had bought my brother a bike he used to ride around in, and I sat at home like . . . *la nena de la casa*, and played with Barbie dolls and did macramé": Switch to the Spanish noun phrase *la nena de la casa* (the little girl of the house), possibly to contrast with Juan's description of his brother as occupying in the family the opposite gender category: *el machito de la casa* (the little man of the house).

16   "I had always sensed my brother's friends thought I was gonna be gay 'cause they would give me these real long adoring looks, and as they grabbed me, I felt *tímida como una nena*, but pretty soon I got up my nerve, and I was grabbing their balls and they were grabbing mine": Switch to the Spanish adjective phrase *tímida como una nena* (shy like a little girl) perhaps to more effectively mark or stress the transformation or change in the subject's shyness that the passage describes ("but pretty soon I got up my nerve . . .") and to underscore this affect's association with the Puerto Rican feminine and domestic spheres. For a more detailed commentary on this affect, see chapter five, "Tímido (*Jíbaro*)."

16   "And finally I moved my hand slowly, and before I knew it my hand was on top of his crotch, *y estaba dura, dura como una maceta*": Change to the Spanish independent clause *y estaba dura, dura como una maceta* (and it was hard, hard like a mallet), possibly to mark or stress the end or result of an action, what Zentella has called a "narrative frame break" (Zentella 94).

16 "And he lay on the floor, *y me le senté ahí*—no lubrication or nothing, it was a very natural thing": Shift to the Spanish independent clause *y me le senté ahí* (and I sat right on it), perhaps to mark and stress what is the climactic point in the narration of this event.

17 "No, the turn on was being aware I was getting clocked by someone I liked—this cute Puerto Rican *cano*": Change to the Puerto Rican Spanish noun *cano* (light-hair, light-skinned boy) to specify a Puerto Rican vernacular racial category.

17 "And whenever I'd run into his older brother, T . . . , in school he'd start walking down the hall *partiéndose* and doing this fag talk and grabbing his crotch like saying, 'Now you can take care of me'": Shift to the Puerto Rican Spanish verb form *partiéndose* (swishing, from the verb *partir*, meaning literally to break or to crack), perhaps to indicate thus the actual break in male body comportment and presentation that the verb suggests.

17 "And I'd say to myself: 'You fucken *bellaquito*, I ain't taking care of your ass, 'cause I don't wanna! And 'cause you ain't got no dick!'": Shift to the Puerto Rican Spanish adjective *bellaquito* (little horny bastard, from the adjective *bellaco*, meaning also sly, unruly, wild), perhaps to literally diminish, with the use of the diminutive *ito*, the other subject's boastful pretensions as macho or male, as the subsequent sentence seems to suggest ("And 'cause you ain't got no dick!").

17 "Their other brother, T . . . , and their cousin were also in the car. And I know it was probably T . . . , who was the most *bocón*, who psyched them into *picking up Juan, taking him up to the Rock, and feeding him dick*. But I said fuck it!": Shift to the Spanish adjective *bocón* (loud mouth), probably to alert the listener that the subsequent phrases (*picking up Juan, taking him up to the Rock, and feeding him dick*) are from the mouth (the loud mouth) of T . . . and that they need, as such, to be treated as quotes, as the change in subject from the first to the third person in this passage suggests. Ironically, though the passage concerns the *pato*'s oral abilities, it is the macho's mouth that the passage underscores. For a more detailed commentary on categories such as *pato* and macho, see chapter five, "Dominant/ Passive; Macho/*Pato* (*Maricón*); Hustler/*Pargo*; Top/Bottom."

18 "He was the baby *y el machito de la casa*, and my father would always spoil him": Shift to the Spanish object noun phrase *y el machito de la casa* (and the little man of the house), most likely to indicate that this phrase is being quoted, that it is a recurrent (explicit or implicit) family phrase which structures gender relations at home. For a more detailed commentary on macho, see chapter five, "Dominant/Passive; Macho/*Pato* (*Maricón*); Hustler/*Pargo*; Top/Bottom."

18 "But every time me and my brother would get into a fight my father would end up beating me, 'cause *yo era el mayor*": Shift to the Spanish dependent clause *yo era el mayor* (I was the oldest) to indicate once again that the speaker is quoting an often-used phrase that structures his relationship with other family members at home, a pattern in Spanish-English code-switching, which Zentella and Torres, among others, have noted (Torres 85; Zentella 94).

18 "Until then my image of gay people were these loud *locas* like M . . . , F . . . , and J . . . They'd walk down the street swishing and shaking their bangles, and if they spooked a boy, and the boy got loud with them, they'd read him and threaten to punch him out. Eventually, they all died—were killed": Shift to the Spanish noun *locas* (queens), most likely to focus on the specific behavior, body language, and transgressive use of space of the local *locas* or queens of Juan's childhood, as the rest of the passage confirms. For a more detailed commentary on this category *loca*, see chapter five, "Dominant/Passive; Macho/*Pato* (*Maricón*); Hustler/*Pargo*; Top/Bottom."

18 "And then I found *The Neuter Rooster*, my first gay nightclub. It had this huge statue of *un pájaro* about to take off, and as you walked in you could hear the club's theme, '*Fly, robin, fly* . . . ,' and you'd see your face reflected in all of these mirrors and all these pretty boys' faces, and I felt . . . like flying, reborn, and I flew, and flew . . . far away": Shift to the Spanish noun *pájaro* (literally a bird and figuratively associated with the term *pato*, queer or faggot), most probably to exploit the ambivalence of the term *pájaro* in order to suggest not only the idea of flying away and rebirth, as the lyrics of the disco song from the Silver Convention, *Fly, Robin, Fly* confirm, but also the recycling and transformation of the degraded category *pato* through new gay forms of relating based on mutuality and sameness, which the disco experience fostered. For a more detailed commentary on *pato*, see chapter five, "Dominant/Passive; Macho/*Pato* (*Maricón*); Hustler/*Pargo*; Top/Bottom." For more on this then emerging "gay" model of sexual practice and identity based on mutuality and sameness, see chapter three, "Clones Go Home!"

19 "And though G . . . was only in his twenties, he looked much older, and was always all dressed up like . . . well . . . like an executive. He had this poised manner about him, *bien parao, pero buena gente*. And

I remember meeting him for the first time and became immediately infatuated": Switch to the Puerto Rican Spanish adjectival expressions *bien parao* and *buena gente* to produce *bien parao, pero buena gente* (uppity but nice), perhaps to exploit the alliteration of p's and b's and their chiasmic structure (*b . . . p, p . . . b*) in order to suggest a sense of "poise" and balance in G . . . 's character, which the text will later undermine and expose to humorous effect.

19 "JR: You see, I later found out that G . . . 's family knew he was gonna be a faggot, 'cause he was *real* tight with this kid who was a faggot—his cousin. AC-M: *Los primos se exprimen . . .*": Shift to the Puerto Rican Spanish saying *Los primos se exprimen* (literally, cousins squeeze each other), which capitalizes on the alliteration *prim . . . prim* to humorously suggest intimacy between cousins.

19 "So his family fixed his marriage to his wife, R . . . , through *brujería,* and I don't know how they did it but by the time the wedding came, his cousin had disappeared . . . like from the face of the earth! Nobody knew where he was. Nobody had heard from him": Switch to the Spanish noun *brujería* (witchcraft, sorcery), perhaps to stress the secretive, coded nature of the way the family arranged G . . . 's marriage, according to Juan.

19 "He unbuttoned his collar, and as we talked I started to notice he had all of these mannerisms, and by the end of the conversation there were *plumas* flying all over the place": Switch to the Spanish noun *plumas* (feathers), most likely as a humorous allusion to *pato* (faggot, literally "duck") and to the idiomatic expression *salírsele las plumas a alguien* (meaning literally for one's feathers to come out, and figuratively to inadvertently reveal or disclose one's [effeminate] gay identity).

19 "And as I painted the house I'd see the shadow of R . . . 's *bata* come in and out of the room with my tray of food, and I could sense that she knew me and her husband were having a fling": Shift to the Spanish noun *bata* (robe), perhaps to allude thus to the R . . . 's control of the domestic, in-this-case-Spanish-speaking sphere.

19 "And then during one of the séances that G . . . 's friend, a medium, was having, he told G . . . that his parents *le habían echao un 'brujo a su casa* to make sure that it wouldn't be sold. 'Cause once sold G . . . would be free to go his way and so would his wife, R . . .": Switch to the Spanish verbal phrase *le habían echao un 'brujo a su casa* (had put a hex on his house), perhaps to signal not only Juan's shift to another's speech, the medium's, which he is quoting, but also to indicate the medium's own reporting or quoting some other voice, that of the spirit or spirits for whom he is a conduit.

20 "And when my parents came in they started yelling at me: '*Tú eres el mayor!* You should know better . . . You should . . . !'": Shift to the Spanish sentence *Tú eres el mayor!* (You're the oldest!), to indicate, as we have already seen, that the speaker is quoting an often-used phrase that structures his relationship with other family members at home, a use of Spanish-English code-switching, which has been noted by Zentella (94) and Torres (85).

20 "I don't know, 'cause I didn't know *nothing* about New York. I guess I was drawn to the City by some unnatural power. I had no *maletas*, all I had was ten dollars": Switch to the Spanish noun *maletas* (suitcases), perhaps to indicate thus the Spanish-speaking familial or domestic sphere, which the subject is here losing.

20 "By then, I mean, I was already a bum, *ya era una bona*. I had come down to the City in dress pants, but by then they were torn and stiff with dirt and caca—I mean, they could've walked home by themselves": Switch to the Spanish independent clause *ya era una bona*, as a translation and repetition (with a difference) of the English "I was already a bum," perhaps to convey and stress through repetition (with a difference) both the idea of transformation and ending of a process that the adverb "already" (*ya*) confirms. The idea of transformation into a new state is further conveyed through Juan's humorous Hispanization and feminization of the English term "bum": *bona*.

Just Telling Stories . . .

21 "We'd come into the City to see *The Wiz*, our graduation present to ourselves, and we'd gone to eat in a Chinese restaurant, and the waiter, *un chino*, came over to us and started talking real clear in Spanish, and I freaked out. It was like going through a time tunnel, or being in *Alice in Wonderland*, or in *The Wiz*—the *chino* didn't speak *chino* but a totally unexpected language": Switch to the Spanish noun *chino* (both Chinese man and Chinese language) to underscore perhaps the strangeness and wonder of Juan's first view of the city, where language and identity often do not match, where language, as often happens in Juan's own code-switching, is rather indicative of a cultural, racial, social, or linguistic contrast (or difference) than expressive of a specific national, cultural, or racial identity.

22 "And as I continued hustling I found out the more domineering you were, the more *pargos* would get off on you. So that there were plenty of *pargos* all I had to do for was a real sexy strip tease act, and by the time I'd take off my clothes they'd already come": Shift to the Spanish noun *pargo* (literally, a porgy or fish, and figuratively, as in English, the gullible, the dupe, the chump), used here to refer to the hustler's client or john, most likely as a way of speaking about the john pejoratively and in a coded, insider's language that is shared only by other Puerto Rican/Latino hustlers. This shift to a coded language that excludes the apparently monolingual john would seem confirmed by the tense racial and class dynamics of the relationship between the hustler and the *pargo* or john during the time Juan hustled in and around Times Square, the late 1970s. See chapter five, "Times Square and the Sex Trade," and "Dominant/Passive; Macho/*Pato* (*Maricón*); Hustler/*Pargo*; Top/Bottom."

22 "And I thought, "Oh, oh, here goes . . . *otro* space cadet!"": Shift to the Spanish adjective *otro* (another), possibly to signal, through the aggravation and emphasis that is often associated with code-switching (Zentella 95–96), reiteration, giving thus *otro* not merely the sense of "another" but of "yet another."

22 "We were by the fireplace, and there were *frisas* on the floor, and in the light N . . . 's body seemed to glow. And I thought, "This is all so bizarre," 'cause he didn't look like the type and this didn't look like the scene"": Shift to the Puerto Rican Spanish noun *frisas* (blankets), perhaps to highlight, through the use of this homey, familial term, the strange and uncanny atmosphere of this apparently ordinary scene ("'cause he didn't look like the type and this didn't look like the scene").

23 "No, in the bathtub, under the golden arches . . . And as the *chorro* hit his body, his dick stood at attention and he started to convulse. A real whacked out trip!"": Shift to the Spanish noun *chorro* (jet or stream of a liquid, in this case, urine), possibly to extend and play on the previous image of urine as "golden arches," with its humorous reference both to golden showers (the popular term for this erotic practice) and to MacDonald's famous trademark, its "golden arches," as well as to stress the strangeness of this scene for Juan ("A real whacked out trip!").

23 "And as I got older, I realized that most people get turned on to me as a dominant. They just seemed to take one look at me and their *patitas* went up in the air . . . looking for some place to paint . . .": Switch to the Spanish diminutive noun *patitas* (little legs), possibly to humorously underscore other people's immediate, physical reaction to Juan as "dominant" by foregrounding this body part's will as a separate, independent entity and its automatic assumption of a "passive" or receptive role, alluded to in the image of "painting [the ceiling]." For a more detailed commentary on the categories "dominant" and "passive," see chapter five, "Dominant/Passive; Macho/*Pato* (*Maricón*); Hustler/*Pargo*; Top/Bottom."

23 "Hustling butchened me up! And it made my life a whole lot easier—*yo que soy un bellaco malo*; all I had to do was play dominant and serve dick": Shift to the Puerto Rican Spanish *yo que soy un bellaco malo* (I who am a real horny bastard), possibly to underscore the quoted or reiterative nature of this humorously boastful phrase.

23 "And he was so *enchulao* with me that he invited me to his house out in the Hamptons": Shift to the colloquial Puerto Rican Spanish adjective *enchulao* (infatuated, smitten, love struck), perhaps to add greater impact to the contrast between the other's state of being *enchulao* or infatuated and its effect ("he invited me to his house . . .").

24 "Yeah, this is the story of the john who didn't really like water sports but liked *meao*." Switch to the Spanish noun *meao* (piss), possibly to contrast between "water sports," or the erotic practice of being urinated on, and the urine fetish of the subject in Juan's story, as well as to contrast and exploit the difference between the euphemistic "water sports" and the more straight-forward and vulgar Spanish *meao*.

24 "But T . . . would always be sitting in the living room watching TV, and I don't know how he managed it, but he'd always have boxing on, and I'd come in and he'd call out to me, '¡Ay, mira, Juanito, ese machito! ¡Mira esos underarms y esa peste! ¡Ay, hijo, mira, Juanito! ¡Mira esa pinga! ¡Ay, Juanito, yo quiero mamar pinga! ¡Juanito, yo quiero mamar! ¡Esa pinga!'* [Oh, Juanito, look, look at that macho boy! Look at those *underarms* and that funk! Oh, Juanito, honey, look! Look at that cock! Oh, Juanito, I wanna suck cock! Juanito, I wanna suck! That cock!] And then he'd ask me to piss in a champagne glass, and as he talked about the boxers, he'd pick up the glass and take a sip, put it back down, and continue the conversation just normal . . .": Switch to the above Spanish sentences to indicate that he is quoting and to stress perhaps the contrast between T . . . 's over-the-top language and actions and his apparently cool, "normal" or ordinary demeanor.

24 "Stories like, 'I met this girl in the street, and I took her home, and she wanted me to suck her pussy . . . ,' and he'd ask, '*Ay, sí, sí* [Oh, yes, yes], and how did you suck her pussy, *papa* [papi]?' 'And how did she suck your *pinga* [cock]?' '*Pues* . . . , *me la mamó así, y me la echó p'atrás, y me agarró las* . . . .' [Well . . . , she sucked it like this, and she pulled it back, and she grabbed my . . . .] And he'd just sit there staring at TV all glassy-eyed and sipping *meao* [piss]": Switch to the above Spanish sentences and back to English to express once more perhaps a contrast between T . . . 's over-the-top actions and language and his affecting a "normal," ordinary, even refined, manner.

24 ". . . and he'd be sipping his cocktail piss. And he'd play with my foreskin, suck on it, pull it, stretch it, and then ask, '*¿Puedes mear hasta llenarlo hasta el* rim, *papa?*' [Can you piss till you fill it to the *rim*, papi?] And I'd say, 'I'll try'": Switch to the Spanish sentence above once again to signal quoted speech and to foreground perhaps a contrast between T . . . 's over-the-top actions and his meticulously exacting behavior, which renders the scene all the more surreal and over-the-top.

25 "T . . . would place me on top of his dining room table, take out a spoon, and start eating his *pee* soup all the while crying out, '*¡Ay, qué rico está esto! ¡Qué rico está este meao!*' And I'd be like, T . . . ?!!'": Switch to the Spanish sentences "*¡Ay, qué rico está esto! ¡Qué rico está este meao!*" (Oh, how delicious this is! How delicious is this piss!), perhaps to foreground once again a contrast between the apparently ordinary form and the extravagant content of T . . . 's actions.

25 "*¡Qué mala!*"[How wicked or cunning (she is)!]: Switch to this Spanish exclamation, perhaps to feminize the subject (*mala*) and to stress thus, by changing language and gender, the performative, imaginative, cunning, rather than authentic or natural, character of his actions.

25 "That's what *las drogas* will do to you": Shift to the Spanish noun *las drogas* (drugs, and by extension, drug culture), perhaps to distance himself from this scene and to render it strange or, as he says, "whacked out."

25 "*¡Qué bicha!*" [What a cunning "bitch"!]: A Puerto Rican Spanish expression that conflates the Cuban Spanish adjective and noun *bicha* (meaning cunning, sly, astute) and the American-English reclaimed noun "bitch" used to refer to the flamboyantly self-assertive, imaginative, over-the-top, and ruthlessly shrewd female characters that began to self-consciously and assertively appear in internationally distributed U.S. soap operas such as *Dynasty* in the 1980s.

25 "¡A *mamabicho bicha!*" [A *bicho*sucking *bicha*]: A Spanish-English bilingual pun that plays on the Puerto Rican Spanish noun *bicho* (dick, cock) and the creative bilingual Spanglish neologism *bicha*, which is described above.

26 "And, yeah, the last time I saw him he actually shit on the bed. It was one of those times you're fucking a john, and he accidentally on purpose . . . *te caga*": Switch to the Spanish verb phrase *te caga* (shits on you), perhaps to underscore the punch line or surprise ending of an action, a use noted by Zentella in her analysis of Spanish-English code-switching (Zentella 94–95).

One of These Days!

27–28 "Central Park was lined up with fags back then—from The Museum of National History to Strawberry Fields! Tons of them. Like garlands. You didn't even have to go inside the park—by the wall, or on the other side of it, by the ditch, there'd be all these *patitos* streeetching their wings . . .": Switch to the diminutive form of the Puerto Rican Spanish noun *patitos* (fags, literally, little ducks), perhaps to transform the pejorative charge of this term through the use of the diminutive *ito* and to play on the literal image of a duck. For a more detailed commentary on categories such as *pato* and macho, see chapter five, "Dominant/Passive; Macho/*Pato* (*Maricón*); Hustler/*Pargo*; Top/Bottom."

28 "And when I looked at him, his eyes sparkled, and he seemed so *enchulao* that I got off": Shift to the colloquial Puerto Rican Spanish adjective *enchulao* (infatuated, smitten, love struck), perhaps to add greater impact to the contrast between the other's state of being *enchulao* or infatuated and the effect this state had on the speaking subject, Juan ("I got off").

29 "So we'd always end up fighting and breaking up, and when I break up, you know, *yo siempre me curo* . . . with someone else, and then he'd come back in the picture all *fresco*, as if nothing had happened, as if we'd never broken up to find me with a new piece, and that would set off the war, become the bone of contention for the next six months": Switch to the Spanish independent clause *yo siempre me curo* (literally, I always heal myself and figuratively, both I recover emotionally and I protect myself), perhaps to emphasize both these meanings, to heal and to protect oneself, and to put emotional distance from the event described. Switch to the Spanish adjective *fresco* (cool, calm, unruffled), possibly to underscore C . . . 's behavior as mere posturing or posing, as a kind of provocation.

29 "And before I could turn around, 'cause he was *so* demented, *me dio una galleta que caí al piso*": Switch to the Spanish independent clause *me dio una galleta que caí al piso* (he slapped me and knocked me down to the floor), perhaps to highlight, through the linguistic break, the "demented" unexpectedness of C . . . 's action.

29 "The past is past! And I stopped being that little Puerto Rican *tímido* kid from Connecticut and started kicking back": Shift to the Spanish *tímido* (timid, shy), most likely to reference Juan's small-town gay Puerto Rican childhood and to signal thus his attempt to overcome a paralyzing affect that he associates both with the stigma of growing up Puerto Rican and gay. For a more detailed commentary on the association between both Puerto-Ricanness and gayness and shyness, see chapter five, "*Tímido (Jíbaro)*." See also chapter four.

30 "And I was such a little *tímido* kid from New Haven when I first met C . . . that, whether I'd kick him back or not, he pulled something out of me that made me feel stronger": Switch to the Spanish adjective *tímido* (shy) to reference once again Juan's small-town Puerto Rican gay childhood. See previous gloss.

30 "And all along he'd be there *cucándome* and saying, 'Why don't you . . . ? Why don't you *hit* me?! *Hit* me!!' But I couldn't, I couldn't . . .": Change to the Spanish verb form *cucándome* (taunting me), perhaps to foreground this action as wildly or uncontrollably independent, self-propelled.

31 "And I was getting dressed, getting ready to leave for my meeting when he said, 'I'd hate to see what happened to your car!' And I was like, *Qué* fucken trip!!": Switch to the Spanish relative pronoun *qué* (what), perhaps to stress even more, or aggravate, the astonishment or outrage already implicit in this exclamation.

31 "Till I finally grabbed him, looked him straight in his *demonic* eyes and said, '*¿Qué te pasa? ¿Tú quieres que te dé?! ¿Es eso?! ¿Tú quieres que te dé?*' [What's the matter with you? You want me to hit you?! Is that it?! You want me to hit you?] And I busted his face": Switch to the above Spanish sentences, probably to underscore or aggravate what are after all, more than real questions, rhetorical questions or affirmations. In addition, notice how these questions are addressed to

C . . . , a monolingual English speaker, confirming thus that they fulfill, more than the speaker's need for veracity or faithful reporting, his rhetorical needs.

32 "Once his mother made me a cake, and we were eating and celebrating *cuando* C . . . *se puso imprudente* . . .": Switch to the Spanish adverbial phrase *cuando* C . . . *se puso imprudente* [when C . . . got disrespectful, rude], probably to quote the language through which Puerto Rican parents request respect from their children (as in the imperative sentence "¡*No seas imprudente!*" [Don't be disrespectful or rude!], for instance).

32 ". . . when T . . . asked me to drive him back, and I said, 'Look, I'm too fucked up, but if C . . . drives, you better hold on to your *panties* . . . !' *¡Y pa' qué fue eso!*": Switch to the Spanish exclamatory sentence *¡Y pa' qué fue eso!* [Why did I say (or do) that for?!], probably to stress even more the unexpectedness of what will follow.

32 "And she could tell her son was being *abusive* . . . abusive to me, and once in the middle of an argument, *el tipo éste se desaparece, se desapareció*, and his mom came in to break up the argument, and I thought it was him, so I turned around to whack him, and I punched out his mom!": Shift to the Spanish independent clause *el tipo éste se desaparece, se desapareció* (and this guy [all of a sudden] disappears, he just disappeared [vanished]), probably to stress, through this linguistic break, the unexpectedness of this subject's disappearance.

33 "Till one day she just got up, picked up a gun, and told him if he didn't go, she'd blow his brains off! And he got *scared* and left, *y nunca más volvió* . . .": Switch to the independent clause *y nunca más volvió* (and he never ever came back), perhaps to mark thus, through this linguistic break, the definitive rupture or change that the clause describes.

33 "And C . . . was in the back and his mom was up in front, but you could still feel *el* hate *que este chamaco le tenía*" [the hate that this kid had for her]: Switch to the Spanish article *el* and to the adjective clause *que este chamaco le tenía*, perhaps to foreground the sentiment of hate, making it almost material and visible.

33–34 "So we finally got to his mom's, and I carried her upstairs, dropped her off, and I remember coming down the elevator to pick up her stuff, and C . . . kept following right behind me, trying to pick on my butt, accusing me of his mom's death, and I couldn't say, couldn't say a thing, couldn't talk, 'cause I had all this . . . *tristeza* I couldn't shake off": Switch to the Spanish noun *tristeza* (sadness, sorrow), perhaps to indicate thus, through this linguistic break, the inability to articulate or talk that the passage describes.

34 "But he was too quick, too quick with his hands, and I was almost out the door when he grabbed me *y me dio tremendo galletazo* . . . pshh . . . pshhh . . . pshhhh!": Switch to the Spanish independent clause *y me dio tremendo galletazo* [he gave me an incredible slap in the face], perhaps to further underscore or aggravate the effect of the slap, which is already described in augmentative terms both by the adjective *tremendo* (tremendous, huge) and the suffix *azo*.

34 "And cops would go by and look at us, '*Mira, mira a esos dos patos peleando!*' '*Go Girl!*'": Shift to the Spanish imperative sentence "*Mira, mira a esos dos patos peleando!*" [Look, look at those two faggots fighting!], perhaps to underscore the speakers' ironically dismissive distance from Juan and C . . . , as both the expletive *pato* and the subsequent switch back to English ("*Go Girl!*") would seem to suggest.

34 "And there was no way of getting this man off me, 'cause every time I'd kick him, he'd turn around and slap me, '*Mira*, you can't leave me! You can't leave *me!*'": Switch to the Spanish imperative *mira* (Look!), perhaps to aggravate the hysterical command, "You can't leave *me!*," which is further underscored by the alliteration of the consonant *m* (*Mira* . . . *me!*).

34 "My clothes were all cut to pieces, the mattress was *stabbed* with a knife, *y la alfombra to'a dañá*": Switch to the Spanish independent clause *y la alfombra to'a dañá* (and the carpet [was] all damaged), perhaps to underscore, through code-switching, the fragmentation and cutting the passage describes.

35 "And my partner, *que era cojonú*, decided to tell them, '*Fuck you!*'": Switch to the Spanish adjective clause *que era cojonú* (who was ballsy) to further specify the subject and to better characterize him perhaps by making his "ballsiness" rhyme with the expletive "*Fuck you!*"

35 "And I looked out the window and guess who was staring at me? C . . . ! And I thought, '*¡A Dioh, carajo, ahora sí que se jodió to'!* . . . '": Shift to the Spanish sentence "*¡A Dioh, carajo, ahora sí que se jodió to'!*" (Oh God, damn, now everything really got fucked up!), most probably to underscore the surprising turn of events and the speaker's uneasy sense of anticipation of further trouble.

36 "And I was shocked to see how fast he'd deteriorated—*él que era flaco* to begin with . . .": Shift to the partial Spanish clause *él que era flaco* to begin with (he who was skinny to begin with), perhaps to underscore the shock of seeing C . . . 's significant physical change.

PARADISE

36 "Larry Levan . . . one of the original DJ divas, the *only* black Buddha, the *only one* who could send me . . . *put* me in a *state* where I'd feel *los negros santeros* dancing all around me . . .": Shift to the Spanish object phrase *los negros santeros* (the black *Santería* gods), possibly to convey, through this very linguistic transformation, Levan's ability, as a kind of musical deity himself, to transform people and space. Metonymical substitution of the word *santero*, or *Santería* priest, for *oricha*, *santo*, or *Santería* deity, conjuring perhaps the very act of possession in which the *santero* or practitioner incarnates the god.

37 "And a month or so later A . . . , this friend of K . . . H . . . , a *cubano*, came over and kinda nervous said to me": Shift to the Spanish vocative *cubano* (Cuban guy), perhaps to indicate both cultural familiarity or intimacy as well as distance or suspicion, as the rest of the passage confirms.

37 "So his posse eventually sneaked out, and we made love, and after we made love, he was *enchulao* . . . 'cause I was top and he was *dominant* . . .": Shift to the colloquial Puerto Rican Spanish adjective *enchulao* (infatuated, smitten, love struck), perhaps to add greater impact to the state of being *enchulao* or infatuated by marking a break between the act (of lovemaking) and its effect. Shift back to English to evaluate or explain that state ("'cause I was . . ."), following a rhetorical pattern identified by Zentella among Spanglish codeswitchers as a "narrative frame break" and by Torres as an "evaluation device" (83–88).

38 "'Cause K . . . didn't rent no rooms; he'd rent *la cocina, la sala*, the whole nine yards . . .": Shift to Spanish object nouns *la cocina, la sala* (the kitchen, the living room), possibly to underscore the counterpoint between the two clauses, "K . . . didn't rent no rooms" and "he'd rent . . . ." As Zentella and the Mexican American linguist Guadalupe Valdés have noted, in code-switching, it is often the contrast itself, sometimes in the form of a counterpoint, rather than the choice of language, that is being exploited to convey meaning (Valdés 102–03; Zentella 111).

38 "And it was funny 'cause every time I'd go home I'd tell my family and friends, '*Gee*, we hung out with Madonna . . . *Gee*, we hung out with Grace . . .' And they'd be like, '*Right*! *Este tipo es un embustero* . . . !'": Switch to the Spanish sentence *Este tipo es un embustero* (This guy's a fibber, a liar), possibly to underscore the contrast with the preceding English exclamation "*Right*!" and to render it ironic.

38 "And I was totally dressed Issey Miyake from head to toe—*toditito de blanco* . . . It was my 30th birthday, and *I was smokin'*!": Switch to the Spanish adverb phrase *toditito de blanco* (completely in white), perhaps to further augment an already superlative English adverb phrase ("totally . . . from head to toe"). Curiously and creatively, the double application of the Spanish diminutive suffix *ito* to *todo* (all, whole) has the opposite effect here of magnifying it, producing an expression akin to the English "every little bit . . . ." The resulting Spanglish alliteration ("<u>to</u>tally . . . <u>to</u>e—*to<u>di</u>tito* . . .") also adds to the sense of progression that culminates in the self-satisfied declaration: "It was my 30th birthday, and *I was smokin'*!"

38 "Well . . . she gets *real patota*! You know how she gets when she gets drunk . . . ? She pushes her way through the crowd holding her drink up, and she looks me *up and down* . . . like in . . . *All about Eve*": Turning to the Puerto Rican (and Caribbean) Spanish expletive *pato* (faggot; literally a duck), here used as an adjective ("faggoty") to denote behavior, rather than personal identity, this switch exploits the gender and aggravation resources of Spanish by both feminizing and augmenting *pato* with the suffix *ota*. The resulting superlative feminine adjective, *patota*, would seem to convey not just "faggoty" but a performative, over-the-top, willfully feminine, or feminine-like behavior, which might be rendered as queeny, bitchy, and campy all at once, as the rest of the passage, with its allusion to the camp classic, Bette Davis's party scene in the film *All about Eve*, confirms. For a more detailed commentary on the category *pato*, see chapter five, "Dominant/Passive; Macho/*Pato* (*Maricón*); Hustler/*Pargo*; Top/Bottom."

39 "And after we went to his studio and there was all this passion brewing . . . *todo se fue a juste*!": Shift to the colloquial Puerto Rican Spanish expression *todo se fue a juste* (all control or restraint went to hell), possibly to convey by thus breaking code the sense of abandon and lack of restraint that the very expression signifies.

40 "And all these homies would come outta nowhere to hang. And whenever he saw a cutie at one of these parties his tail would start *wagging como un perro sato* . . . and lose control . . .": Shift to the

Spanish adverb phrase *como un perro sato* (like a [horny] street mutt), possibly to foreground this metaphoric tail's behavior here as automatic, independent, out-of-control, as the rest of the sentence confirms.

42 "I remember once everyone smoking pot at the Whitney—*hasta las viejitas*": Switch to the Spanish adverb phrase *hasta las viejitas* (even the little old ladies), possibly to stress the speaking subject's sense of surprise.

43 "And as I was holding her up, she started *sweating . . . y se prendió Grace . . . se prendió*, and the whole skirt started *smelling . . . a toto!*": Switch to the Spanish independent clause *y se prendió Grace . . . se prendió* (and Grace got turned on . . . she got turned on), and to the Puerto Rican Spanish adverb phrase *a toto* (like pussy), possibly to stress once more a behavior that is perceived as detached from the subject, automatic, beyond its control.

44 "He was a pretty young boy but kinda *tímido*, you know, *un jíbarito*, when Keith first met him": Switch to the Spanish *tímido* (timid, shy), possibly to underscore a relationship between timidity or shyness and Puerto-Ricanness through the mediating term *jíbaro* or *jíbarito* (little country boy). For a more detailed commentary on this association, see chapter five, "Tímido (Jíbaro)."

44 "And then the day finally came when the project was supposed to start, and this gorgeous woman, taller than Keith, shows up. *Y esa mujer era bella*, I mean, *bella!*, *pero laaarga . . . como el cielo*. And real sexy": Switch to the Spanish sentence *Y esa mujer era bella*, I mean, *bella!*, *pero laaarga . . . como el cielo* (And that woman was beautiful, I mean, beautiful!, but looong (tall) . . . like the sky), possibly to emphasize and augment a quality, such as gorgeous (gorgeous . . . *bella* . . . I mean, *bella* . . .), through its translation and reiteration in Spanish.

45 "And the cops were getting angrier, and people kept gathering while this woman kept posing—*to the right, to the left, a lo loco . . .*": Switch to the Spanish adverb phrase *a lo loco* (wildly), perhaps to foreground the subject's performance's increasing independence and detachment from the scene and scandal that it is causing.

45 "And D . . . knew my cooking 'cause she'd been to our apartment in New York *con el hijo de Pablo Picasso*, Claude": Switch to the Spanish prepositional phrase *con el hijo de Pablo Picasso* (with Pablo Picasso's son), perhaps to denote a kind of familiarity that the rest of the passage confirms.

45 "*Algo boricua*, you know, *arroz blanco, habichuelas colorás, ensalada de aguacate, pollo frito*—what I'd always cook for Keith": Switch to the Spanish object phrase *Algo boricua*, you know, *arroz blanco, habichuelas colorás, ensalada de aguacate, pollo frito* (Something typically Puerto Rican, you know, white rice, red beans, avocado salad, fried chicken) to reference a typical or authentically Puerto Rican meal, as the use of the indigenous term for Puerto Rican, *boricua*, suggests.

46 "And the rice wasn't totally burned, *pero olía a quemao . . .*": Switch to the Spanish independent clause *pero olía a quemao* (but it smelled like it was burning), perhaps to stress a contrast, as the conjunction *pero* (but) suggests.

46 "And there I was *en la cocina tó mojao*, 'cause I'd rushed out of the bathroom, no shirt, no shoes on, being introduced to the princess of Monaco, and feeling like the *only pendejo . . .*": Switch to the Spanish adverb phrase *en la cocina tó mojao* (in the kitchen all wet), most likely to contrast with the subject's grand expectations, as the rest of the sentence and the use of the Latin American Spanish adjective *pendejo* (sucker, chump) suggest.

46 "And they'd smoke and get high, *y querían chichar . . . a la mala!*": Use of the Puerto Rican Spanish independent clause *y querían chichar . . . a la mala* (and they wanted to fuck . . . by force), possibly to stress an unexpected action or result.

47 "And you could tell she was getting giddy and *girly*, sticking out her tongue, and opening her legs, *y la mujer se estaba calentando*, and getting ready to attack": Switch to the Spanish independent clause *y la mujer se estaba calentando* (and the woman was getting horny), perhaps to stress and add suspense to the process of transformation that is being narrated in this passage.

48 "And when I got to Customs they couldn't understand how I'd flown around the world without a fucken *maleta*": Switch to the Spanish noun *maleta* (suitcase), possibly to contrast with the English noun "world" and express through this referent to the familial or domestic sphere, as on page 20, the loss of home.

49 "And if he got horny, he'd just shut the door, watch his videos, *y se acabó*": Switch to the Spanish independent clause *y se acabó* (and that was it), perhaps to stress the ending of an action.

49 "No, but *maybe . . .* And in this relationship had I stayed on *a la mala*, had I been more *cojonú*, had I battled with him . . .'Cause with

Taurus men, you know, you have to wave that red cape and hit'em upside the head to keep'em interested! And maybe I was *too* nice . . .": Switch to the Spanish adverb *a la mala* (by force) and the adjective *cojonú* (or *cojonudo*: ballsy, forceful), perhaps to stress or aggravate the already forceful action described.

49   "'Cause I could always sense the more *cojonú* I was the more he'd desire me . . . 'Cause Keith was always like *that*—he always wanted what he couldn't have, or be. Like Gil . . .": Switch to the Spanish adjective *cojonú*, once again to further stress an already underscored quality, as the adverb "more" suggests.

49   "*Y él hasta le hizo un libro a ese chamaco*, and dedicated it to him: Gil Vazquez . . .": Switch to the Spanish independent clause *Y él hasta le hizo un libro a ese chamaco* (And he even made a book for that boy), perhaps to highlight the speaker's surprise, as the adverb *hasta* (even) suggests.

50   "And sometimes Grace would be in the car, and she'd be screaming at the top of her lungs, '*Sácale el pie al pedal ése. Sácale el pie*!!'": Switch to the Spanish imperative sentences "*Sácale el pie al pedal ése. Sácale el pie*!!" (Take your foot off that pedal. Take it off!!), perhaps to aggravate the command and express thus its urgency. Interestingly, in Juan's recollections English speakers often appear speaking Spanish, especially when giving commands, or situations that transpired in one language are often reported in another, even in direct or quoted speech, confirming thus that code-switching is most frequently triggered, as Zentella, Torres, and Valdés have argued, by rhetorical needs rather than the desire to be linguistically faithful to an original source.

52   "And he said, 'Don't worry, I know—I've got them. Just come by my house.' *Pero ese perro ya me había mordío* [But that dog had already bitten me], so I went back to the restaurant instead": Switch to the Puerto Rican Spanish expression *ese perro me mordió* (that dog already bit me), used to ironically express that one is aware that the addressee is trying yet again to scam or con one.

53   "And, yeah, it was nice, 'cause we spread Keith's ashes on top of a hill in a corn field where Keith used to play, and as we spread them, the sun went down, and the sky turned red, and a flock of *pájaros* flew overhead": Switch to the Spanish noun *pájaros* (birds), most likely to allude thus to the Puerto Rican term *pato* (faggot, literally a duck) and to transform and reclaim it, as Juan consistently does throughout his interview. For a more detailed commentary on the category *pato*, see chapter five, "Dominant/Passive; Macho/*Pato* (*Maricón*); Hustler/*Pargo*; Top/Bottom."

53 "Yeah, I developed wasting syndrome—*yo que siempre he sido flaco pero duro*—was looking gaunt and spent": Switch to the Spanish independent, parenthetical clause *yo que siempre he sido flaco pero duro* (I who have always been skinny but solid), perhaps to contrast the speaker's present deteriorated physical condition with his previous healthy state and to underscore his shock. For a more detailed explanation of wasting syndrome, see chapter five, "Wasting."

53–54 "'Cause I'd put myself in a state of mind . . . *que no, que no queda más na'* . . . *y uno esperando la muerte* . . ." [that [I thought] no, there's nothing left . . . [except] one waiting for death . . .]: Shift to the Spanish clauses above, most likely to mark a change from first-person narration or dialogue to a free indirect style (*style indirect libre*) of reporting, which simulates an interior monologue.

54 "'Cause they say when we die we go to hell, but I was thinking—*here I've been living a hell*. And I kept thinking, *¿Dios mío, por qué me tienes aquí metío en este* hell?: Switch to the Spanish question *¿Dios mío, por qué me tienes aquí metío en este* hell? (My God, why have you put me here in this *hell*"), most likely to mark a difference once again between spoken speech or dialogue and interior monologue, as the independent clause "And I kept thinking" indicates. Shift back to English ("hell") to return to spoken speech or dialogue and underscore the speaker's present moment and condition.

55 "And the world around me looked like I was looking at it through *una pecera*, and the guard was talking, but I couldn't hear him—like in a silent film": Switch to the Spanish noun *una pecera* (a fish tank), to further stress the strange, uncanny, and surreal point of view Juan is often forced to adopt in many of the contexts he describes in his interview.

"I'M JUANITO XTRAVAGANZA": AN EPILOGUE

55 "They had always wanted me to walk *banjee*, or street hoodlum, with *face*, 'cause they thought I'd no face problems and would just look *flawless* walking up the runway . . . with the fresh sneakers . . . the beads . . . the bangles . . . the *cara de palo* . . . the *yo!-yo!-whatsup?!*:" Switch to the Spanish idiomatic expression *cara de palo* (deadpan or stone-faced, literally wooden face), perhaps to foreground the very act or performance of the category "banjee" or street hood that Juan both exemplifies for the ball audience and simulates.

57 "And they were shouting and calling me, *Tío... Tío...* AC-M: And you? Were you shouting back? JR: Yeah... *Bendición... Bendición... Bendición...* ": Switch to the Spanish kinship term *tío* (uncle), and to the traditional Puerto Rican Spanish noun with which Puerto Rican children ask for a blessing from their adult relatives, *Bendición* (Blessing), here transformed into the adults' reply, most probably to stress the familial bond that the drag ball houses promote. For a more detailed commentary on the drag ball houses, specifically, the House of Xtravaganza, see chapter five, "Xtravaganza, the House of."

REFERENCES

Aletti, Vince. "An Interview with Keith Haring." In *Keith Haring: Future Primeval*. Normal, IL: Illinois State University Galleries. 91–104.

Algarín, Miguel and Miguel Piñero, eds. 1975. *Nuyorican Poetry: An Anthology of Puerto Rican Words and Feelings*. New York: William Morrow & Company.

Almaguer, Tomás. 1993. "Chicano Men: A Cartography of Homosexual Identity and Behavior." In *The Lesbian and Gay Studies Reader*, ed. Henry Abelove, Michèle Aina Barale, and David M. Halperin. New York and London: Routledge.

Aponte-Parés, Luis. 1995. "What's Yellow and White and Has Land All Around It?: Appropriating Place in Puerto Rican Barrios." *Centro: Journal of the Center for Puerto Rican Studies* 7 (1): 8–19.

———. 1999. "Lessons from *el Barrio*—the East Harlem Real Great Society/Urban Planning Studio: A Puerto Rican Chapter in the Fight for Urban Self-Determination." In *Latino Social Movements: Historical and Theoretical Perspectives*, ed. Rodolfo D. Torres and George Katsiaficas. New York and London: Routledge.

Austin, Joe. 2001. *Taking the Train*. New York: Columbia University Press.

Baker, Russ. 1990. "Breaking the Faith: A Close Look at *Covenant House*." *Village Voice* 35 (12): March 20.

Basch, Michael Franz. 1976. "The Concept of Affect: A Re-Examination." *Journal of the American Psychoanalytic Association* 24: 759–77.

Berman, Marshall. 1982. *All that Is Solid Melts into Air*. New York, London: Penguin Books.

———. 1997. "Signs of the Time." *Dissent*. <www.findarticles.com>.

Bianco, Anthony. 2004. *Ghosts of 42nd Street: A History of America's Most Infamous Block*. New York: William Morrow.

Blinderman, Barry. 1990. "Close Encounters with *The Third Mind*." In *Keith Haring: Future Primeval*. Normal, IL: Illinois State University Galleries. 15–21.

Bottoms, Stephen J. 2004. *Playing Underground: A Critical History of the 1960s Off-Off-Broadway Movement*. Ann Arbor: University of Michigan Press.

Bourgois, Philippe. 1995. *In Search of Respect: Selling Crack in El Barrio*. Cambridge: Cambridge University Press.

Bowles, Peter. 2005. "Mayor: Stay Open during Puerto Rican Day Parade." *New York Newsday*. June 10, 2005. <www.NYNewsday.com>.

Briggs, Laura. 2002a. "*La Vida*, Moynihan, and Other Libels: Migration, Social Science, and the Making of the Puerto Rican Welfare Queen." *CENTRO Journal* 14 (1): 75–101.

―――. 2002b. *Reproducing Empire: Race, Sex, Science, and U.S. Imperialism in Puerto Rico*. Berkeley: University of California Press.

Brown, Aaron Pierre. 1999. "What Is Vogue?" <www.balls.houseof enigma.com>.

Buckley, Perter G. 1991. "Boundaries of Respectability: Introductory Essay." In *Inventing Times Square: Commerce and Culture at the Crossroads of the World*, ed. William R. Taylor. New York: Russell Sage Foundation. 286–96.

Burns, Ric. 2002. *Coney Island* (Film). Program description: <www.pbs.org/ wgbh/amex/coney>.

Burroughs, William S. and Brion Gysin. 1978. *The Third Mind*. New York: Viking Press.

Butler, Judith. 1993. *Bodies that Matter: On the Discursive Limits of "Sex."* New York and London: Routledge.

―――. 1997. *The Psychic Life of Power: Theories in Subjection*. Stanford: Stanford University Press.

Cabranes, José A. 2001. "Some Common Ground." In *Foreign in a Domestic Sense: Puerto Rico, American Expansion, and the Constitution*, ed. Christina Duffy Burnett and Burke Marshall. Durham and London: Duke University Press.

Cameron, Dan. 2005. "It Takes a Village." In *East Village USA*. Ed. by Dan Cameron, Liza Kirwin, and Alan W. Moore. New York: New Museum of Contemporary Art.

Carrillo, Héctor. 2002. *The Night Is Young: Sexuality in Mexico in the Times of AIDS*. Chicago: The University of Chicago Press.

Castells, Manuel. 1983. *The City and the Grassroots: A Cross–Cultural Theory of Urban Social Movements*. Berkeley, LA: University of California Press.

Certeau, Michel de. 1988. *The Practice of Everyday Life*. Trans. Steven Rendall. Berkeley: University of California Press.

Chauncey, George, Jr. 1991. "The Policed: Gay Men's Strategies of Everyday Resistance." In *Inventing Times Square: Commerce and Culture at the Crossroads of the World*, ed. William R. Taylor. New York: Russell Sage Foundation. 315–28.

―――. 1994. *Gay New York: Gender, Urban Culture, and the Making of the Gay Male World, 1890–1940*. New York: BasicBooks.

Cheren, Mel. 2000. *Keep on Dancin': My Life and the Paradise Garage*. (As Told to Gabriel Rotello and with Assistance from Brent Nicholson Earle.) New York: 24 Hours For Life, Inc.

Clark, Larry. 1983. *Teenage Lust: An Autobiography*. Meridien, CT: Meridien Gravure.

Collin, Mathew with John Godfrey. 1997. *Altered State: The Story of Ecstasy Culture and Acid House*. London: Serpent's Tail.

Cooper, Martha and Henry Chalfant. 1984. *Subway Art.* New York: Holt, Rinehart and Winston.

Cortázar, Julio. 1970. *Ceremonias.* Barcelona: Seix Barral.

Crimp, Douglas. 2002. "Mario Montez, for Shame." In *Regarding Sedgwick: Essays on Queer Culture and Critical Theory,* ed. Stephen M. Barber and David L. Clark. New York and London: Routledge.

Cruz, Celia. 2003. "Yo Viviré" (I Will Survive). *Regalo del Alma.* Composed by Frederick Perren and Dino Fekaris; adapted by Oscar Gómez. Miami Beach, FL: Sony Discos TRK 70620.

Cruz-Malavé, Arnaldo. 1996. "What a Tangled Web!: Masculinity, Abjection, and the Foundations of Puerto Rican Literature in the United States." *differences* 8 (1): 132–51.

Cunningham, Michael. 1993. "The Slap of Love." *Open City* #6. <www.opencity.org/cunningham>.

Dávila, Arlene. 2004. *Barrio Dreams: Puerto Ricans, Latinos and the Neoliberal City.* Berkeley and Los Angeles: University of California Press.

Deitch, Jeffrey. 1985. "East Village Art Grows Up." *International Herald Tribune.* October 15: 13.

Delaney, Samuel R. 1999. *Times Square Red, Times Square Blue.* New York and London: New York University Press.

Deleuze, Gilles. 1990. *The Logic of Sense.* Ed. Constantin Boundas. New York: Columbia University Press.

Denson, Charles. 2002. *Coney Island: Lost and Found.* Berkeley: Ten Speed.

Dieckmann, Katherine. 1990. "Tag Team: LA II Remembers the Guy Who 'Draws Babies on the Door.'" *The Village Voice.* May 15.

Duberman, Martin. 1993. *Stonewall.* New York: Dutton.

Eisener, Bruce. 1989. *Ecstasy: The MDMA Story.* Berkeley: Ronin.

Fiedler, Leslie. 1960. *Love and Death in the American Novel.* New York: Criterion Books.

Fikentscher, Kai. 2000. *"You Better Work!": Underground Dance Music in New York City.* Hanover and London: Wesleyan University Press.

Flores, Juan. 2000. *From Bomba to Hip-Hop: Puerto Rican Culture and Latino Identity.* New York: Columbia University Press.

Flores, Juan and Wilson A. Valentín-Escobar, eds. 2004. "Puerto Rican Music and Dance: RicanStructing Roots/Routes." *Centro Journal* 16 (2) (Fall).

Foucault, Michel. 1978. *The History of Sexuality.* New York: Pantheon.

Freud, Sigmund. 1953–74. *The Ego and the Id. The Standard Edition of the Complete Psychological Works of Sigmund Freud.* Ed. James Strachey. 24 vols. London: Hogarth. 19: 16.

Friedman, Josh Alan. 1986. *Tales of Times Square.* New York: Delacorte Press.

Friedman, Mack. 2003. *Strapped for Cash: A History of American Hustler Culture.* Los Angeles: Alyson Books.

Garber, Eric. 1989. "A Spectacle in Color: The Lesbian and Gay Subculture of Jazz Age Harlem." In *Hidden from History,* ed. Martin Duberman, Martha Vicinus, and George Chauncey. New York: NAL Books. 318–31.

Gilbert, James. 1988. *Cycle of Outrage: America's Reaction to the Juvenile Delinquent in the 1950s*. Oxford: Oxford University Press.

Gilfoyle, Timothy J. 1991. "Policing Sexuality." In *Inventing Times Square: Commerce and Culture at the Crossroads of the World*, ed. William R. Taylor. New York: Russell Sage Foundation. 297–314.

Glasser, Ruth. 1995. *My Music Is My Flag: Puerto Rican Musicians and Their New York Communities 1917–1940*. Berkeley and Los Angeles: University of California Press.

———. 1997. *Aquí Me Quedo: Puerto Ricans in Connecticut*. Trans. José Rodríguez Sellas, Racquel Requena, and María de Lourdes Martínez. New Haven, CT: Connecticut Humanities Council.

Goude, Jean-Paul. 1981. *Jungle Fever*. Ed. Harold Hayes. New York: Xavier Moreau, Inc.

———. 2005. *So Far So Goude*. With Patrick Mauriès. New York and Paris: Assouline.

Gruen, John. 1966. *The New Bohemia: The Combine Generation*. Photographs by Fred W. McDarrah. New York: Shorecrest.

———. 1991. *Keith Haring: The Authorized Biography*. New York: Fireside.

Gruen, Julia. 1999. "Haring All-Over." <www.haring.com/cgi–bin/essays>.

———. 2007. "No Boundaries." <www.haring.com/cgi–bin/essays>.

Gutmann, Mathew C. 1996. *The Meanings of Macho: Being a Man in Mexico City*. Berkeley and Los Angeles: University of California Press.

Guzmán, Pablo. 1998. "*La Vida Pura*: A Lord of the Barrio." *The Puerto Rican Movement: Voices from the Diaspora*, ed. Andrés Torres and José E. Velázquez. Philadelphia, PA: Temple University Press. 155–72.

Halberstam, Judith. 2005. "Shame and White Gay Masculinity." *Social Text* 84–85 (Fall/Winter): 219–33.

Haring, Keith. 1984. "Introduction." *Art in Transit: Subway Drawings*. Photographs by Tseng Kwong Chi. With an introduction by Henry Geldzahler. New York: Harmony Books. Also <www.haringkids.com/art/subway/index.html>.

———. 1997. *Keith Haring Journals*. Introduction by Robert Farris Thompson. New York: Penguin Books.

Hebdige, Dick. 1993. "Welcome to the Terrordome: Jean-Michel Basquiat and the 'Dark' Side of Hybridity." In *Jean-Michel Basquiat*, ed. Richard Marshall. New York: Whitney Museum of American Art.

Herlihy, James Leo. 1965. *Midnight Cowboy*. New York: Simon and Schuster.

Hoban, Phoebe. 1998. *Basquiat: A Quick Killing in Art*. New York: Penguin Books.

Hodgkinson, Will. 2007. "Snap Shot: Grace Jones." *The Guardian*. January 9.

Hogan, Steven and Lee Hudson. 1998. *Completely Queer: The Gay and Lesbian Encyclopedia*. New York: Henry Holt and Company.

hooks, bell. 1992. "Is Paris Burning?" *Black Looks: Race and Representation*. Boston: South End. 145–56.

Hubert, Jeffrey T. and Mary L. Gillaspy. 2000. *Encyclopedic Dictionary of AIDS-Related Terminology*. New York: Hawoth Information.

Huncke, Herbert. 1990. *Guilty of Everything*. New York: Paragon House.

Immerso, Michael. 2002. *The People's Playground*. New Brunswick, NJ: Rutgers University Press.

Kasson, John. 1978. *Amusing the Million: Coney Island at the Turn of the Century*. New York: Hill & Wang.

Kershaw, Miriam. 1997. "Postcolonialism and Androgyny: The Performance Art of Grace Jones." *Art Journal* 56 (4) (Winter): 19–25.

Koestenbaum, Wayne. 1993. *The Queen's Throat: Opera, Homosexuality and the Mystery of Desire*. New York: Poseidon.

———. 2001. *Andy Warhol*. New York: Viking.

Kolossa, Alexandra. 2004. *Keith Haring (1958–1990): A Life for Art*. Köln, London, Los Angeles, Madrid, Paris, and Tokyo: Taschen.

LaFountain-Stokes, Lawrence. 2003. "Gay Shame, Latino/a Style: A Critique of White Queer Performativity." Author's manuscript.

Lancaster, Roger N. 1992. *Life Is Hard: Machismo, Danger, and the Intimacy of Power in Nicaragua*. Berkeley, LA: University of California Press.

———. 1997. "Sexual Positions: Caveats and Second Thoughts on Categories." *The Americas* 54 (1) (July): 1–16.

Lauria, Mickey and Lawrence Knopp. 1985. "Toward an Analysis of the Role of Gay Communities in the Urban Rennaisance." *Urban Geography* 6 (2): 152–69.

Lawrence, Tim. 2003. *Love Saves the Day: A History of American Dance Music Culture, 1970–1979*. Durham and London: Duke University Press.

Levinas, Emmanuel. 1969. *Totality and Infinity: An Essay on Exteriority*. Trans. Alphonso Lingis. Pittsburgh, PA: Duquesne University Press.

Levine, Martin P. 1992. "The Life and Death of Gay Clones." In *Gay Culture in America*, ed. Gilbert Herdt. Boston: Beacon Press.

Lewis, Oscar. 1965. *La Vida: A Puerto Rican Family in the Culture of Poverty—San Juan and New York*. New York: Random House.

———. 1975. *Five Families: Mexican Case Studies in the Culture of Poverty*. New York: Basic Books.

Ludlam, Charles. 1992. *Ridiculous Theatre: Scourge of Human Folly: The Essays and Opinions of Charles Ludlam*. Ed. Steven Samuels. New York: Theatre Communications Group.

Magnuson, Ann. 1997. "The Prime Time of Our Lives." In *Keith Haring*, ed. Elisabeth Sussman. New York: Whitney Museum of American Art. 124–32.

Makagon, Daniel. 2004. *Where the Ball Drops: Days and Nights in Times Square*. Minneapolis: University of Minnesota Press.

Marotta, Toby. 1981. *The Politics of Homosexuality*. Boston: Houghton Mifflin Company.

Martí, José. 1975 (1881). "Coney Island." *Obras completas*. Havana: Editorial de Ciencias Sociales. 9: 123–28.

McNamara, Robert P. 1994. *The Times Square Hustler: Male Prostitution in New York City.* West Port, CT and London: Praeger.

Mele, Christopher. 2000. *Selling the Lower East Side: Culture, Real Estate, and Resistance in New York City.* Minneapolis: University of Minnesota Press.

Melendez, Miguel. 2003. *We Took the Streets: Fighting for Latino Rights with the Young Lords.* New York: St. Martin's Press.

Menchú, Rigoberta. 1984. *I, Rigoberta Menchú: An Indian Woman in Guatemala.* Ed. Elisabeth Burgos-Debray. London: Verso.

Mercer, Kobena. 1994. "Reading Racial Fetishism: The Photographs of Robert Mapplethorpe." *Welcome to the Jungle.* London and New York: Routledge. 171–219.

Minton, Henry L. 2002. *Departing from Deviance: A History of Homosexual Rights and Emancipatory Science in America.* Chicago and London: University of Chicago Press.

Mintz, Sidney. 1974. "Caribbean Peasantries." *Caribbean Transformation.* Chicago: Aldine Publishing Co.

Montejo, Esteban. 1968. *The Autobiography of a Runaway Slave.* Ed. Miguel Barnet. New York: Pantheon Books.

Montez, Ricardo. 2006. "'Trade' Marks: LA2, Keith Haring, and a Queer Economy of Collaboration." *GLQ: A Journal of Lesbian and Gay Studies* (12) (3): 425–40.

Morales, Iris. 1996. *¡Palante, Siempre Palante! The Young Lords* (Documentary Film).

———. 1998. "¡Palante, Siempre Palante!: The Young Lords." In *The Puerto Rican Movement: Voices from the Diaspora,* ed. Andrés Torres and José E. Velázquez. Philadelphia, PA: Temple University. 210–27.

Morris, Gary. 1999. "Two Early Works: *Restaurant and Screen Test #2.*" *Bright Lights Film Journal* (24). <brightlightsfilm.com>.

Morrison, Toni. 1989. "Unspeakable Things Unspoken: The Afro-American Presence in American Literature." *Michigan Quarterly Review* 28 (1): 1–34.

———. 1993. *Playing in the Dark.* New York: Vintage.

Moynihan, Colin. 2002. "Keith Haring's Silent Partner." *The Village Voice.* July 24–30.

Mulvey, Laura. 1985. "Visual Pleasure and Narrative Cinema." In *Film Theory and Criticism: Introductory Readings,* ed. Gerald Mast. New York and Oxford: Oxford University Press.

Muñoz, José Esteban. 1999. *Disidentifications: Queers of Color and the Performance of Identity.* Minneapolis: University of Minnesota Press.

Muñoz-Laboy, Miguel. 2001. "The Organization of Sexuality of Bisexually Active Latino Men in New York City." Ph.D. Dissertation, Columbia University.

Negrón-Muntaner, Frances. 2004. *Boricua Pop: Puerto Ricans and the Latinization of American Culture.* New York: New York University Press.

Olalquiaga, Celeste. 1992. *Megalopolis: Contemporary Cultural Sensibilities.* Minneapolis: University of Minnesota Press.

Owen, Frank. 2003. *Clubland Confidential.* London: Ebury.

Parker, Richard. 1990. *Bodies, Pleasures, and Passions.* Boston: Beacon.

Paz, Ocatvio. 1959. *El laberinto de la soledad.* Mexico City: Fondo de Cultura Económica.

Pedraza, Pedro. 1997. "Puerto Ricans and the Politics of School Reform." *Centro: Journal of the Center for Puerto Rican Studies* 9 (1): 75–85.

Pérez, Hiram. 2005. "You Can Have My Brown Body and Eat It Too!" *Social Text* 84–85 (Fall/Winter): 171–91.

Pérez-Firmat, Gustavo. 1995. *Bilingual Blues (Poems, 1981–1994).* Tempe, AZ: Bilingual Press/Editorial Bilingüe.

Phillips, Patrick. 2004. "Richard Johnson: Many Journalists View Gossip Columnists as 'the Dirty, Seemy Side' of the News Business." *I Want Media.* <www.iwantmedia.com>. May 9.

Quintero Rivera, Angel G. 1998. *Salsa, sabor y control: sociología de la música tropical.* México: Siglo Veintiuno.

Ramírez, Rafael L. 1993. *Dime capitán: Reflexiones sobre la masculinidad.* Río Piedras, Puerto Rico: Ediciones Huracán.

Ramos, Josell. 2005. *Maestro.* Artrution Productions.

Rechy, John. 1963. *City of Night.* New York: Grove.

Register, Woody. 2001. *The Kid of Coney Island: Fred Thompson and the Rise of American Amusements.* Oxford: Oxford University Press.

Reynolds, Simon. 1999. *Ecstasy Generation: Into the World of Techno and Rave Culture.* New York: Routledge.

Ricard, Rene. 1981. "The Radiant Child." *Artforum* 20 (December): 35–43.

Ritter, Bruce. 1987. *Covenant House: Lifeline to the Street.* New York: Doubleday.

———. 1988. *Sometimes God Has a Kid's Face: The Story of America's Exploited Street Kids.* New York: Covenant House.

Rivera, Raquel Z. 2003. *New York Ricans from the Hip Hop Zone.* New Directions in Latino American Cultures. Series edited by Licia Fiol-Matta and José Quiroga. New York: Palgrave Macmillan.

Roemer, Rick. 1998. *Charles Ludlam and the Ridiculous Theatrical Company.* Jefferson, NC: McFarland.

Rondón, César Miguel. *El libro de la salsa: crónica de la música del Caribe urbano.* Caracas: Editorial Arte.

Rose, Tricia. 1994. *Black Noise: Rap Music and Black Culture in Contemporary America.* Middletown, CT: Wesleyan University.

Rosenbaum, Marsha. 2002. "Ecstasy: America's New Reefer Madness." *Journal of Psychoactive Drugs* 32 (2) (April–June): 137–42.

Sánchez, Luis Rafael. 1979. "Cinco problemas al escritor puertorriqueño." *Vórtice* 2 (2–3): 117–21.

———. 1994. *La guagua aérea.* San Juan: Cultural.

Sánchez Korrol, Virginia E. 1994. *From Colonia to Community: The History of Puerto Ricans in New York City.* Berkeley and Los Angeles: University of California Press.

Sandoval-Sánchez, Alberto. 1997. *"West Side Story:* A Puerto Rican Reading of 'America.'" In *Latin Looks: Images of Latinas and Latinos in the U.S. Media,* ed. Clara E. Rodríguez. Boulder, CO: Westview.

Sartre, Jean-Paul. 1956. *Being and Nothingness: An Essay on Phenomenological Ontology.* Trans. Hazel E. Barnes. New York: The Philosophical Library.

Saussure, Ferdinand de. 1966. *Course in General Linguistics.* New York, Toronto, and London: McGraw-Hill.

Scarano, Francisco A. 1996. "The *Jíbaro* Masquerade and the Subaltern Politics of Creole Identity Formation in Puerto Rico 1745–1823." *American Historical Review* 101 (5) (December): 1398–431.

Schneider, Carl D. 1977. *Shame, Exposure, and Privacy.* Boston: Beacon Press.

Sedgwick, Eve Kosofsky. 1993. "Queer Performativity: Henry James's *The Art of the Novel." GLQ* 1 (1): 1–16.

———. 1995. "Shame and Performativity: Henry James's *New York Edition* Prefaces." In *Henry James's New York Edition: The Construction of Authorship,* ed. David McWhirtes. Stanford: Stanford University Press. 206–39.

———. 1996. "Queer Performativity: Warhol's Shyness/Warhol's Whiteness." In *Pop Out: Queer Warhol,* ed. Jennifer Doyle, Jonathan Flatley, and José Esteban Muñoz. Durham and London: Duke University Press.

Senelick, Laurence. 1991. "Private Parts in Public Places." In *Inventing Times Square: Commerce and Culture at the Crossroads of the World,* ed. William R. Taylor. New York: Russell Sage Foundation. 329–53.

Ševčenko, Liz. 2001. "Making Loisaida: Placing *Puertorriqueñidad* in Lower Manhattan." In *Mambo Montage: The Latinization of New York,* ed. Agustín Laó-Montes and Arlene Dávila. New York: Columbia University Press.

Sheff, David. 1989. "Keith Haring: An Intimate Conversation." *Rolling Stone.* August 10. <www.haring.com/archives/interviews>.

Silcott, Push and Mireille. 2000. *The Book of E: All about Ecstasy.* London: Omnibus.

Sischy, Ingrid. 1997. "Kid Haring," *Vanity Fair.* July 1997. <www.haring.com/archives/press/vanityfair>.

Smith, Jack. 1997. *Wait for Me at the Bottom of the Pool: The Writings of Jack Smith,* ed. J. Hoberman and Edward Leffingwell. New York: High Risk.

Somerville, Siobhan. 2000. *Queering the Color Line: Race and the Invention of Homosexuality in American Culture.* Durham: Duke University Press.

Sommer, Doris. 1999. *Proceed with Caution, When Engaged by Minority Writing in the Americas.* Cambridge: Harvard University Press.

———. 2004. *Bilingual Aesthetics: A New Sentimental Education*. Durham and London: Duke University Press.

Stoler, Ann Laura. *Race and the Education of Desire: Foucault's* History of Sexuality *and the Colonial Order of Things*. Durham: Duke University, 1995.

Sussman, Elisabeth, ed. 1997. *Keith Haring*. New York: Whitney Museum of American Art.

Thomas, Piri. 1968. *Down These Mean Streets*. New York: New American Library.

Tomkins, Silvan. 1995. *Shame and Its Sisters: A Silvan Tomkins Reader*, ed. Eve Kosofsky Sedgwick and Adam Frank. Durham and London: Duke University Press.

Torres, Lourdes. 1997. *Puerto Rican Discourse: A Sociolinguistic Study of a New York Suburb*. Mahwah, NJ: Lawrence Erlbaum Associates.

Traub, James. 2004. *The Devil's Playground: A Century of Pleasure and Profit in Times Square*. New York: Random House.

Turner, Joan. 1984. "Building Boundaries: The Politics of Urban Renewal in Manhattan's Lower East Side." Ph.D. Dissertation, City University of New York, New York.

Valdés, Guadalupe. 1981. "Code Switching as Deliberate Verbal Strategy: A Microanalysis of Direct and Indirect Requests among Chicano Bilingual Speakers." In *Latino Language and Communicative Behavior*, ed. R.P. Durán. Norwood, NJ: Ablex Press. 95–108.

Varnedoe, Kirk and Adam Gopnik. 1991. *High and Low: Modern Art, Popular Culture*. New York: The Museum of Modern Art.

Warhol, Andy and Pat Hackett. 1980. *POPism: The Warhol Sixties*. San Diego, New York, and London: Harcourt.

Watstein, Sarah and Stephen E. Stratton. 2003. *Encyclopedia of HIV & AIDS*. 2nd ed. New York: Facts on File.

Whitaker, Rick. 1999. *Assuming the Position: A Memoir of Hustling*. New York/ London: Four Walls Eight Windows.

Woodlawn, Holly with Jeffrey Copeland. 1991. *A Low Life in High Heels: The Holly Woodlawn Story*. New York: St. Martin's Press.

Yamagiwa, Seiji. "The World of *Shojo*: Militantly Cute." *Kateigaho: Japan's Art and Culture Magazine* 12 (Summer): 70.

Yarbro-Bejarano, Yvonne. 1994. *Race and Representation in* Tongues Untied, The Last Generation, *and* Paris Is Burning. Stanford, CA: Center for Chicano Research, Stanford University.

Young Lords Party and Michael Abramson. 1971. *Palante: Young Lords Party*. New York: McGraw-Hill.

Zentella, Ana Celia. 1997. *Growing Up Bilingual: Puerto Rican Children in New York*. Malden, MA and Oxford: Blackwell Publishers.

INDEX

Page numbers in *italics* indicate illustrations.

relationship with Grace Jones, 43, 160–2
relationship with Japan, 48, 89–90, *see also under* Japan
relationship with Juan Dubose, 40, 86, 152–3
relationship with graffiti writers and hip-hop, 6–7, 44, 60, 64, 68, 70–81, 83, 88, 91, 124
relationship with Juan Rivera, 3–4, *4*, 6, 36–55, *56*, 90–3, 171
relationship with Kenny Scharf, 42, 165–6
relationship with L.A. II, 44, 76–9, 162–4
relationship with Madonna, 43, 87, 150, 152
relationship with the mass media, 59–60, 72–4, 88–90
relationship with Warhol, 59, 82, 87, 89, 150
Spectacolor Billboard, 79–81, *80*
subway art, 72–5, *73*
at the School of Visual Arts (SVA), 64
The Ten Commandments, 41, 88
at the Whitney Museum, 42
the will of, 51, 93, 174–5
Harlem, 63
Hebdige, Dick, 151
Herlihy, James Leo, 138
Hernández, Rafael, 126
hip-hop, 6, 44, 60, 63–4, 70, 70–81, 83, 88, 91, 124, 131, 134–6, 162–4
graffiti, 6–7, 40, 42, 44, 59, 60, 64, 68, 131, 134–6, 162–4: on canvas, 75, 135–6; and the East Village underground, 134–6; and the Metropolitan Transit Authority (MTA), 75; as modernist, 74; and

technology, 74; wild style, 74; *Wild Style*, the film, 135; as sign of urban crisis, 7, 75, 79
style, definition of, 64
HIV/AIDS, 3, 35, 36, 40, 48–9, 51–4, 56–7, 60, 71–2, 86, 90, 92–3, 122, 129, 146–7, 148, 153, 155, 158, 162, 166–7, 174–5, 178
Hoberman, J., 114
Hodas, Martin, 144–5
Holly Solomon Gallery, 75
Holzer, Jenny, 68
Horn, Trevor, 162
hooks, bell, 181
Hughes, Langston, 179
Huncke, Herbert, 141
hustling, 5–6, 20–27, 49, 51–2, 54, 140–7, 170–1
on 14th St., 141
on 42nd St., *see* Times Square
on 53rd St. and Third Ave., 27, 140
bars, 27, 146
and nostalgia, 141–2, 146, 170–1
and the *pargo*, or john, 22–6, 30, 140–1, 143–4, 146, 170–1
and Puerto Ricans, 53, 141–2, 145–7, 170–1
and "trade," 66, 107–8, 140, 145–6, 170–1
see also under Juan Rivera, sexuality, and Times Square

Ibiza, 173
Iman, 38, 41, 42
Institute of Contemporary Art, 88
Invasion of the Body Snatchers, 71

Jagger, Bianca, 38
Jagger, Mick, 38
James, Henry, 176